DVOŘÁK

His Life and Music

Also by Gervase Hughes

THE MUSIC OF ARTHUR SULLIVAN

COMPOSERS OF OPERETTA

GREAT COMPOSERS OF THE WORLD

ANTONÍN DVOŘÁK

DVOŘÁK

His Life & Music

by Gervase Hughes, M.A., B.Mus. (Oxon.)

DODD, MEAD & COMPANY
NEW YORK

ML
410
D99
H79

Contents

1 INTRODUCTORY   *1*
— *Czech Names*   *4*

2 DVOŘÁK'S HOMELAND   8
— *Topography*   *9*
— *Early History*   *12*
— *An Age of Oppression*   *14*
— *Signs of National Resurgence*   *17*
— *The Revolutions of 1848*   *19*

3 CHILDHOOD AND STUDENT DAYS *21*
— *School*   *24*
— *Widening Horizons*   *27*

4 TEN YEARS OF STRUGGLE   *31*
— *Early Compositions*   *33*
— *Hard Work and not Much to show for It*   *38*
— *Interlude for Smetana*   *41*

5 A 'WAGNERIAN' PERIOD   44
— *Wagner versus the Rest*   *47*

6 UPS AND DOWNS   *52*
— *Mainly Operetta*   *54*
— *Mainly Chamber Music*   *57*
— *Symphony No. 5 in F Major*   *60*
— *Down rather than Up*   *62*
— Stabat Mater   *64*

7   RECOGNITION   66
— *Moravian Duets*   67
— *A Mixed Bag*   69
— The Peasant a Rogue   72
— *Symphonic Variations*   73
— *Reaction and Recovery*   75
— *Slavonic Dances*   76
— *Eight Eventful Months*   79

8   CONSOLIDATION   83
— *Publication Problems*   84
— *Violin Concerto in A Minor*   86
— Gipsy Songs   88
— *An Easy-going Spring and Summer*   90
— *Symphony No. 6 in D Major*   92
— *Something for Everyone*   94
— Dimitrij   98

9   INTERNATIONAL FAME   103
— Scherzo Capriccioso   104
— *Bohemia–Vienna*   106
— *Bohemia–London*   108
— *Bohemia–Worcester*   111
— *Symphony No. 7 in D Minor*   114
— *Bohemia–Birmingham*   117
— *Bohemia–Leeds*   119

10   FURTHER CONSOLIDATION   124
— *Chamber Music and a Mass*   126
— *Piano Quintet in A Major, op. 81*   129
— The Jacobin   131

11 HONOURS AT HOME AND
      ABROAD   *135*
      — *Symphony No. 8 in G Major*   *136*
      — *Out and About*   *138*
      — *A Requiem Mass*   *140*
      — *Professor and Doctor*   *142*
      — *Concert–overtures*   *145*
      — *Invitation to New York*   *147*
      — *Preparations and Farewells*   *149*

12 NEW YORK—AND THE MID-
      WEST   *153*
      — *First impressions of America*   *155*
      — *Symphony No. 9 in E Minor*   *160*
      — *Holiday Plans*   *162*
      — *Spillville*   *164*

13 BACK AND FORTH ACROSS THE
      ATLANTIC   *170*
      — Biblical Songs   *172*
      — *Summer at Home*   *174*
      — *New York Again*   *176*
      — *Cello Concerto in B Minor*   *178*
      — *Chamber-music Culmination*   *180*

14 CONCENTRATION ON BOHEMIA *184*
      — *Symphonic Poems*   *185*
      — *Public and Private Affairs*   *192*
      — The Devil and Kate   *194*
      — Rusalka   *198*

15   THE CLOSING YEARS   204
     — Armida   206
     — *Illness and Death*   212

16   IN CONCLUSION   217
     — *The Weakness*   217
     — *The Strength*   222
     — *The True Worth*   225

Appendix I   Some Significant Biographical Events   227
Appendix II   A Few Notes on the Bibliography   231

INDEX OF DVOŘÁK'S COMPOSITIONS 235

GENERAL INDEX   240

CHAPTER ONE

Introductory

Most of the well-known composers who practised their art during the nineteenth century, including those whose active careers overlapped it to any appreciable extent at one end or the other, belonged by birth as well as vocation to what are commonly called the 'professional' classes. The fathers of Cherubini, Beethoven, Weber, Rossini, Bellini, Offenbach, Johann Strauss, Brahms, Bizet, Sullivan, Puccini, Elgar and Richard Strauss all earned their living in some corner or other of the musical field. The fathers of Schubert, Chopin, Bruckner, Fauré and Janáček were schoolmasters or tutors. Berlioz and Sibelius were begotten by doctors; Meyerbeer and Mendelssohn by bankers; Schumann by a publisher; Glinka and Liszt bv estate-managers; Wagner (probably) by an actor; Gounod by a painter; Franck, Tchaikovsky and Massenet by engineers of one sort or another; Lalo and Mussorgsky by army officers; Balakirev, Bruch, Saint-Saëns, Chabrier and Grieg by civil servants; Rimsky-Korsakov by a naval officer. Exceptionally, Borodin's father was a prince and Delibes' a postman, and the fathers of Donizetti, Smetana, Wolf, Mahler and Debussy were tradesmen in (respectively) wool, beer, leather, prune-brandy and china. The fathers of Verdi and Dvořák were lower in the social scale; they came of peasant stock—Italian in the one case and Bohemian in the other—but being blessed with a measure of opportunity and initiative each, in due course, rose to become landlord of a village pub.

It was therefore no coincidence that Giuseppe Verdi and Antonín Dvořák should have had many characteristics in common. Both were industrious; both were shrewd, with the canniness of a peasant; both were good at heart but bluff and occasionally gruff in manner; both were modest by nature and yet by temperament sensitive to criticism; both were home-lovers and apt to feel ill-at-ease, Dvořák especially, in unfamiliar surroundings. Admittedly their theological views were diametrically opposed, but Dvořák was as sincere in his unquestioning acceptance of the Catholic faith in which he had been nurtured as was Verdi in his profound distrust of *any* religious dogma. (Verdi's attitude may have been partly intuitive, but it was fostered during adolescence by his mentor Ferdinando Provesi, who although a church-organist and choirmaster had no time for the clergy.)

Verdi and Dvořák never met face to face, and although Dvořák was a great admirer of Verdi's music he only here and there showed signs of having been consciously influenced by it. What is more to the point is that for Dvořák music was a *raison d'être* to precisely the same extent as it was for Verdi; while being far and away the most compelling interest in life, it was not the only one. Verdi's nationalistic outlook encouraged him to take part in politics and during his late forties and early fifties he was actually a member of parliament. Dvořák, although equally devoted to his homeland, found relaxation in watching trains and breeding pigeons; had he lived beyond the age of sixty-two, he might in his declining years have become a regular contributor to popular journals such as the *Railway Magazine* and *The Racing Pigeon*.

Every musical genius, it may be presumed, is also a human being with human failings. Where Verdi and Dvořák differed from some other great composers was that for the most part they kept genius and humanity in separate compartments, so that the attributes of genius remained unhampered by human imperfections—or for the matter of that unsustained by human virtues. The music they wrote might be superb or at the opposite extreme it might barely pass muster; but its quality was no criterion of the mood in which they found themselves at the time of its creation. And indeed it was only rarely that they allowed personal feelings to be reflected even in its style or temper; when on top of the world they were as likely to produce music that was sombre as music that was joyous; when in the throes of depression (unless the depression were so extreme as to deter them from composition altogether) they were as likely to produce music that was cheerful as music that was gloomy.

It is not to be wondered at that such objectivity of approach became second nature to Verdi in his specialization on opera, where music has no lasting value unless attuned to the plot and the stage-characters and the successive dramatic situations in which they find themselves. And although not all his biographers would agree with me, I maintain that Dvořák achieved the same detachment not only in his operas (which was to be expected) but also (except very occasionally) in his 'absolute' music—symphonies and string quartets and so forth. While it is proper to point out that his music, taken as a whole, derived much of its spontaneity from a normally uninhibited attitude towards psychological and philosophical problems (he was a spiritual descendant of Haydn), it would be inappropriate, in nine cases out of ten, to relate individual works to his humour of the moment, let alone discuss them in the high-flown phraseology to which some commentators have recourse when attempting to convey in words the emotional ebb and flow of masterpieces conceived or contrived by composers with a more complex personality. Antonín Dvořák was a straightforward chap who led a straightforward life and composed (mostly) straightforward music; I have therefore done my best to recount that life and describe that music in a straightforward manner.

'I do not write opera from a desire for glory,' Dvořák once affirmed, 'but because I consider it the most beneficial for the people.' This declaration provides a significant clue

to his outlook on music in general. Like Haydn and Verdi
—and also (coming down by no more than a peg or two)
like Sullivan—he provided music that was intended to
entertain rather than uplift; music that would appeal to
ordinary folk who sprang from origins as socially and intel-
lectually humble as his own. He was a practising democrat
—and therein lay his true worth. Yet the fact remains that
much of his music is unknown to the present-day counterparts of those for whose enjoyment it was primarily
designed: the devoted but not necessarily sophisticated
lovers óf music who nightly throng concert-halls and opera-
houses.

This book is therefore addressed not so much to professional musicians (among whom only very few could be
discovered whose enthusiasm for Dvořák falls far short of
my own) as to laymen in all walks of life who instinctively
appreciate good music but may have had no opportunity
to study more than the rudiments and little opportunity to
set their own value on Dvořák's outstanding contributions
to the art—with the exception of a handful of works which
are deservedly popular but not all of which are truly representative of his genius. I have therefore eschewed music-type
examples, and those who understandably wish to delve into
the aesthetics of Dvořák's music, or his technical methods,
should ferret out and examine for themselves any passages
to which specific attention is drawn in the text; many of the
published scores (although I am afraid not all) may quite
possibly be found on the music-shelves of the nearest public
library.

CZECH NAMES

When speaking or writing English it would be as ridicu-
lous to call Praha anything but Prague as it would be to call
Firenze anything but Florence. With this solitary exception

I have throughout used the Czech (Bohemian) names for towns and villages situated in Bohemia and indeed in the whole of what is today Czechoslovakia, but in many instances I have inserted in brackets the German names by whĭch they were more often known abroad during Dvořák's lifetime. On the same principle I have as a general rule adopted the Czech spellings of the names of men and women born in Bohemia, although at the risk of appearing inconsistent I have retained the more familiar German spellings for some comparatively well-known figures belonging to the eighteenth and early nineteenth centuries.

Czech operas, cantatas, symphonic poems, songs and so on, whether composed by Dvořák or anyone else, are named in both Czech and English on their first mention in the text; thereafter (and in the index of Dvořák's compositions) I have stuck to English. In the absence of published translations of Dvořák's operas (leaving aside a few detachable items), I have myself ventured here and there to render a line or two into our own language. In doing so I have sometimes found it desirable to give more consideration to the verbal context and the underlying rhythm of the melody than to the literal meaning of a short phrase as it stands.

A non-Slav can never hope to pronounce Czech names one-hundred-per-cent correctly, and indeed a conscientious attempt to do so might well result in a dislocated jaw. From an English standpoint the phonetic structure of Czech is almost as forbiddingly complicated as its grammar, but it may nevertheless be worth while to indicate a few peculiarities of pronunciation which can be recognizably reproduced by Anglo-Saxons in a relaxed manner of speech without undue facial distortions.

(1) There is *always* a stress on the first syllable: Smetana is *Smett*ana.

(2) Vowels are pronounced much as they would be in French, with an acute accent broadening the sound—except that an unaccented *a* is *very* short and approximates

to the *u* in 'but': thus for practical purposes Bratislava is
*Brutt*isluvva. (In the case of the Czech *u* a small circle—*ů*—
performs the same function as an acute accent.)

(3) The diphthong *ou* is sounded like the *oa* in 'moat', and
c without an accent like the *ts* in 'moats', so that Olomouc is
*Oll*omoats.

(4) The letter *j* (as in German) equals the English *y* in
'yard'; *č*—note the 'hook' accent—equals the *ch* in 'chat':
Janáček is therefore *Yunn*ahchek.

(5) When *s* and *z* have hook accents they become *sh* and
zh: Tomašek is *Tomm*ashek and Žak is Zhuk.

(6) When *r* has a hook accent it becomes *rzh* (or the *rge*
of 'bourgeois'), and Dvořák himself can safely be called
*D*vorzhahk (the *r* is slightly rolled)—although the initial *D*
should be so nearly elided that *V*orzhahk will do.

(7) When *e* has a hook accent it becomes the *ye* of 'yes',
and when *n* has one it becomes the *ny* of 'canyon': the
surname of Dvořák's maternal grandfather is written sometimes as Zdeněk and sometimes as Zdeňek; in either case
it is pronounced *Zden*yek.

(8) When an *l* or an *r* occurs as the *middle consonant of
three*, as in Vltava or Brno, the *first two* constitute a separate
syllable—V'l-tava, B'r-no; here the *V'l* and the *B'r* incorporate a vowel-sound as indeterminate as that in the *vel*
of 'travel' or the *ber* of 'barber', and since the first syllable
must be stressed we get something like *Vŏŏl*tava and
*Bŏŏr*no.

It should be added that in the Czech language ladies'
surnames, even those of foreign ladies, are accorded the
feminine suffix 'ová' (John Smith's wife Jane and daughter
Mary are Jane Smithová and Mary Smithová); that the
Czech name for Bohemia is Čechy (the *ch* being sounded as
in the Scottish 'loch'); and that the Czech name for Czechoslovakia is Československo (where besides the invariable
stress on the first syllable there is also a slight but perceptible
stress on the *slov*). Finally it must be pointed out that the

accepted English transliteration of Čech as Czech is logically indefensible, since such a conjunction of the letters c and z exists in neither language (although characteristic of Polish); however regretfully, one must in this instance bow to long-established orthographical convention.

CHAPTER TWO

Dvořák's Homeland

In a broadcast to the British nation on 27 September 1938, at a period of great tension between Nazi Germany and Czechoslovakia, our then Prime Minister described the Czechs as 'a people of whom we know nothing' and their land as 'a far-away country'. A month previously the man who was later to succeed him in that high office, and who had done his homework more thoroughly, had publicly declared that 'an attack [by Hitler] upon Czechoslovakia would be an outrage against the civilisation and freedom of the whole world'; he could have gone on to remind his listeners of some of the salient facts in the history of the country that had led to its becoming (in his own words) a 'faithful ally', and to point out that Prague, its capital, is not appreciably farther away from London than are the Shetland Isles, Copenhagen, Berlin, Milan, Marseilles—or Munich.

It is believed that the Czechs, a Slav race, originally moved west from the plains of Russia or Poland about A.D. 600. By 1938 we should all of us have known that since A.D. 900 they have been firmly settled in those regions of central Europe now known as Bohemia and Moravia. Hemmed in too closely for comfort on the south and west and north (but not on the east) by Germans, they themselves have always constituted a substantial and menacing Slav penetration into territory otherwise almost entirely German-speaking and German, or Austro-German, both in culture and (broadly) in political affiliation. A somewhat similar situation might have developed in England, fraught with equally embarrassing potentialities, had Pictish tribes from Scotland established themselves a thousand years ago as the permanent occupiers of Cumberland, Westmorland, Lancashire, Cheshire and north Staffordshire.

TOPOGRAPHY

Bohemia (and here I am using the term in its historical sense to cover *all* Czech districts) has no sea-coast—although Shakespeare accorded it one in *The Winter's Tale*—and its countryside, generally speaking, is undulating and fairly well-wooded. It is divided into Bohemia proper (to the west) and Moravia (to the east) by an upland slab which forms part of a European watershed and thereby ensures that most of Bohemia proper belongs to the basin of the Elbe (North Sea) and most of Moravia to the basin of the Danube (Black Sea). From the map on page 10 it will be seen that the river Vltava (at one time more familiarly known abroad by its German name of Moldau) rises in the extreme south of Bohemia near the Austrian border and joins the Elbe (locally called the Labe) about twenty-five miles north of Prague. Farther north still, their combined waters force a passage into what is now East Germany through a narrow gap in the otherwise continuous chain of mountains that forms a semi-circular physical barrier between Bohemia on the inside and the German lands of Bavaria and Saxony and Silesia on the outside. Here and there these mountains reach a height of some 5,000 feet above sea-level, and their scenery for the most part resembles that of the Vosges or the Jura. They provide a natural frontier—much as the Pennine Chain would have done in my hypothetical British parallel—and from time immemorial have nearly always embodied a political frontier as well. Non-Slavs are therefore logically entitled to call them the Böhmerwald (Bohemian Forest), Erzgebirge (Ore Mountains), Lausitzergebirge (Lusatian Mountains), Riesengebirge (Giant Mountains) and Adlergebirge (Eagle Mountains) rather than Šumava, Krušné hory, Lužické hory, Krkonoše and Orlické hory; the more so because many of the slopes *on the Bohemian side* have over

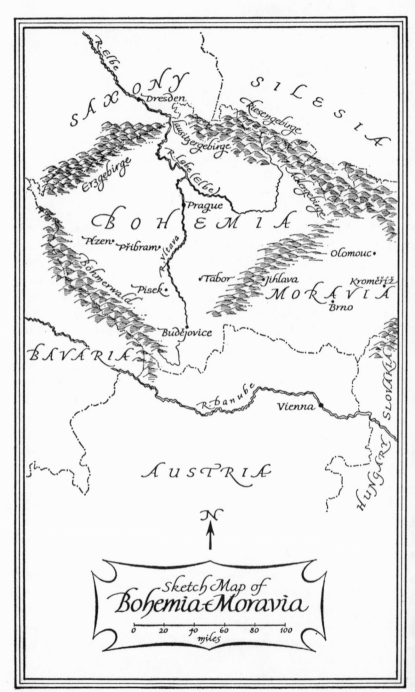

Sketch Map of
Bohemia & Moravia

0   20   40   60   80   100
miles

N

the centuries been populated not by descendants of the originally intruding Slavs but by descendants of a residue of Germanic tribes who stayed on there—in the same way that a residue of Anglo-Saxon tribes might have stayed on in east Lancashire or in the Eden valley district of Cumberland.

(In 1938 Adolf Hitler, who didn't really care two hoots about the welfare of the 'Sudeten Germans', contentedly enough ensconced in the Bohemian foothills of the Lausitzergebirge and the Riesengebirge, incited German irredentism among them so that he could use them as pawns in the opening gambit of a nefarious game of chess in which he was soon to outwit his joint-opponents Neville Chamberlain and Édouard Daladier—not having yet come up against Winston Churchill or Stalin. More recently a communist Government in Prague has pursued a policy of bit-by-bit expulsion of Sudeten Germans to German soil, where they may be less likely to provide some future Hitler with a specious excuse for provoking another international 'incident'.)

In Moravia, too, there have always been pockets of hereditary Germans or Austrians, but instead of being concentrated round the fringes, as in Bohemia proper, they have contained themselves in isolated enclaves and have never hit world headlines. It is more to the point that Moravia belongs topographically to eastern rather than western Europe; nearly all its rivers are tributaries or sub-tributaries of the Danube (downstream from Vienna), but in its eastern corner lies the source of the river Oder, which flows north into Silesia and eventually reaches the Baltic.

From the Jablonica (Jablunka) Pass, near the Silesian border, which marks the western extremity of the main range of the Carpathian Mountains, a lower range of hills —sometimes called the White Carpathians—extends southwestwards towards the Danube valley and separates Moravia to the west from Slovakia to the east. The Slovaks are racially allied with the Czechs and speak a dialect of the same language, so that there were sound ethnographical and etymological as well as political reasons for the incorporation of their homeland (previously part of Hungary) in the Republic of Czechoslovakia that came into being on the collapse of the Austro-Hungarian Empire in 1918 at the end of the First World War. But since most of the region had comparatively poor communications with the west—there was only one main-line railway link with Moravia as against five with the 'Great Hungarian Plain', for which Slovakia serves, geographically, as a northern buttress—one feels that possibly the long-term *economic* consequences of the arrangement were not fully taken into account by the treaty-makers. Be that as it may, and however much one may feel tempted to enlarge upon Slovakia's scenic attractions (which are not unlike those of inland Wales, although more varied), the fact remains that prior to 1918—that is to say until fourteen years after Dvořák's death—its associations lay not so much with Bohemia as with Hungary. The treatment meted out to the natives by their Magyar overlords was not noticeably sympathetic—but that is another story: the Slovaks cannot be allowed to trespass further on our present context; we must get back to Dvořák's own people, the Czechs.

EARLY HISTORY

The first Prince of Bohemia was a young man called Wenceslas (of which the Czech equivalent is Václav), who was born in the year 907. His name is known to millions of people who have not the slightest idea who he was or what he did or when and where he lived. 'Good King Wenceslas' was presumably 'good' since he was subsequently canonized, but he was never actually a 'king', and his reign as a prince, even, was very short: at the age of twenty-two (long before he had a chance to become the benign figure sometimes represented on Christmas cards) he was murdered by a jealous brother. Nevertheless, he was posthumously awarded a symbolical crown, and across the centuries Czech patriots, in moments of emotional fervour, have made frequent reference to 'the Lands of the Crown of Saint Wenceslas'.

During the latter part of the Middle Ages, Bohemia (again using the term in its wider connotation) survived as one of several semi-independent states in the loose and catalyctic but powerful federation known as the Holy Roman Empire, of which it was a constituent 'kingdom', with Prague as its capital city. Its most notable figure of those days was Jan Hus, who like our own John Wyclif (a fairly close contemporary) planted many of the seeds from which the Reformation was later to spring. He was burnt at the stake for heresy in 1415, but his influence did not die with him, and in due course his countrymen proved themselves equally receptive to the teachings of Martin Luther and John Calvin. Indeed it was as much a religious as a political dispute between Austria (predominantly Catholic) and Bohemia (predominantly Protestant) that led to fighting between the two countries in the early stages of the Thirty Years War (which eventually involved, for different reasons, a much wider area of Europe). Unfortunately for the Czechs, they suffered a heavy military defeat in the Battle of the White Mountain (at the gates of Prague) in 1620, and thereafter their country found itself struck off the map as a political entity. (Two of the minor curiosities of European history are that Anne, daughter of King Charles of Bohemia, married King Richard II of England, and that the last Queen of independent Bohemia was Elizabeth, daughter of England's reigning monarch King James I. Evidently Prague was not so 'far-away' in the fourteenth and seventeenth centuries as it was in the early twentieth.)

AN AGE OF OPPRESSION

For the next one hundred and eighty-five years a succession of Holy Roman Emperors, all but one of whom belonged to the Habsburg dynasty, made it their policy to hold the Czechs in utter subjugation. For a start, any member of the Bohemian aristocracy lucky enough to escape execution after the Battle of the White Mountain had his property confiscated, the big estates being handed over to noblemen (or in some cases to jumped-up adventurers) who hailed from Bavaria, Austria or Hungary. The populace was deprived of every form of civil right. The use of the Czech language for official purposes was banned. Leading Protestants were drastically persecuted, and education, in religion and everything else, was entrusted to imported Jesuit priests who performed their task conscientiously and largely succeeded in stamping out—or at any rate driving underground—the heretical notions of Hus and Luther and Calvin. So far as the vast majority of its inhabitants was concerned, the land of Wenceslas soon became—and long remained—a land of hard-done-by peasants. Even an Edict of Toleration, which was published in 1781 by the comparatively enlightened Emperor Josef II and nominally abolished serfdom, improved their lot only marginally, although restrictions on the use of the Czech language were thereafter somewhat relaxed.

As a matter of administrative convenience Prague all along served as the headquarters of a 'provincial district' of the Empire, but its cultural life during this period was almost exclusively Austro-German at second hand. This is a point one should always bear in mind when reading of visits to Prague by internationally-known musicians. Although the first performance of Mozart's *Don Giovanni* took place in their own capital (in 1787), there can have been very few genuine Czechs present on that occasion: the gilded audience was largely composed of a bevy of Austrian and Bavarian notabilities, together with a sprinkling of German-speaking bureaucrats.

Meanwhile, during this dark age in their country's history, nearly all Bohemian-born composers (among those whose names are remembered) left their native land at the earliest opportunity and spent their working lives elsewhere. Heinrich von Biber found a niche in Salzburg and J. D. Zelenka in Dresden. František Benda plumped for Prussia and his brother Jiři for Thuringia, while F. X. Richter and Jan Stamitz travelled farther afield to establish the 'Mannheim school' of symphonists. Vienna gave hospitality to J. B. Vanhall, F. L. Gassmann, Leopold Koželuh, Paul Vranický, Benedict Žak and Anton Kraft (who is credited by some authorities with a cello concerto normally attributed to Haydn). Josef Mysliveček went to Italy (where his name was pronounced Venatorini). Josef Kohout and J. B. Krumpholz settled in Paris. J. L. Dussek—more correctly Dušík—and Adalbert Gyrowetz roamed all over the place. A Czech word of praise (perhaps *blahopřáni* would be appropriate) is therefore due to Josef Seegr (1716–1782) and F. X. Brixi (1732–1771), who stuck things out at home. Like most of the others they were Jesuit-trained, and both earned their livings as organists. Their compositions, mainly though not exclusively concerned with church ritual, rarely amounted to much more than a mixture of Haydn and water—but that was a great deal better than nothing.

It should be stressed at this juncture that in their schools and colleges the Jesuit mentors, to their credit, maintained a high level of general education by contemporary standards, not least in music. That distinguished historian of the art, Charles Burney (1726–1814), a penetratingly observant traveller, discovered this for himself when he visited Bohemia in September 1772. In one village he 'went into the school, which was full of little children of both sexes from six to ten or eleven years old, who were reading, writing, playing on violins, hautbois, bassoons, and [there were] four clavichords, with little boys practising on them all.' (The overall sound-effect must have been very similar to that which assails one's ears in a corridor of the Royal College of Music when doors have inadvertently been left ajar.)

While Burney was having dinner at an inn one evening, he was entertained by a passing band of itinerant musicians playing conventional dance tunes, but 'the performance of them added little to the beauty of the compositions'. (When in July 1931 I paid my first visit to Czechoslovakia in the congenial company of the late Leslie Heward, who had recently been appointed conductor of the City of Birmingham Orchestra, we had a similar experience while partaking of a snack lunch at a roadside pub a few miles south of Prague; the 'band' comprised two clarinettists, who tootled something very much like the opening passage of Dvořák's symphony in F major. They were rewarded with a glass apiece of *pivo*, the excellent beer for which Bohemia is famous; one likes to think that Burney's serenaders, although more numerous, were treated more handsomely.)

After making further inquiries of Seegr and others Burney was driven to conclude that in Bohemia 'those among the poorer classes, who are taught music in their infancy, have no occasion to pursue it in riper years, and seldom advance further than to qualify themselves for the street, or for servitude.' He went on to explain that 'many of those who learn music at school go afterwards to the plough, and to other laborious employments; and then their knowledge of music turns to no other account than to enable them to sing in their parish-church, and as an innocent domestic recreation.' One regrets that apparently he was never present at village merry-making on a feast-day. On such occasions the humble peasants were not discouraged from performing their traditional folk-songs and dances; their polkas and skočnás and furiants incorporated melodic and rhythmic characteristics very different from the formal lilts to which Burney was accustomed, and it would have been interesting to know what he thought about them.

SIGNS OF NATIONAL RESURGENCE

The political structure of Europe underwent a series of upheavals during the twenty-five years of almost continuous and widespread military strife (the 'Napoleonic wars') that followed the internationally provocative French Revolution (1789) and the subsequent establishment in France of the 'First Republic' and, later, the 'First Empire'. A particularly decisive date for central Europe was 2 December 1805, when the mercenary troops of the Holy Roman Emperor Franz II were decisively defeated by the mercenary troops of the (unholy) French Emperor Napoleon I—by then well on his way to becoming master of Europe —in a battle which raged round the Moravian village of Slavkov, seven miles south-east of Brno (Brunn) and six hundred and fifty miles due east of Paris. (Slavkov is better know to historians as Austerlitz.) By the subsequent Treaty of Pressburg (Pressburg being the German name for Bratislava) the Holy Roman Empire was dissolved, and Franz II found himself reduced to the level of a mere king; he was reluctant to relinquish his title, however, and insisted on still being called an emperor, albeit only Emperor of Austria.

His troubles were not yet over: French troops occupied Vienna in 1809, and the tide did not turn irrevocably against Napoleon until 1815, when (ten miles south of Brussels and thanks to the English and the Prussians) he became the first man in history to meet his Waterloo—a name afterwards immortalized (like Austerlitz) in the railway world. At the Congress of Vienna later in the same year, it was recognized and confirmed that the territories over which the Habsburgs would henceforth hold sway, although considerably less extensive than those of the now defunct Holy Roman Empire (which in its heyday had stretched from the North Sea and the Baltic to Naples), nevertheless included Austria proper, the Czech homelands of Bohemia and Moravia, Galicia (a sizable chunk of historic Poland with a population partly Russian), and a more southerly district where it did not matter that the inhabitants were Italians or Slovenes so long as it afforded Vienna the valuable commercial asset of access to the sea at the Adriatic port of Trieste.

Conscripted to fight in wars which ravaged Bohemia as thoroughly as anywhere else but were unlikely, whatever their outcome, to result in any betterment of the conditions under which the common people had to live, even in peacetime, many Czechs had meanwhile become restive. The initial success in 1789 of the formerly downtrodden French masses provided an impetus and aroused aspirations, but the Czechs, relatively few in numbers and effectively held in thrall, found no leader strong enough to overcome the almost insuperable difficulties of organizing a political revolt. Round the turn of the century, however, there were signs of a revival of their *cultural* ideals, led in the first instance by the writer and lecturer Josef Dobrovský (1753–1829) and in another field by Václav Tomašek (1774–1850), an excellent all-round musician. Their hard road ahead became less uphill after 1809, when the Emperor's new Foreign Minister, Prince Metternich (1773–1859), in pursuance of his policy of strong opposition to German—as distinct from Austrian—nationalism, began to encourage the budding cultural revival in Bohemia in the hope that it would help to keep the Czechs tolerably quiet under Austrian rule.

And so it came about that from 1811 onwards Prague had its own Conservatoire of Music; that in 1823 a Viennese *Singspiel* (operetta) was played in Prague's 'German

Provincial Theatre' in a Czech translation—a revolutionary innovation; that in 1826 there was the first-ever production of a Czech opera, *Drátenik* (*The Tinker*), by František Škroup (1801–1862). Škroup followed up with half a dozen more in as many years, but apart from their libretti they held no specifically Bohemian characteristics, and although he wrote the tune later used for the national anthem of Czechoslovakia he was neither sufficiently accomplished as a composer nor sufficiently whole-hearted as a nationalist to encourage others to follow in his footsteps. None the less, *The Tinker* provided a significant signpost for Bedřich Smetana, two years old at the time, who was destined to become the first musician of his race ever to aspire to greatness. (I shall have plenty to say about Smetana later on.)

THE REVOLUTIONS OF 1848

Presently Czech nationalists found two inspiring *political* champions—František Palacký (1798–1876) and František Rieger (1818–1903). Palacký, having spent much of his early life abroad, was both more cosmopolitan in his outlook and more diplomatic in his dealings with authority than were some of his equally enthusiastic but less tactful colleagues; this was a good thing, since it assured him, to a certain extent, of the favour of Metternich. He said comparatively little about 'the Lands of the Crown of Saint Wenceslas'; for the moment what he strove for, though vainly, was the conversion of the Austrian Empire into a federation: not a federation like the Holy Roman Empire in which there had been one master-race and several subject-races, but one in which Germans and Slavs would share absolute equality. Alternatively he looked forward to some form of Slav union, embracing not only the Czechs and Slovaks but also the Serbs and Croats (who inhabited districts south of the Danube in what is today Yugoslavia) and possibly the Poles. Early in 1848, however, revolutions more violent in character than any that either Palacký or Rieger had in mind broke out first in France and then, a month later, in Austria—which was soon in a state of complete turmoil.

There is no need to recount here the confused course of the events that followed one another thick and fast during that momentous year; we are concerned only with their outcome in so far as the Czechs were affected. Those unhappy people came no nearer to regaining their independence (they had to wait another seventy years for that), since a local rebellion of their own, in June, was nipped in the bud by swift action on the part of Austrian troops. This attempt on the part of the Czechs to seize the initiative may have been morally justified, but was too hastily conceived and too badly organized to have any hope of success. Furthermore, it was ill-timed from a psychological point of view: imbued as they were with patriotic fervour and influenced as they were by Palacký's pan-Slav propaganda, the Czech insurgents failed to realize that racial irredentism was not strictly relevant to the revolutionary movements then sweeping Europe, which in their most significant aspects represented not so much an uprising of nationalists against imperial or monarchical autocracy as an uprising of proletarians against patrician autocracy. (It was in Vienna itself that some of the heaviest street-fighting took place.)

In Austria the proletariat did eventually score a notable short-term victory for democracy: a Constituent Assembly (parliament) was convened, which almost immediately passed an Act of Emancipation granting equal civil rights to all within the Empire, regardless of rank, and a measure of official status to the 'minority languages'—which included Czech. The news reached Prague on 8 September 1848; not many miles away Antonín Dvořák was celebrating his seventh birthday.

CHAPTER THREE

Childhood and Student Days

Even to this day many innkeepers in the rural districts of northern Italy resemble Giuseppe Verdi's father in that they sell not only wine (for consumption on or off the premises) but also groceries and other comestibles. The 'osteria ed alimentari' has its counterpart elsewhere in central Europe: anyone who keeps his eyes open while motoring through southern Germany or German-speaking Switzerland can hardly fail to notice that in many villages the compound word 'Gasthaus-Metzgerei' is painted in large letters on at least one house-front, indicating that the establishment combines the functions of inn and butcher's shop. During the nineteenth century the same sign was equally in evidence throughout Bohemia, where German was the official language. (Nowadays one has to look for a 'hostinec a řeznický'.)

A visitor to northern Bohemia during the late autumn of 1840 who happened to light on the *Gasthaus-Metzgerei* at the village then called Mühlhausen, whether in search of a glass of beer or a joint of meat, would have been served by a good-looking and broad-shouldered fellow of twenty-six named František Dvořák or possibly by his twenty-year-old bride Anna. (They had been married on 17 November.) A chance traveller who turned up there on the evening of 8 September 1841 might have had his fill of good beer and good meat—and good cheer and good company—free of charge, for Anna had that day provided František with a son and heir, shortly to be christened Antonín, and all and sundry were invited to celebrate the happy event in the traditional Bohemian manner with drinking, feasting, music and dancing. (There had been one slight hitch in the proceedings: a small fire had broken out in the inn about an hour after Antonín's birth, and he and his mother had had to be hurriedly evacuated to a cottage on the other side of the road. Fortunately the fire was soon extinguished and the contretemps was not allowed to interfere in any way with the evening's rejoicings.)

Until 1620 this village had been known as Nelahozeves, and so it has been known ever since 1918, when, after three hundred years of Habsburg domination, arbitrarily imposed German place-names such as Mühlhausen were thrust into deserved obscurity—except on maps and in travel-literature published in Germany or in what remained of once-proud Austria. Overlooked by an ugly but imposing eighteenth-century castle, Nelahozeves lies on the left bank of the Vltava about eighteen miles north and downstream from Prague, close to the point where the river is crossed by the main Prague–Dresden highway (today Trunk Road no. 8). Being itself just off the main road, the village still retains, superficially at any rate, some sleepy backwater character-istics that seem to belong to a bygone age, despite the nearby encroachment of the industrialism upon which the rulers of present-day Czechoslovakia are endeavouring to build and maintain their country's economic prosperity.

Although as the years went by Antonín Dvořák was to have occasional disagreements with them, he would have been the first to admit that he was fortunate in his parents. His father František came of sturdy peasant stock, *his* father having been imbued with a spirit of enterprise that eventu-ally enabled him to raise his status from that of farm labourer to that of innkeeper; František himself, by the time he reached his middle twenties, had proved himself fully capable of taking over the job. It remains to be added that like many others among his countrymen he had an instinctive love for music, which in his case evinced itself in the enthusiasm with which he played polkas on the violin and sang folk-songs in a robust baritone to his own accompaniment on the zither, an instrument which superficially resembled the guitar but had about thirty strings rather than six. (The names of both instruments derive from the κιθατα of ancient Greece.)

Antonín's mother was of no less humble origin, but she had spent her girlhood in more dignified surroundings: her father Josef Zdeněk, although born into the peasantry, rose to become bailiff to Prince Lobkowitz at the local castle. Now Lobkowitz is a name that crops up as frequently in musical biographies as does that of Esterházy. One member of the Esterházy clan was Haydn's patron for nearly thirty years and gave him the opportunity to demonstrate his genius; another engaged the nineteen-year-old Schubert to teach music to his children; a third at one time had Liszt's parents on his pay-roll. Turning to the Lobkowitzes, we find that one prince employed Gluck's father as head-forester and that another contributed towards an annuity for Beethoven. The latest in line of succession owned most of the wide area of Bohemian countryside that came under the local government jurisdiction of what might be called the Slány (Schlan) Rural District Council, in which Nelahozeves was situated and of which the town of Slány (marked on all large-scale maps) was the administrative centre. Prince Lobkowitz rarely came to stay at Nelahozeves (which was only one of his many stately homes) and between-whiles Josef Zdeněk was a faithful steward of his interests. Anna herself grew up to be a woman with no nonsense about her. In adolescence she knew her place as the daughter of a jumped-up peasant who had eventually become a salaried retainer of a feudal aristocrat. In youth and middle-age she knew her place as an innkeeper's wife. In due course she came to know her place as the mother of an illustrious composer. I never think of her without recalling a character in one of Aldous Huxley's stories. 'The core of her being remained solidly peasant; but the upper and conscious part of her mind was, so to speak, only loosely fastened to the foundation, so that it could turn freely this way or that, without strain or difficulty, according to changing circumstances.'

Ever since the virtual extinction of Protestantism in Bohemia during the seventeenth century the ancestors of both the Zdeněks and the Dvořáks had been pious Catholics; Anna and František carried on the family traditions, and their children (they had fourteen all told, of whom five boys and three girls survived infancy) were brought up in that faith. Like every other child born before the first Kindergarten was opened, they did not go to school until they were about seven years old: Antonín, their firstborn, began his formal education in 1848.

SCHOOL

The passing of the Act of Emancipation in September 1848 engendered bright hopes for the future of the Czech people, but in the event the Act had a short life and the bright hopes remained unfulfilled. The man primarily responsible for the volte-face was Metternich's successor as Foreign Minister, Count Felix Schwarzenberg (1800–1852), who prevailed upon the reigning Emperor Ferdinand (virtually an imbecile) to abdicate, replaced him with his young nephew Franz Josef (who was to occupy the throne for nearly seventy years) and inaugurated military countermeasures against the numerous but ill-organized supporters of democracy. The details need not be recounted here; suffice to record that Schwarzenberg quickly achieved his main objective: the restoration of the *status quo ante* throughout the Austrian dominions. (Perhaps it should be mentioned, however, that the disunited Czechs played into his hands to a certain extent: the moderate pan-Slav Palacký group on the one hand and the more extreme nationalists on the other were at loggerheads amongst themselves.) What concerns us now—or, rather, what concerned Antonín Dvořák then—is that from 1849 onwards conditions once again prevailed in Bohemia in which any Czech youngster who wished to raise himself above the level of a manual labourer had to speak and understand German at least sufficiently well to be able to carry on a normal conversation in that language.

Thanks to Charles Burney we know that in rural Bohemia primary education had for long been as much concerned with music as with reading and writing and arithmetic. More often than not the village schoolmaster was incidentally the village organist—although when speaking of a country in which music meant so much one should perhaps put it the other way round and say that more often than not the village organist was incidentally the village school-master. He might sometimes be a man of good general education who took up organ-playing in order to qualify for a regular job, but he was more likely to be a musician with just sufficient command of the three R's to be entrusted with the task of inculcating them to eight-year-olds.

Josef Spic, organist and schoolmaster at Nelahozeves during the eighteen-forties and eighteen-fifties, belonged to the latter category. He endeared himself to the villagers not only as a competent organist but also as a spirited feast-day entertainer on violin, oboe, trumpet and zither, but how far his scholastic attainments matched his musical prowess one cannot tell: any records he may have kept of his own or his pupils' proficiency in Latin or German or mathematics went up in smoke when fire destroyed the schoolhouse some forty years later. One is left with no reliable evidence even as to how long Dvořák was a pupil at Spic's school, but it was certainly for more than the bare minimum of two years' compulsory education upon which the Austrian Government insisted.

The easy-going Spic was content to develop the musical

ability which Antonín had inherited from his father, and failed to instil any worth while knowledge of that most essential of all subjects—German. So when the summer of 1853 came round Antonín's parents decided to send him to live with a childless aunt and uncle (Anna's brother Antonín Zdeněk) at Zlonice (Zlonitz), a small town in the centre of a coal-mining district about fifteen miles away to the west, where the headmaster of the local school, Antonín Liehmann (1808–1879), although a Czech, had the reputation of being both a fine German scholar and a strict disciplinarian.

Anna's and František's expectations of Liehmann were not from their point of view fully realized. He was bilingual in Czech and German, but his main interest in life (like Spic's) was music. He did not spare the rod, but at the age of forty-five was far from being a crotchety old pedagogue and was quite prepared to spoil the child in whom he could detect signs of genuine musical talent. He was so well satisfied with his new pupil's rapid progress on the organ, piano, violin and viola that he soon encouraged him to study harmony and counterpoint as well—to the inevitable neglect, once again, of his German. At Zlonice Antonín's twelve-year-old eyes were opened to a new world, and he decided in his own mind that for him there could be only one future career—that of professional musician.

But he was soon to be driven out of a delightful cloud-cuckoo land in which stuffy textbooks on German grammar and syntax could lie neglected. In the autumn of 1854, little more than a year after he had sent his eldest son there, František Dvořák himself moved house to Zlonice: his brother-in-law, Antonín's temporary guardian, had suggested that he could make higher profits as the proprietor of a *Gasthaus-Metzgerei* in an up-and-coming industrial town than as the proprietor of a *Gasthaus-Metzgerei* in an off-the-beaten-track village. No sooner had the Dvořáks settled in their new home than František discovered that Antonín's command of German was hardly any greater than it had been when he left Nelahozeves. Being a sincere chap who always did his best, according to his lights, on behalf of his children, he came to the conclusion that in the circumstances he had better pack Antonín off to some German-speaking district of Bohemia where a deaf ear would be turned to him if he persisted in talking Czech.

The place eventually chosen was Česká Kamenice (Böhmische Kamnitz), a small Sudeten town lying fifty miles due north of Prague and in the foothills of the Lausitzergebirge (see map on page 10). Antonín's host was a miller named Ohm. Probably he had been a regular customer of František Dvořák at Nelahozeves when taking sacks of flour from Kamenice to Prague; the two families would at any rate seem to have been on terms of acquaintance, since the Dvořáks simultaneously extended exchange hospitality to one of Ohm's sons. It is not clear in what way Ohm expected *his* young hopeful to benefit from residence at Zlonice; perhaps the lad had ambitions to become a licensed victualler and František undertook to teach him how to serve beer and slice carcasses.

WIDENING HORIZONS

Dvořák all his life regarded German as an alien tongue forced upon the Czechs by an overbearing master-race. But at Kamenice, while still in his early teens, he found that the only alternative to speaking German was to relapse into utter torpitude. To relapse into utter torpitude was foreign to his temperament, and he soon came to recognize the truth of the old adage that needs must when the devil drives; perhaps to realize, too, that any hopes he might cherish of making a permanent mark in the world of music were doomed from the start unless he could converse in German with those who were in a position to further his prospects. So he promptly buckled down to acquire rather more than the rudiments of the language, and his first tangible reward came when he made sufficient progress to win the favour of Franz Hancke, the local choirmaster, who thereafter from time to time allowed him to deputize for him. Antonín welcomed this opportunity to try his hand at training and conducting a church choir—singing in German —which indeed provided valuable experience for him.

While Antonín was faring reasonably well at Kamenice, his family was not prospering at Zlonice, and František was beginning to wonder whether after all he had been wise to leave Nelahozeves, where although he had not made a fortune he had had a monopoly of the local clientèle, such as it was, and had never run into financial difficulties. At Zlonice, the landlord whom he had displaced immediately opened another pub in opposition, and being a popular character in the neighbourhood contrived to attract thereto the bulk of the custom upon which František was relying. Within a year or so he found himself unable to balance his budget; since the establishment was a comparatively large one he was obliged to employ an assistant, and now that he could no longer afford to pay wages there was only one thing for it: Antonín must come home and help in the shop.

And help in the shop is just what Antonín did during most of the next two years, but he was now once more within the sphere of influence of the admirable Liehmann, who arranged whenever possible for him to visit nearby villages on feast days to play the organ in church and the violin in the streets. On these occasions young Dvořák may now and again have slipped in a composition or two of his own: apparently nobody else would tackle them, not even Liehmann himself, because they were too difficult! Meanwhile Liehmann went on teaching him all that he himself knew about music (and since he was a composer in his own right that was quite a lot) and eventually persuaded the reluctant František that his first-born's talents were being wasted at Zlonice. So not long after his sixteenth birthday, with a small financial allowance from his kindly-disposed uncle and the rather grudging consent of his parents (let it not be forgotten that they *did* consent) Antonín Dvořák begged a lift on a neighbour's hay-cart and made his way to Prague to become a full-time student of music.

During his first two years there, Antonín paid a small sum for board and lodging to Jan Plevý, a cousin-by-marriage of his father, who was a tailor by profession, and he lived with his family in what is now Husova (Hus Street). He enrolled not at the Conservatoire (which as already noted had been founded in 1811) but at the Organ School —which had been founded in 1830 by the rather grandiloquently-named Association for the Improvement of Church Music in Bohemia. This decision was taken on Liehmann's advice: he thought the Organ School more likely to provide good training in all-round musicianship than the Conservatoire, which at the time concentrated mainly on turning out singers and virtuoso instrumentalists. (Thirty-two years later the two institutions were merged into one.)

The director of the Organ School was a German, Karl Pitsch (1786–1858), who was a great admirer of Handel and Bach and conservative enough to insist that so far as theory went all instruction should be based on strictly classical models. He seems to have been an aloof character who maintained little contact with the *alumni*, and for practical purposes the furtherance of Dvořák's studies was the responsibility of three professors who were all Czech by birth: he was taught the organ by Josef Förster (1833–1907), singing by Josef Zvonař (1824–1865), harmony and counterpoint by František Blažek (1815–1900).

When Dvořák had been at the Organ School for about a year Pitsch died; he was succeeded as director by Josef Krejčí (1821–1881), who at the age of thirty-seven was unusually young to be appointed to such an important post, He was a short-tempered fellow and unpopular with the students, but although (despite being a Czech) he regarded German music as the only music worthy of the name he did at least use a new broom to sweep away some of the dead wood left by his predecessor: he brought the curriculum fairly well up-to-date and tried to take a personal interest in those with whose welfare he was entrusted. (Perhaps that was one reason why he was unpopular with them!) Krejcí evidently thought highly of Dvořák, since he gave him private lessons; and although Dvořák did not cotton on to him either as a man or a teacher he must have been gratified when in August 1859 he was presented by him with a 'leaving certificate' testifying that he was now fully competent to perform the duties of organist and choirmaster.

There were other ideas at the back of his mind, however. Being able to play both violin and viola reasonably well, he had joined an amateur orchestra, sponsored by the 'Saint Cecilia Society', which rehearsed nearly every evening and gave regular public concerts under the baton of Antonín Apt (1815–1887), a conductor whose taste in music was considerably more catholic than that of either Pitsch or Krejcí; indeed he specialized on Schumann, Liszt and Wagner. Dvořák had shared a desk in this orchestra with Adolf Čech (1842–1903), who was himself to become a conductor and whom we shall meet in later chapters. With this experience behind him he decided that for the time being he would forget about organs and choirs—and *scrape* for a living.

Meanwhile, his father had left Zlonice, and early in 1860 took over the management of a *Gasthaus-Metzgerei* at the small town of Kladno. This lies only twelve miles west of Prague, so that Antonín was able to slip off and spend an occasional week-end with his parents.

CHAPTER FOUR

Ten Years of Struggle

If Dvořák had been fortunate in his parents he was not less so in his aunts and uncles. The financial assistance of Antonín Zdeněk had enabled him to come to Prague in the first place; when he left the Organ School in the summer of 1859 and that allowance ceased, a married sister of his father, Josefa Dušková, came forward with an offer, eagerly accepted, of free hospitality (which, however, did not include lunch or dinner except on special family occasions) at her home near the city centre in the large open square known today as Karlovo Náměsti (Charles Square). There was no piano in the flat, but Dvořák had become friendly with Karel Bendl (1838–1897), a young man in comparatively easy circumstances and already beginning to make his mark as a conductor and composer, who allowed him to use *his* piano and also lent him a pile of musical scores.

It was not long before Dvořák secured a regular job as viola-player in a small professional orchestra directed by Karel Komzák (1823–1893), popular figure in Prague. His orchestra was engaged to play in turn at all the larger restaurants and beer-gardens of the city, and its repertory consisted mainly of dance music and 'gems from the operas' —operas which as likely as not had been composed by Mozart, Rossini, Verdi (up to and including *Rigoletto*), or even Wagner (up to and including *Lohengrin*). Dvořák's salary was meagre: he could buy only the bare necessities of life and even had he wished to do so could not afford to indulge in any form of youthful extravagance. Komzák rehearsals in the morning; lunch at some cheap café; the studying of scores (borrowed from Bendl) in the afternoon; Komzák 'concerts' in the evening and meanwhile a snatched bite of food; then back to aunt Josefa and uncle Václav for bed and breakfast: this was his normal daily routine for the next three years.

They were three years during which the Czechs, for perhaps the first time in their history, derived indirect benefit from a war which did not directly concern them—a war between Austria and Italy. In 1860, after several years of *risorgimento*, the Italians, led by Count Cavour (1810–1861) and taking full advantage of political dissensions between the French and the Austrians (who had long regarded themselves as joint-trustees for Piedmont and Lombardy and Venetia) secured the 'unification' of their country. In a short but conclusive campaign, Austrian troops had proved themselves no match for their southern neighbours; at the subsequent Truce of Villafranca, Emperor Franz Josef was compelled to cede to Italy some—though not all—of the Italian territory over which he had never had any moral right to rule. Following this set-back to imperial ambitions there was a swift reappraisal in Vienna of the situation *north* of the Danube, where Prussian nationalism (soon to be personified by Otto von Bismarck) was beginning to rear its sinister head, and it was decided that it would be expedient, in order to avoid future trouble in that quarter, to propitiate Bohemia in advance by relaxing restrictions on pro-Slav activities and admitting Czech delegates to the Imperial Council. Not since the days of the short-lived Constituent Assembly of 1848 had the Czechs been allowed any say in the government of the empire of which their homeland was a constituent part.

These political developments gave an impetus to those who were striving to revive the *cultural* glories of ancient Bohemia ('the Lands of the Crown of Saint Wenceslas'). In 1861 the Hlahol Choral Society was founded in Prague by Dvořák's singing-teacher Josef Zvonař. ('Hlahol' is a Czech word meaning a clanging sound.) In 1862 a 'Czech National Theatre' was inaugurated; previously there had only been a

'German Provincial Theatre'. For the moment an edifice truly worthy of Bohemian dramatic and operatic aspirations remained a pipe-dream, but meanwhile plays and operas were staged at a 'Provisional (or Interim) Theatre'. (Any reference to the National Theatre in this and the next few chapters must therefore be taken to apply to the National Theatre *organization*, temporarily housed in the Provisional Theatre *building*.) When it came to finding a resident orchestra the management asked the well-established Karel Komzák to provide the nucleus: Dvořák thus found himself, *ipso facto*, in the orchestral pit of the National Theatre from the word go; he was to stay there for eleven years. His earnings immediately received a modest but welcome boost: although there were rehearsals on most mornings, operas or plays with music were given on only three or four evenings a week, and at other times members of the orchestra were free to accept outside engagements in restaurants or beer-gardens or anywhere else. From time to time, too, the orchestras of the Czech National Theatre and the German Provincial Theatre forgot political differences and joined forces to give 'Philharmonic' concerts.

EARLY COMPOSITIONS

The opus-numbering of Dvořák's early works (and indeed of some of his later ones, too) is chaotic: some bear no opus number at all; others bear two or three different ones; now and again the same opus number is applied to two or three different works. This was far from the composer's original intention: from the age of nineteen he punctiliously headed each successive composition op. 1, op. 2, etc. If on completion he decided, however, that it was unworthy of him, he threw it aside with no expectation that it would ever be picked up—and used the same opus number over again; but since sometimes he subsequently retrieved a discarded work and revised it he soon got into a tangle with his numbering, losing count of what was worth keeping for its own sake and what was worth revising and what wasn't worth keeping at all. Furthermore, when many years later some of his comparatively youthful compositions were printed for the first time, their publisher took it upon himself to accord them new opus numbers that were relevant solely to the date of publication: a work originally inscribed as op. 18, for instance, eventually appeared in print as op. 77. Throughout this book Dvořák's works will generally speaking be discussed in what so far as I have been able to ascertain was their order of composition; I shall often have occasion to refer to them by recognized opus numbers as a means of identification, but I hope I have made it clear that in some cases these may not hold much chronological significance.

Every biographer of Dvořák and indeed every lover of his music owes a deep debt of gratitude to his compatriot and champion Otakar Šourek (1883–1956), who did all that any man could do to spread abroad the gospel of his greatness. Yet not even the painstaking Šourek succeeded in unearthing, in its entirety, any composition that is known for certain to belong to Dvořák's childhood or student days. A quintet in A minor for two violins and two violas and cello, dated 18 June 1861, ranks as the earliest of several 'ops. 1'; it comprises three very long movements, each of which suffers from lack of variety in the thematic material. The original 'op. 2' was a string quartet (two violins, viola, cello) in A major, composed in March of the following year (1862) while he was awaiting call-up to serve his term as a conscript in the Austrian army. (It is a curious fact that in the event this apparently healthy young man was rejected by the military authorities on medical grounds.) This quartet, like the quintet which preceded it, was of inordinate length, but showed slightly more initiative: although the first movement derived from Haydn and the second was an immature attempt to emulate middle-period Beethoven, one can perceive in the third and fourth occasional quirks of melody and rhythm that foreshadowed, if only to a tiny degree, what the future held in store.

As time went on Dvořák began to find life with the Dušíks somewhat frustrating. His kind aunt and uncle (with young sons and daughters of their own) were a very religious and highly respectable couple who expected him to keep as regular home-hours as his duties at the theatre or elsewhere would permit, but being a normal twenty-three-year-old he preferred to spend at least *some* leisure moments in the more congenial company of his like-minded contemporaries; moreover, in the absence of a piano (and he couldn't always be dashing off to beg permission to play on Bendl's) he was finding it difficult to concentrate as much as he hoped to on composition. So from November 1864 onwards he agreed to share the modest rent of a flat in the Žižkov district of Prague with five other men of about his own age. The milieu was probably not unlike that so vividly depicted by Puccini in the first and last acts of *La Bohème*, but at least there was a piano, and Dvořák was the only one of the six who was likely to want to use it regularly. One of his garret-companions was Mořic Anger (1844–1905), a first-violinist (and subsequently deputy-conductor) at the National Theatre; another was Karel Čech (1844–1913)—brother of Adolf Čech—who at the time was a medical student but later (spurred on, perhaps, by Dvořák and Anger) took up singing as a career and made quite a name for himself.

By now Dvořák had begun to augment his earnings by teaching, and before long he found himself emotionally involved with a young lady pupil—Josefa, daughter of Jan Čermák, a prosperous jeweller to whose family he gave piano lessons; she was barely sixteen years old at the time and his ardent pleadings made no noticeable impression. This apart, he was in a fairly contented frame of mind, since in due course, as he had hoped, the Anger–Čech ménage proved more conducive to creative work than had the Dušík household. During the two and a half years which had elapsed since the string quartet in A major, he had written nothing except a polka and a kvapík (galop) for piano (published together seventeen years later as op. 53 !) But as soon as 1865 was under way he got down to business. By March he had completed a symphony in C minor, a work of no more lasting consequence than Haydn's very first essays in the symphonic field but sufficiently formal and innocuous to disarm criticism. As an afterthought Dvořák added a title, *Zloniké zvony* (*The Bells of Zlonice*) and indeed this work can best be regarded as a tribute to his former preceptor Antonín Liehmann, who in Zlonice days had done so much to foster his talent and spur his ambition.

Dvořák followed up his first symphony with a 'concerto' for cello and piano in A major which, however, was lost to sight until sixty-four years later, when it was dug out of obscurity and 're-edited' and orchestrated by the German composer Günther Raphael (who was one year old at the date of Dvořák's death). The first movement of this Dvořák-Raphael collaboration is a haphazard affair mainly in march rhythm; the second depends almost entirely upon an extended *cantabile* melody for the soloist; the only feature of interest in the finale is the occasional clashing of a 3/4 rhythm against the prevailing 6/8.

Next came a song-cycle based on a collection of verses by Gustav Pfleger-Moravský (1833–1875) entitled *Cypřiše* (*The Cypresses*). The settings are presumed to have been instigated by their composer's passion for Josefa Čermáková, but no impact was made in that quarter and perhaps Dvořák never expected there to be: he dedicated the work not to Josefa but to his friend Karel Bendl (to whose music library he still had access). Of the eighteen songs of *The Cypresses* four were published in 1882 as another op. 2 and eight more in 1888 as op. 83, *Písně milostné* (*Love Songs*). Dvořák is said to have revised them before presenting them to the public, but on internal evidence the revision cannot have amounted to much: some of the piano accompaniments, in particular, are almost unbelievably perfunctory. All these songs are sentimental in character and several are reminiscent of Schumann, notably op. 83 no. 1, *Ó naší lásce nekvete to vytoužene štěstí* (*Never will love lead us to that glad goal*), which judged as a song rather than as representative Dvořák is the best by a long chalk.

His ambitions were evidently still largely concentrated on instrumental music however, for in August of the same year he embarked on a second symphony—in B flat major. Here he cast aside the acceptable Haydnesque conventionality of *The Bells of Zlonice*, apparently in order to give the impression that he was an angry young man—although he really had not much to be perturbed about except in his rôle of rejected suitor. This second symphony was disjointed in construction, and only in the slightly Schubertian third movement (*allegro con brio* in 3/4 time) can one detect any homogeneity of style. A shortened version of this work was played in Prague in 1888, but neither of Dvořák's first two symphonies was published during his lifetime, and in truth they can both be regarded as little more than academic curiosities.

In the autumn of that year (1865) Dvořák moved house again. One account says that his fellow-lodger Mořic Anger had objected to his monopolizing the piano at all hours of day and night. It is just as likely that Dvořák had after all found himself temperamentally unsuited to *la vie de Bohème* in a communal bedsitter. Whatever the reason or reasons for the flit, now that his teaching activities were bringing in sufficient revenue to enable him to hire a piano for his own exclusive use, he was content to eat humble pie and creep back, with a piano under his arm, to his Dušík aunt and uncle. He had to share a room with two other lodgers, however.

HARD WORK AND NOT MUCH TO SHOW FOR IT

In June 1866 Otto von Bismarck (1815–1898), the King of Prussia's 'iron chancellor', launched a morally unjustifiable but long-expected attack on Austria. (Morally unjustifiable because it was inspired by a lust for power: as Bismarck himself conceded, 'Prussian linen is not always of the cleanest'. Long-expected because Emperor Franz Josef's advisers had no illusions about Prussia's ultimate objective—the domination of central Europe.) Austrian troops, trained in old-fashioned methods of warfare, were unable to cope with an army most efficiently led by Count von Moltke (1800–1891), who had introduced modern weapons and made full use of recently-constructed railways for the purpose of military transport. (It had apparently escaped the notice of the War Office in Vienna that such things as railways now existed.) The campaign lasted only a few weeks, the decisive battle being fought on 3 July at Sadová (Sadowa) near Hradec Králové (Königgratz), sixty miles east of Prague.

Bismarck was by now on his way to becoming the strong man of Europe, and on this occasion it suited his book to be generous to defeated opponents; many German historians have regarded this generosity as having been not only uncharacteristic but also misjudged. He demanded no territorial concessions from Austria on Prussia's behalf, but in return for support given him by Italy he insisted that Austria should relinquish those districts in the Italian province of Venetia that had up to date remained part of the Austrian Empire. In the outcome, therefore, this war, although fought on Bohemian soil, had little effect one way or the other on Bohemia—nor did the subsequent establishment of the 'dual' Austro-Hungarian monarchy, a linking of interests between Austria and Hungary which in the long run proved itself strong enough to deter Prussia from attempting further aggression in central Europe. The Czechs retained the political advantages which they had gained in 1860 but gained nothing further. The National Theatre in Prague continued to flourish; Antonín Dvořák was still a member of its orchestra, still lived with the Dušíks—and still gave piano lessons in the Čermák household.

Since Josefa Čermáková continued to turn a deaf ear to protestations of undying love, Antonín in due course transferred his affections to her younger sister Anna—who soon showed signs that she was likely to prove more co-operative. From about 1869 onwards she herself was employed at the National Theatre as a chorus-singer and occasional small-part soloist, so that there may well have been opportunities for surreptitious billing and cooing in office hours as well as outside them. Unfortunately Jan Čermák did not favour an impecunious musician as a son-in-law. Dvořák respected his motives and was prepared to bide his time: he was convinced that he would soon establish himself as a successful composer and thereby overcome parental objections to a wedding. It was a good omen that now and again he was commissioned by the National Theatre to provide entr'actes and incidental music for straight-play productions, but although this was probably the first time that his name had been brought to the notice of the public he did not bother to retrieve the scores, all but a few fragments of which found their way into the theatre's dustbin as soon as they had served their short-term purpose. It is of more retrospective importance that during this period he also completed a Mass, two concert-overtures, a clarinet quintet, perhaps half a dozen string quartets, a cello sonata, and an opera—*Alfred*. Most of these works he burnt, but *Alfred* (dated 1870 and coming up for discussion in the next chapter) escaped the holocaust. So did a few passages from the cello sonata (in F minor) and three complete string quartets (in D major, E minor and B flat major) which were rediscovered after the composer's death and have recently been published in Prague.

All three of these quartets suffered from the long-windedness that had characterized the quintet in A minor and the quartet in A major normally identified as op. 1 and op. 2. The third movement of the D major marked the first occasion (so far as one knows) on which Dvořák allowed patriotic sentiment to intrude on art: it was based on a currently popular song entitled *Hej, Slované!* (which might be translated as *Hiya, Slavs!*). He showed a readiness to experiment when he constructed the E minor quartet in five interlinked sections instead of the conventional four separate 'movements'. (One 'section' was later rearranged, to good purpose, as a *Nocturne* in B major for string orchestra and was published as op. 40.) He foreshadowed a subsequent bent in the finale of the B flat major quartet when he combined its main theme in counterpoint with the unexpectedly reintroduced main theme of the first movement.

But by and large the publication of these quartets has done little more than confirm what one already suspected: that Dvořák, so far from being an infant prodigy like Mozart or Mendelssohn, had even by the time he reached the age of twenty-nine shown few signs that his talent as a composer was anything out of the ordinary. No middle-class nineteenth-century parent of marriageable daughters would have blamed Anna's papa for adopting an unsympathetic attitude whenever the question of a possible nuptial union came up for discussion at the family dinner-table: so far as he was concerned her devoted and beloved Antonín was merely a common-or-garden viola-player with the poorest of long-term prospects.

INTERLUDE FOR SMETANA

A few paragraphs must now be spared for a brief résumé of the career so far of a man whom Dvořák had first met in 1863 and who thereafter exercised considerable influence over him.

Bedřich Smetana was born in 1824 at Litomyšl (Leitomischl), a small town in eastern Bohemia not far from the borders of Moravia. His father was the manager of a brewery (in those regions of Europe one is frequently aware of the significance of beer) and discouraged him from adopting music as a profession. But Bedřich, who even as a boy had displayed remarkable proficiency on both piano and violin, struck out on his own and at the age of twenty secured a reasonably lucrative post as music-master in the feudal household of Count Leopold Thun, who owned one magnificent mansion in Prague and half a dozen others in various country districts of Bohemia. Count and music-master parted company in 1848, when Smetana, who all his life was a devoted Czech nationalist, joined other equally enthusiastic compatriots in the abortive June rebellion of that year. In 1849 the young firebrand settled down and married Kateřina Kolařová, a daughter of old friends of the Smetana family and herself an accomplished pianist; between the two of them they established a private music-school in Prague. This modest venture, sponsored by Franz Liszt, was sufficiently successful to bring Smetana's name to the notice of musicians outside Bohemia, and in 1856 he accepted the directorship of the Göteberg Philharmonic Society. During the next seven years he was therefore obliged to spend most of his time in Sweden, where he produced his first compositions of importance: three symphonic poems entitled *Richard III*, *Wallenstein's Camp* and *Haakon Jarl*, all of which paid tribute to Liszt in their manner and to Wagner in their matter.

Smetana's wife Kateřina died in 1859, but about a year later he married again, and in 1863 returned to Prague, where he soon began to play a prominent part in the cultural revival which had been set in motion in 1860 and by now was getting well under way. His name became closely associated with Czech musical organizations such as the Hlahol Choral Society and the National Theatre, by both of which he was often engaged as guest conductor—thereby becoming aware for the first time of Dvořák's existence. He even composed a Czech opera, *Braniboři v Čechách* (*The Brandenburgers in Bohemia*), which after many frustrating delays was eventually produced on 5 January 1866. But although Smetana the man was an ardent nationalist, Smetana the composer was at the time a suspect cosmopolitan: the libretto of *The Brandenburgers* appealed to Czech patriotic instincts, but the music could only be regarded as an attempt to emulate early Wagner; consequently the work made little more impact on the public than a revival of Wagner's *Rienzi* might have done. (It is only fair to add that nevertheless *The Brandenburgers in Bohemia* has now and again been revived in Prague during the hundred years since its first production.)

Annoyed by the comparatively poor reception given to his first opera, Smetana, who let it be admitted right away was a hyper-sensitive and somewhat ill-tempered fellow, tried to revenge himself on the good people of Prague by dashing off an operetta, a 'trivial' affair which he thought only boors would be likely to appreciate. 'I composed it without ambition, straight off the reel, in a way that beat Offenbach himself hollow.' Whatever Smetana's motives, *Prodaná nevěsta* (*The Bartered Bride*) showed him in a much more favourable light than any of his previous works. This indeed was Smetana straight off the reel; Liszt and Wagner might never have been born; here was jolly folk-style music that the Czech people understood and loved. It should be explained, however, that *The Bartered Bride* which we know today differs in many respects from *The Bartered Bride* which captivated Prague when first played there on 30 May 1866. (Dvořák, of course, was doing his stint in the orchestra.) In its original form Smetana's new stage-piece comprised no more than eight detached musical numbers separated by dialogue; it needed three subsequent revisions before its status was raised from that of a two-act operetta to that of a three-act opera. Personally, I still prefer to regard it as belonging to the more unassuming category: judged as an opera (an *opéra comique*) *The Bartered Bride* has its shortcomings; judged as an operetta, despite the irritating intrusion of conventional recitative in place of the original dialogue, it ranks as a masterpiece. (The additions included a polka and a furiant—both of which have enriched our appreciation of Bohemian dance-rhythms—and the lovely soprano aria in Act III which in Rosa Newmarch's English translation begins with the words 'Our dream of love how fair it was'.)

In September 1866 Smetana was appointed permanent musical director of the Czech National Theatre. It was still occupying its 'provisional' headquarters, but to celebrate the ceremonial laying of the foundation stone of a new National Theatre building on 16 April 1868 he was invited to compose a new opera. Presumably because he thought this too solemn an occasion for anything but 'music drama' he eschewed the light-heartedness of *The Bartered Bride* and produced forthwith another pseudo-Wagnerian essay: *Dalibor*. *Dalibor* is a better opera than *The Brandenburgers in Bohemia*, standing in the same relation thereto as does *The Flying Dutchman* to *Rienzi*, but a curious sidelight is thrown on Smetana's mentality when one recalls that even at the age of forty-three this ardent Czech nationalist saw fit to adopt a largely alien idiom in a work specifically composed to mark a milestone in the progress of a *Bohemian* cultural enterprise.

CHAPTER FIVE

A 'Wagnerian' Period

During his student days Dvořák had fallen under the romantic spell of Weber and early Wagner, and for many years
thereafter he was wont to spend spare hours and spare cash
at the German Provincial Theatre in Prague absorbing *Der
Freischütz* and *Tannhäuser* and the rest. Yet what survives
of his creative output of the eighteen-sixties, much of it
chamber music, showed few signs of Weber's influence
and fewer still of Wagner's. When in 1870, without
saying a word to any of his friends or colleagues, he set
to work on—and completed—an opera, it was a different
story.

For many years he had been playing regularly under the
conductorship of Smetana, and it was perhaps only natural
that in due course he should come to share his boss's view
that the proper prescription for a serious Czech opera was to
choose a libretto with a strongly Bohemian slant and then
set it to music *à la* Wagner. But Dvořák, who with characteristic modesty wanted to keep his operatic ambitions a close
secret, did not like to approach either Karel Sabina (1813–
1877), the librettist of *The Brandenburgers in Bohemia* and
The Bartered Bride, or any other Czech writer. Instead he
chose a German story by the short-lived Karl Theodor
Körner (1789–1813) entitled *Alfred der grosse*. He evidently
saw nothing incongruous in symbolizing his country's
struggle for autonomy by picturing—in German—events
which had taken place in England during the year 878.

It is possible that a British composer steeped in the west-
country atmosphere (the name of Rutland Boughton springs
to mind) might have fashioned a plausible opera from the
simple tale of how King Alfred (of the cakes) vanquished
Danish invaders at the battle of Ethandune (Edington).

44

Dvořák, at the unconscious behest of his deceased collaborator, made a hash of the whole affair by introducing
improbable irrelevancies: for instance the Danish leader
Harald (tenor), although accompanied throughout the
campaign by his wife Gothron (contralto), was apparently
not so much concerned with fighting Alfred (baritone) as
with seducing Alfred's wife Alvina (soprano). Such garbled
nonsense only served to clutter the plot and involved Dvořák
in the necessity of splitting the opera into about a dozen
separate and disconnected scenes, thereby destroying any
sense of dramatic unity.

The *musical* unity of *Alfred*, such as it was, depended upon
the use of Wagnerian *Leitmotive* (guiding themes). In his
monumental *Život a dílo Antonína Dvořáka (The Life and
Works of Antonín Dvořák)* Otakar Šourek, always anxious to
make out a good case for his idol, commented that in
assigning the main interest to the orchestra at the expense
of the singers Dvořák was merely following in Wagner's
footsteps. (Fair enough.) He also quoted no less than
twenty-nine excerpts in music-type for our edification:
twenty-five of them (eight of which are *Leitmotive*) suggest
nothing more than that Dvořák was striving to emulate the
stereotyped melodic and harmonic and rhythmic progres-
sions of Wagner's early operas; the remaining four are
taken from what must have been the lyrical high-spot, a
love duet for Alvina and Alfred in which the composer
seems to have escaped momentarily from the wizard's spell
and found a more individual mode of expression.

For many years Dvořák kept very quiet about *Alfred*, but
he never destroyed the manuscript. After his death it was
discovered by his pupil and friend and fellow-composer
Oskar Nedbal (1874–1930), who in 1905 conducted the
overture at a concert in Prague and later arranged for it to be
published as the *Dramatic* overture—although it is more
often called the *Tragic* overture. The opera itself had its
first performance at Olomouc (Olmütz) on 10 December

1938—ten weeks after the signing of the Munich Agreement.

No sooner had Dvořák completed an opera with a German text than he set to work on an operetta with a Czech text provided by Bernhard Guldener (1836–1877), who wrote under the pseudonym of Lobeský. This time Dvořák was less secretive about his intentions but nearly as unfortunate in his choice of librettist. The plot of *Král a uhlíř* (*King and Collier*) need not long detain us. Matěj, the 'collier' of the title—who is not a collier but a charcoal-burner—has a pretty daughter, Liduška. Her sweetheart Jeník misconstrues the attentions paid to her by a mysterious stranger to whom Matěj has given hospitality, and falling prey to violent jealousy he goes off in a huff. The mysterious stranger, however, turns out to be a king in disguise, and Matěj and Liduška are invited to court, where they are sumptuously entertained. Jeník reappears unexpectedly as a member of the king's private guard, and is rewarded for his loyalty by being given Liduška's hand in marriage.

Dvořák, still relying on Wagner so far as the theatre was concerned, tried to turn this rather silly tale into a sort of miniature *Mastersingers*. Even Šourek, although he analysed the work in detail and was once again lavish with music-type examples, could not raise much enthusiasm for a musical idiom which, although conceivably suited to an heroic opera like *Alfred*, was utterly out of place in an operetta. (Šourek points out, incidentally, that one of the 1865 *Cypresses* songs was incorporated.) Small wonder that when Dvořák sent the score to Smetana for his opinion that worthy returned it without comment. (Later, however, he relented to the extent of conducting the overture at a public concert.) The National Theatre management was at first slightly more encouraging than Smetana had been, and actually allowed the work to go into rehearsal, but eventually concurred with Smetana's judgment that it was unplayable in its present form and declined to proceed with a production. And that was the end of *King and Collier* for the time being.

WAGNER VERSUS THE REST

It has already been recorded that Dvořák discarded many compositions belonging to his twenties, and to be frank most of those which have since then been rediscovered and published might well have been allowed to rest in obscurity. By the time he reached his thirties he was beginning to find his feet, but nevertheless he ultimately destroyed several works dated 1871, 1872 and 1873. Among them were a violin sonata; a trio for violin, cello and piano; an octet for the curious combination of two violins, viola, double-bass, clarinet, bassoon, horn and piano; three *Nocturnes* for orchestra (not to be confused with the *Nocturne* in B major for string orchestra mentioned previously); and a concert-overture, *Romeo a Julie*. (You should be able to figure out that title for yourself.)

These lost works did not, however, constitute his total output of those three years. For instance, a dozen or so songs composed during 1871 and 1872 have survived: four were settings of Serbian folk-verses translated into Czech, and six others were settings of poems from a probably spurious mediaeval Czech manuscript alleged to have been discovered at Králové Dvůr (Königinhof) in north-eastern Bohemia. Few of these songs hold much interest let alone much merit, but nos. 3 and 5 of the Králové Dvůr collection, *Skřivánek* (*The Lark*) and *Kytice* (*The Nosegay*), are in their simple way reasonably competent affairs with persistent semiquaver piano accompaniments. A choral work composed during the early summer of 1872 was of greater importance and indeed set Dvořák on the high road to public recognition. This was the *Hymnus*, a short cantata based on a patriotic hymn by Vítězslav Hálek (1835–1874) entitled *Dědicové Bílé Hory* (*The Heirs of the White Mountain*), which called upon the Czechs to realize their unity as a nation despite the oppression they had so long endured. (For the significance of the White Mountain in the history of Bohemia see page 13.)

Hálek's poem had been written in 1869 and as it happened soon acquired topicality. In February 1871 the new Austrian Prime Minister, Count Hohenwart (1824–1899), who was German by birth and mistrusted his adopted country's close association with Hungary, went so far as to propose a watered-down version of František Palacký's earlier plan for turning Austria into a federation: Vienna to be the capital of the Austrian sector and Prague of the Czech sector (which would also include Galicia, inhabited by Poles and Russians). But Franz Josef was not only Emperor of Austria; by this time he was King of Hungary as well, and his Prime Minister in Budapest, Gyula Andrássy (1823–1890), was violently opposed to any such concession to pan-Slav interests. For one thing it would weaken Hungary's position in the dual monarchy; for another, it would make it more difficult for the Hungarian government to maintain proper control over the Slav peoples of Slovakia. Andrássy won the day: Franz Josef dismissed Hohenwart in October 1871—and Czech ambitions were once again frustrated.

Dvořák set Hálek's hymn, which comprised seven four-line stanzas, for chorus and orchestra. For the first four stanzas the *tempo* is fairly slow, *andante con moto* in 6/4 time occasionally crossed with 3/2 rhythm, and the predominant key is E flat major. However, at the line 'Již klěnme z srdcí živou matce střechu' ('With valiant breast be we our mother's shielding'—and here, as almost throughout, the published English translation is inadequate) Dvořák bursts into a stirring *allegro non tanto* in C major, which persists until there is a final and emphatic return to E flat major to round things off. The work alternates between moods of solemnity without pessimism and patriotic ardour without blatancy, and although it can hardly be accounted a master-piece it was unquestionably Dvořák's finest and most individual achievement up to date (June 1872): it contained few traces of Wagner's influence and many foreshadowings of its composer's mature style. The *Hymnus* was given its first performance on 9 March 1873—by the Hlahol Choral Society under the baton of Dvořák's good friend Karel Bendl.

Another survivor from 1872 is a three-movement piano quintet (string quartet plus piano) in A major, which like one or two of the early string quartets was played in public shortly after completion. The piano sets things going with a vigorous tune, in octaves, but thereafter neither of the quin-tet's first two movements is innocent of Wagner's influence. There is a touch of enterprise, however, in the handling of modulations (a 'modulation' being a transition from one key to another): one finds, for instance, an abrupt digression from A major to G major in the first movement and another from F major to F sharp minor in the second. The finale is entirely uninhibited: it is a light-hearted *allegro con brio* in tripping 6/8, and at the time Dvořák was blamed, not entirely without justification, for introducing an inappro-priately trivial element to the chamber-music medium. Contemporary critics were by now becoming sufficiently interested to tug him this way and that: although he may not have been conscious of it, the fact remains that he was still torn in doubt as to whether he was musically speaking a Slav or a Teuton.

Only three of Dvořák's (surviving) compositions date from the following year, 1873: a symphony in E flat major and two more string quartets—in F minor and A minor. Thanks to a reawakening of interest in his music as a whole, the E flat major symphony gets an occasional performance nowadays—and there can be no complaint about that. But it is difficult to follow the reasoning of the anonymous commentator who on the sleeve of the Supraphon gramophone recording has expressed the view that this work represents Dvořák's 'total emancipation from the external influences of the neo-romantic music of Liszt and Wagner': to my mind it represents, rather, the *climax* of what might be called his Wagnerian period.

This symphony, like the piano quintet of the previous year, has only three movements. The first is far and away the best. For one thing it is unusually concise (by Dvořák standards). For another, Wagner was after all a very great composer and not too much blame need be attached to anyone who could reproduce the spirit of Wagner (along with a soupçon of Mendelssohn) as competently as Dvořák did here. The slow movement, however, is a depressing affair, whether regarded as third-rate original Dvořák or second-rate imitation Wagner. The finale restores the balance to some extent: it is at least lively, although the liveliness seems to derive not so much from Dvořák's spontaneous exuberance as from an attempt to capture the rather forced exuberance of Liszt and Wagner in their less-inspired moments and (dare one add?) the rather forced exuberance of Beethoven in some of *his* less-inspired moments. Whatever today's judgment may be, Smetana, who had so uncompromisingly turned down *King and Collier*, was impressed by this symphony and was later to conduct its first performance.

Of Dvořák's two string quartets belonging to 1873, that in F minor is quite an accomplished piece of work. The first movement (*allegro*, 3/4) is typically long-winded but sufficiently well-constructed upon pleasant thematic material to hold one's attention. As for the second movement, a somewhat Mendelssohnian *andante con moto* in A flat major and 6/8 time, one need only record that Dvořák thought so highly of it that he used it six years later as the basis of a 'romance' for violin and orchestra (which to this day remains in the repertory of his great-grandson, the violinist Josef Suk). The third movement begins and ends in waltz time, but also includes an exceptionally charming middle section in 2/4. The finale (*allegro molto*, 2/4) seems to demand an orchestra to make its full effect.

The A minor string quartet of 1873 is by comparison rather a naïve affair. It was designed, like the earlier E minor quartet, to be played without a break; its most noteworthy feature is an attractively expressive melody (*poco adagio*, E major, 2/4) which provides the nucleus of the second 'section'.

All in all, 1873 was a year upon which Dvořák could look back with satisfaction. He had continued as a happy tenant of the Dušíks, who had meanwhile moved into a larger flat in the same square where he had been allocated a room of his own overlooking a garden. One of the Králové Dvůr songs had achieved publication, the first of his compositions to do so. Several of his chamber works had been played in public, and one of the three *Nocturnes* for orchestra (all subsequently lost or destroyed) when given at a Philharmonic concert, had earned a word of praise from no less a personage than Richard Wagner, who happened to be on a visit to Prague at the time. The *Hymnus* had been performed by the Hlahol Choral Society and had made a favourable impression. The symphony in E flat major had yet to be played, but the normally critical Smetana was already showing interest in it. There was yet another cause for gratification: following the death of the stubborn Jan Čermák in February, his widow Klotilda raised no objection to a marriage, and at St. Peter's Church, Prague, on 17 November 1873, Antonín pressed a wedding-ring on his Anna's finger. It was thirty-three years to the day since the marriage of his own parents.

CHAPTER SIX

Ups and Downs

Dvořák's marriage, like nearly everyone else's, marked a turning point in his domestic career. It also marked a turning point in his musical career. Therefore, before proceeding further, it will be as well to remind ourselves what the compositions of his bachelor days had amounted to.

Ignoring those which have been lost altogether or survive only in fragmentary form, he had up to date completed one opera, one operetta, one choral work, three symphonies, nine chamber works, two piano pieces and about twenty-five songs. Although the choral work (the *Hymnus*) and a handful of the rest were not devoid of merit, the fact remains that his present-day reputation would hardly be a whit different from what it is had the whole lot gone up in smoke on his wedding-day. Schubert—who left eight completed operas or operettas, about forty-five choral works, thirty-five orchestral works, forty-five chamber works, two hundred and fifty piano pieces and six hundred songs—died at the age of thirty-one. By contrast Dvořák's creative life, so far as posterity need really concern itself, may be said to have begun at thirty-two.

When he married he left the National Theatre orchestra, in which he had played the viola for eleven years, to become organist at St. Adalbert's Church, a post which left him more time for composition and also raised his status in the eyes of his mother-in-law. It was she who during the next three months extended to the bride and bridegroom the hospitality of the commodious Čermák residence *na Florenc* (in Florence Street), which was situated just behind the railway station then known as the 'Staatsbahnhof', between the wars as the 'Masaryk nádraží' and today as 'Praha-střed'—*i.e.* Prague Central. (This is primarily a suburban-line station: the only express trains to use it are those to and from the Dresden direction.)

While the Dvořáks were living with Klotilda Čermáková, Antonín composed a fourth symphony—in D minor—which whatever its shortcomings owed less to Wagner than had his E flat major symphony of 1873. One can trace Wagner's influence in the theme upon which the second movement was based and in the middle section of the third and again in parts of the finale, but much of the music was recognizable Dvořák, in manner if not always in matter. The opening of the first movement was genuinely impressive, the initial mutterings on the lower strings foreshadowing the opening bars of a far greater symphony in the same key which he was to compose eleven years later, but thereafter it became an interminable and inconclusive duel between early-period Dvořák and middle-period Beethoven. The second movement comprised long-drawn-out 'variations' on a theme almost comically reminiscent of *Tannhäuser*'s pilgrims. The third was a classical scherzo, well-constructed but somewhat repetitive. In the finale there were two good tunes, appropriately contrasted, but Dvořák let them run riot in some inexpert 'development', and although he once again called upon the aid of Beethoven and Liszt and Wagner those three worthies could do little to help mitigate the tedium. (The scherzo was played later the same year, but the first performance of the work as a whole did not take place until 1892.)

How is one to reckon this symphony alongside the previous one? I would say that the E flat major deserves to be played now and again if only for the sake of its Wagnerian but commendably concise first movement; that the D minor deserves to be played now and again because here Dvořák was at last beginning to strike out on a line of his own. But he had not yet learnt—and perhaps he never did learn—to keep a sufficiently tight rein on his natural volubility, a volubility which rivalled Schubert's. George Grove, founder and first editor of the *Dictionary of Music and Musicians*, once referred, appropriately enough, to Schubert's 'heavenly lengths'; I am afraid one would have to use a different adjective to describe the 'lengths' of Dvořák's fourth symphony.

For several reasons February and March 1874 were memorable months for Dvořák: he completed his new D minor symphony; Smetana conducted the first performance of the E flat major symphony at a Philharmonic concert; Anna told him she was pregnant; and the young couple found a home of their own (not far from the Dušík dwelling) at 14 Rybníček (Teichgasse).

MAINLY OPERETTA

Although by this time Dvořák had escaped from a theatre orchestra he had not escaped from the lure of the stage: in April 1874 he retrieved the libretto of *King and Collier* and began to set it to music all over again. (He always allowed it to be believed that he had destroyed the original setting, but it was unearthed after his death and devotees arranged a production in 1929.) The second *King and Collier* relied not so much on Wagner and the Smetana of *Dalibor* as on Weber and the Smetana of *The Bartered Bride*. If the construction was rather slipshod that was partly the librettist's fault, and certainly Dvořák here proved, for the first time, that he could write 'democratic' music without sacrificing individuality; consequently the saga of charcoal-burner Matěj and his daughter Liduška and her jealous swain Jeník became almost plausible. For instance there was a duet in Act I for Liduška (soprano) and Jeník (tenor) which started in a mood of teasing charm but presently developed into a sentimental love-scene; Dvořák emphasized the contrast by switching from jog-trot four-bar phrases to more lyrical (and unexpected) five-bar phrases at the words 'Přijdeli, pak po všem je věta' ('Should that be so, then all is over'). The score as a whole, much of it in either lively polka-rhythm or gentle *Ländler*-rhythm, made such an impression on the management of the National Theatre that at the end of August the work was accepted for production later the same year. All that remained for Dvořák to do was to write an overture, but there was no hurry about that: Anna had just presented him with a son and heir (Otakar), so in September he promptly let off steam with an orchestral *Rhapsody* in A minor—and then relaxed with a string quartet in the same key.

The *Rhapsody* (op. 14), which demanded a larger orchestra than any of his previous compositions, was an obvious and largely unsuccessful attempt to emulate Liszt. The music is disjointed and noisy and full of cheap instrumental effects: in one passage, for instance, marked 'quasi recitative', two trumpets and two trombones blast out in unison against a background of *tremolando* strings. Having got this indiscretion off his chest Dvořák wisely locked it up in a secret drawer, although he later scratched out the original title and substituted 'Symphonic Poem'—without venturing to provide a 'programme'.

Nothing could have provided a greater contrast than the immediately following string quartet in A minor (op. 16), which holds little character but is unassuming and innocuous and easy on the ear. Here Dvořák, so far as construction was concerned, adhered to classical precedent almost throughout: the first movement, for instance, was in strict sonata form. (In the classical era sonata form, or something like it, was *de rigueur* for the opening movement of a full-length instrumental work. Its basis was as follows: an exposition in which a 'first subject' and a 'second subject' were presented, each in a different key; next a 'development section' in which the hidden potentialities of what had gone before were developed to the best of the composer's ability; this led to a recapitulation in which the original first and second subjects reappeared, this time both in the same key; sometimes there was a 'coda', or tailpiece, to round things off.) The only challenge to academic tradition in Dvořák's op. 16 occurred at the beginning of the finale, where there was an emphatic assertion of the key of F major instead of the A minor or A major that might have been expected. (This whim of starting a movement in a 'wrong' key later became almost a mannerism.)

Towards the end of October *King and Collier* went into rehearsal and the composer provided it with an overture, an appropriately cheerful piece based on tunes from the operetta itself but carefully composed and not just a mere pot-pourri. The three-act *King and Collier* was loudly applauded on its first performance (27 November 1874) and received enthusiastic press notices; greatly encouraged, Dvořák, during the next month or so, completed another operetta: *Tvrdé palice*, a one-act curtain-raiser. (Literally, *tvrdé palice* means no more than 'hard stubbornness', but the accepted English title is *The Pigheaded Peasants*.) The librettist, Josef Štolba (1846–1930), knew his job much better than did Lobeský (Guldener), and produced a well-constructed little play about two peasant lovers, Lenka and Toník (the diminutive of Antonín), who were pigheaded enough to oppose their parents' plans for a wedding until Řeřicha, a shrewd and kindly-disposed neighbour, resorted to subterfuge on their behalf. Dvořák was delighted with the libretto and fittingly enough *The Pigheaded Peasants* ranks possibly as the most praiseworthy and certainly as the most spontaneous of all his compositions up to that date.

The overture, after a slow introduction, sets the pace: its sparkling 'development section', in accordance with the highest classical precedents, is exceptionally well-contrived. In the operetta itself the action is so swift (as in *King and Collier* there is no dialogue and not much recitative) and the music bubbles along so exuberantly that only the sternest critic need notice that now and again it lapses into something like triviality. There are excellent ensembles for various permutations of the five principal characters, three of whom are also given an opportunity to display vocal prowess in more or less formal arias. In these Lenka, the soprano, comes off best: her 'Jak jest mi jen?' ('What about *me*, then?') is a melodic gem. The only noticeable dramatic weakness is that a superfluous chorus is dragged in, for no other purpose than to take part in the dénouement.

Unfortunately the close of 1874 marked a temporary setback to Dvořák's operetta ambitions. *King and Collier*, despite its first-night success, failed to stay the course, mainly because of the feeble libretto. (We shall renew acquaintance with it in a later chapter, however.) Nor did the National Theatre, surprisingly enough, show any interest in *The Pigheaded Peasants*, which had to wait more than six years before achieving public presentation.

MAINLY CHAMBER MUSIC

Dvořák soon had good cause to forget his disappointment over *King and Collier* and *The Pigheaded Peasants*. About twelve years previously Emperor Franz Josef (or some influential official in his Ministry of Culture) had been sufficiently enlightened to establish a State Commission to provide financial assistance, in the form of annual grants, to promising artists and musicians who had been born in the Austrian Empire but were debarred, by reason of poverty, from pursuing their natural bent to best advantage. Dvořák passed safely through the means test, and the compositions he submitted, which included the E flat major symphony of 1873, secured him an award for 1875. It will mean little to my readers to learn that this amounted to 400 gulden (long since an obsolete currency); suffice to say that it was more than three times as much as he earned in a whole year as organist.

The judges on the State Music Commission were well qualified to assess the merits of musical composi- tions. One was Eduard Hanslick (1825–1904), the learned but ultra-conservative music critic of the *Neue Freie Presse* (whom Wagner had lampooned in *The Mastersingers* as Beckmesser). Another was Johann Herbeck (1831–1877), director of the Vienna Court Opera, but about this time he was succeeded by that sincere character and great composer Johannes Brahms (1833–1897). Dvořák's entries con- tinued to earn approval, and he was given this state award for three years in succession, so that when 1877 came round he could afford to give up organ playing as a means of liveli- hood. For the moment, however, we are still concerned with 1875.

His first composition of that year (completed in March) was a quintet in G major for two violins, viola, cello and double-bass, a combination hitherto the virtual preserve of George Onslow (1784–1853), a prolific composer of cham- ber music who was of British parentage but born in France. It can be said right away that Dvořák used the unwieldy double-bass adjunct to the normal string quartet with great discretion and indeed from time to time with considerable effect. This quintet (originally op. 18), although somewhat unsubstantial, is charming throughout: all four movements, even a *poco andante* (placed third), are characterized by a tripping operetta-like delicacy that is comparatively rare in Dvořák's instrumental music. The whole affair might almost have been contrived by the Sullivan of *Trial by Jury* (also dated March 1875) had that composer subsequently taken a spring holiday in Bohemia and developed an interest in the national idiom.

Next came four duets for soprano and tenor (op. 20), to which I shall have occasion to make further reference presently, and then in quick succession three works which were comparable in scale with the quintet—although not all three were comparable in quality. They were a *Serenade* for string orchestra in E major (April), a piano trio in B flat major (May) and a piano quartet in D major (June).

The *Serenade* (op. 22) was aptly entitled, since at least four of its five movements (the second of which was a delightful waltz) displayed an elegant touch suggestive of gracious living accompanied by 'serenading' in the stately home of some eighteenth-century aristocrat; in the finale alone did the composer discard periwig and lace cuffs, and even here the junketing, though lively, was well-bred, and in the closing moments there was a delicious return to the courtliness of the opening. Pastiche perhaps, but what excellent pastiche! Since Dvořák was as yet only on the threshold of developing an individual style, it is perhaps not surprising that this slightly uncharacteristic but extremely accomplished and enjoyable *Serenade* is the earliest of his compositions in which a detached listener is likely to discover *enchantment*.

If by contrast the B flat major piano trio (op. 21) is *dis*enchanting, that is mainly the fault of its first movement, which is both commonplace and dull from start to finish. The second movement is attractively lyrical in mood without achieving distinction; the third and fourth might with justice be described as inoffensively trivial. The D major piano quartet (op. 23) is even more of a disappointment: the short melodic phrases upon which the first movement is based (there is nothing long enough to be called a 'tune') are incapable of sustaining interest throughout the ten minutes of its duration; the second comprises a few characterless 'variations' on a vapid theme; the third and last is an unsuccessful attempt to combine in one movement the functions of scherzo and finale. The shortcomings of these two works appear all the more palpable when set alongside the merits of the 'double-bass' quintet and the *Serenade* which so closely preceded them. Within a matter of weeks, however, Dvořák was to restore the balance.

SYMPHONY NO. 5 IN F MAJOR
at one time called No. 3

Of all the works that Dvořák composed during the first
two years of his married life the best-known is his fifth
symphony, in F major, the first of the 'big five' which
nowadays are numbered, on a sensible chronological basis,
5, 6, 7, 8 and 9. But since none of the preceding four had
yet reached the printing-press (and indeed did not do so
during Dvořák's lifetime) the 'big five' were labelled by
their eventual publisher, Fritz Simrock, as nos. 1, 2, 3, 4
and 5. Furthermore it so happened that the symphony in F
major, although the first in order of composition (July
1875) and of performance (March 1879) was only the *third*
in order of publication (1888); consequently it became
'no. 3'—and so remained for more than half a century. To
help clarify the matter it may be as well, at this juncture,
to tabulate the correct numbering of Dvořák's symphonies

DVOŘÁK'S SYMPHONIES

Year of compo-sition	Key	Correct number in chrono-logical sequence	Number by which known until about 1955	Original 'opus number'	'Opus number' on pub-lication
1865	C minor	1		3	
1865	B flat major	2		4	
1873	E flat major	3		10	
1874	D minor	4		13	
1875	F major	5	3	24	76
1880	D major	6	1		60
1885	D minor	7	2		70
1889	G major	8	4		88
1893	E minor	9	5		93

side by side with the arbitrary numbering (arbitrary, that is to say, from any point of view except that of the publisher) which was tolerated for so many years and is perpetuated on the title-pages of most orchestral scores and on the labels of gramophone records issued prior to about 1955.

(Apologists for Simrock have pleaded that he was justified in publishing the F major symphony as op. 76 rather than op. 24 because it was revised just prior to publication, but the excuse will not hold water: for one thing the 'revision' consisted of little more than touching up the orchestration here and there; for another this consideration can have carried little weight, since he followed up by performing the same disservice for the 'double-bass' quintet op. 18, which he issued as op. 77. Dvořák was justly incensed: he would much have preferred to let posterity judge these works by the standards of 1875 rather than by the standards of 1888—by which time he had reached the age of forty-six and established himself with a host of works more finely wrought than any belonging to his early thirties. He was right to make his protest; and let it be added that anyone who feels an instinctive admiration for his music should listen carefully to this delightful and comparatively early symphony before attempting to savour the more sophisticated masterpieces of his maturity.)

Although no. 5's first movement may owe something to Smetana and its second to Schubert and its third to Mendelssohn, there is hardly anywhere a trace of the Wagner who had dominated no. 3 and reared his head occasionally in no. 4: by now Dvořák had cast off Teutonic shackles and was becoming conscious of his *national* responsibilities. The pastoral quality of the first movement and the alternating moods of the second (despite the occasional Schubertian touch) and the liveliness of the third (despite the occasional Mendelssohnian touch) all supplied proof that at last another outstanding *Czech* composer had arrived, worthy to pick up the mantle which Smetana was soon to lay down. As regards the finale, however, one's feelings are mixed. Cellos and double-basses set things going with a fine vigorous tune, not in the main key of F major but in A minor (cf. the finale of the string quartet op. 16) and so long as this remains to the forefront no one can complain; the rest of the thematic material, unfortunately, is somewhat commonplace, and one is left with the overall impression that whatever the merits of this finale they hardly match those of the three preceding movements in a symphony which taken by and large typifies the Dvořák *of 1875* at his best.

DOWN RATHER THAN UP

His next large-scale composition typified the Dvořák of 1875 at his worst, or at least (let us be charitable) at his most unfortunate. It was another opera on the *Alfred* scale and was entitled *Vanda*.

Composers of heroic operas have often had to cope with unsuitable libretti, but few can have been as intractable as that of *Vanda*: the jejune plot, which concerned an obscure episode in the history not of England this time but of Poland, was somehow or other spun out to occupy five acts. The original Polish text was by Juljan Surzycha (1820–1882); it was translated and adapted by František Zakrejs (1839–1907) and Václav Beneš-Šumavský (1850–1927). *Vanda* was played a few times by the National Theatre company (the first performance took place on 17 April 1876) but thereafter went the way of *Alfred*; it was obviously killed stone-dead by its inept libretto. As regards the music, this too was in the *Alfred* manner and actually reproduced a tune or two from the earlier work; Šourek was probably right when he referred to several impressive choral scenes as the high-spots. The overture alone has survived to this day; it is competently constructed but little else can be said in its favour except to concede that it is poor *genuine* Dvořák rather than poor Dvořák-cum-Wagner.

Meanwhile Anna had presented her husband with a second child, Josefa, but she died when only a few days old. This unhappy occurrence, which in those days was by no means an uncommon one, does not seem to have greatly affected Dvořák's outlook on life; at any rate his next two compositions, a piano trio in G minor and a string quartet in E major both completed during January and February 1876, exhibited no signs of depression. The piano trio (op. 26) was as characteristically long-winded as the symphony in D minor of 1874, and it was only in the expressive slow movement and the lively scherzo that the best of Dvořák occasionally peeped through. The E major quartet (originally op. 27 but later published as op. 80) can more fittingly be ranked alongside the F major symphony of 1875: it was Dvořák's most mature piece of chamber music so far. The first movement was based largely on one healthy tune, often treated 'canonically', and was reasonably concise. The second, in A minor but later breaking into A major, was a piece of inspired lyricism; although the construction was conventional, Dvořák here displayed a *technical* facility in the string-quartet medium equal to that of the most illustrious of his contemporaries. The scherzo and the finale were less noteworthy, but the former contained some attractive syncopation in the Schumann manner.

Next came a few unimportant piano pieces and part-songs (ops. 28 and 29) and a big choral work—*Stabat Mater*. Although Dvořák did not actually complete this score until October 1877, the bulk of it was composed between February and May 1876, and it can properly be regarded as belonging to that year.

'STABAT MATER'

Stabat Mater was the title of a Latin poem written in the Middle Ages by Jacopone da Todi; it depicted the emotions of Mary the mother of Jesus on witnessing from afar the crucifixion of her Son, and later became accepted as part of the Catholic missal; many composers have chosen it as a text for a sacred choral work. I am not qualified to express an opinion as to what extent Dvořák's setting is satisfactory from a liturgical point of view, but when judged as music there is plenty to be said in its favour—and a certain amount to be said in detraction.

Not that the work could truly be described as inconsistent in quality: on the contrary each separate item with the solitary exception of no. 6 ('Fac me vere tecum flere'), which is perfunctory and somewhat unworthy of its composer, holds moments of beauty, 'absolute' beauty. Yet it is difficult to find many traces of the *spiritual* beauty that might have been expected of an accomplished composer serving the Church to which he was such a faithful adherent. Perhaps Dvořák was here consciously striving to adopt an appropriate tone of high seriousness which did not as yet come naturally to him; possibly on this occasion he allowed personal sorrow—on the recent death of his baby daughter —to affect his approach. However that may be, there is throughout rather too much facile 'chromaticism' of the type to which Tchaikovsky was prone in his self-pitying moods, and it is the three items in which this tendency is pushed comparatively into the background that remain the most satisfying: no. 3 ('Eia mater' for chorus)—a rare instance of indebtedness to Verdi; no. 5 ('Tui nati vulnerati' for chorus) —which is marred, however, by somewhat clumsy orchestration; and no. 9 ('Inflammatus et accensus' for contralto solo) —where the opening, at any rate, is almost Handelian in its forthrightness.

Anyone hearing this work for the first time should not be put off by the opening chorus, interspersed with solos, in which despair persists for a full quarter of an hour or more; if he listens carefully to the remainder he will realize that although Dvořák's *Stabat Mater* may not be completely characteristic it nevertheless represents a conscientious and reasonably successful attempt to reconcile the art to which he was devoted with the religious faith to which he was devoted.

CHAPTER SEVEN

Recognition

At this stage (May 1876) let us take a quick look at what Bedřich Smetana had been doing since he conducted the first performance of Dvořák's E flat major symphony in March 1874. In that same year he had completed *Dvé vdovy* (*Two Widows*)—an operetta which although it never achieved the same popularity as *The Bartered Bride* was nevertheless lively and entertaining—and had begun work on a series of six symphonic poems collectively entitled *Má vlast* (*My Country*). It is not part of my present purpose to review *My Country*, but it should be pointed out that while *Vltava* is deservedly the best-known item *Šárka* is an almost equally fine piece of work and that the other four are all at least as impressive as most of Liszt's symphonic poems. Most regrettably Smetana, from 1875 onwards, became increasingly deaf (as did Beethoven from 1800 onwards and Fauré from 1905 onwards): a string quartet dated 1876 and entitled *Z mého života* (*From my Life*) was an attempt to express in 'intimate' music the extent to which the affliction affected him; the letters he wrote at the time to his friend Josef Srb-Debrnov give a clear notion of the frustration he was suffering.

Although Dvořák was in the long run to prove himself a greater composer than Smetana, he never quite equalled let alone surpassed him in the field of 'programme music'; none the less, he owed it largely to the promptings of *My Country* and *From my Life* that he could elsewhere adopt the idiom of the mature Smetana to his own purposes and perhaps here and there improve on it. It was in the latter part of 1876 and in 1877 that he first did so.

MORAVIAN DUETS

In March 1875 (see page 58) Dvořák had composed four vocal duets (op. 20); they were rather characterless settings of traditional Moravian poems, but he did a good stroke of business for himself when he dedicated them to Marie, wife of Jan Neff, a prosperous Prague merchant in whose household he gave piano lessons. She was delighted with them and begged him to carry on the good work. Dvořák duly obliged with five more in May 1876, ten more in July 1876, and four more in September 1877. There were thus twenty-three of these duets all told, but the title *Moravian Duets* (or alternatively *Airs from Moravia*) is usually taken to apply to a collection of thirteen of them, all belonging to the summer of 1876. Neff and Dvořák shared fifty-fifty the cost of having them privately published later that year as Dvořák's op. 32, and Neff, without informing Dvořák of his kindly intentions, sent copies to many distinguished personalities in the musical world—including Brahms.

The duets of op. 20 had been for soprano and tenor; those of op. 32 were for soprano and contralto. It should be pointed out however that no. 7 of this set, *Voda a pláč* (*Brooklet and Tears*), was virtually a contralto solo: the soprano joined in only for the three concluding bars. As it happened this particular item came somewhere near thirteenth out of thirteen in order of merit: it consisted merely of a rather trite melody sung three times over to different words. No. 12, *Neveta* (*Consolation*), was similarly constructed, but here Dvořák had the initiative to introduce a new melodic and harmonic pattern into the third verse. The same formal and slightly irritating repetition cropped up again in no. 13, *Štpek* (*The Wild-flower*), but taking it all in all *The Wild-flower* rounded off this duet-cycle very acceptably. On the debit side it only remains to record that no. 11, *Zajatá* (*The Female Prisoner*, or to be less literal *The Captured Bride*), strikes a detached listener as owing more to Robert Schumann than it does to folk-song sources.

So much for nos. 7, 11, 12, 13. The remaining nine, when judged by appropriate standards, demand collective praise rather than individual criticism. To what extent the traditional characteristics of Moravian folk-song—which are said to have influenced Dvořák—differed from those of the folk-music of Bohemia proper only an expert could tell. On the internal evidence of his op. 32 one might express the view that Moravians seem to have been wedded to the 2/4 rhythm of the polka and skočná rather than the quick 3/4 rhythm of the furiant: the former, slow or fast, puts in a frequent appearance. Fair enough: Dvořák did not regard himself as a Bohemian in the merely narrow sense of the term but as a Slav, and by now he had a determination to prove himself a true Slav rather than a Teuton hanger-on. What is perhaps rather more to the interest of posterity is that in these duets he used the two voice parts to the best possible advantage, often introducing one after the other, not necessarily in 'strict canon' but in extremely effective 'free canon'. Of the nine duets with which this paragraph is concerned each one has something to be said in its favour, and I need only give my personal opinion that no. 4 is the pick of the bunch. Its Czech title is *V dobrým sme se sešli* (which has been rendered both as *Ere we part, love, kiss me* and *Gaily as I met thee*); it remains a small-scale masterpiece: the mood is that of Brahms's *Vergebliches Ständchen*—a mood which suited a Czech better than it suited a German.

Dvořák submitted the *Moravian Duets* as an entry for the Austrian state scholarship award of 1877 and thereby won it for the third year in succession. Moreover, Brahms was so much impressed that he sent a copy of the work to the Berlin music publisher Fritz Simrock, along with a covering letter in which he extolled its excellence. Simrock took the hint, bought the *Moravian Duets* from Dvořák for rather less than he thought they were worth and rather more than the composer expected, published them in a German translation—and made a heap of money out of them. (They were lapped up in all German-speaking countries.) Thereafter he not unnaturally became extremely interested in Dvořák, who from his point of view was obviously a good bet. But Dvořák was no fool: as the years rolled by and he gradually became better established and more financially independent he was able (as we shall see presently) to argue over terms with Simrock rather than allow Simrock to dictate them. He remained deeply conscious, however, of his indebtedness to Brahms, but for whose interest and practical help many years might have had to elapse before his reputation could be spread beyond the confines of Bohemia and Moravia.

A MIXED BAG

Following the success of the *Moravian Duets*, Dvořák managed to persuade three separate firms to purchase and publish between them eleven song settings of items selected from a slim volume of poems by Vítězslav Hálek (who had provided him with the *Hymnus*) entitled *Večerní písně* (*Evening Songs*). As a result of the division of responsibility between three different publishers, four of these songs survive as an op. 3, two as part of an op. 9 and the remaining five as op. 31—but let that pass: they are sufficiently homogeneous to be regarded as constituting a self-contained song-cycle. There are no masterpieces here, but neither are there any utter flops, and although the average level of inspiration may be somewhat below that of the *Moravian Duets* it is only an occasional flash-back to Schumann that prompts one to question Šourek's assumption that they were all composed during that same period—May to July 1876. The most striking among them is op. 3 no. 4, *Když Bůh byl nejvíc rozkochán* (*When God was in a merry mood*), where the extraordinarily venturesome piano accompaniment fore-shadows the chromatic inclinations of Richard Strauss.

While this burst of song writing was going on, Anna presented her husband with another daughter, Růžena, so that there were now once again two children in the Dvořák household, but his next *artistic* production, as it happened, was the least satisfying of all his best-known instrumental works—a piano concerto in G minor (op. 33, August/September 1876). Here there was a surfeit of piano and a deficiency of concerto, a surfeit of padding and a deficiency of inspiration. The only melody with any character of its own crops up in the finale (at bar 103 in the first instance), and the whole affair sounds not so much like true Dvořák as like a parody by some ill-disposed rival who was deter-mined to draw attention to his weaknesses. (Yet the work still seems to hold some attraction for virtuoso pianists.)

Two pieces for piano solo, both composed during that autumn, are more interesting: a dumka in D minor and a *Theme with Variations* in A flat major. The word 'dumka' has no exact equivalent in English: perhaps 'elegy' is as near as one can get. The name indicates a type of composi-tion which originated in the Ukraine (the south-western corner of what is today the Union of Soviet Socialist Republics); it may be vocal or instrumental or both at once, its main characteristic being a continued alternation between two deliberately conflicting moods, often submission and despair on the one hand and agitation or exaltation on the other. Reputable dumka exponents, such as Dvořák, sometimes but by no means always use the same basic theme through-out, changing its complexion as required to suit the atmos-phere of each contrasted episode. The form is indigenous to Slav countries, and is so typically expressive of one aspect of the Slav temperament that westerners are apt to find it slightly exotic; when the musical content is provided by a Dvořák the taste becomes easy to acquire. It must be admitted, however, that this particular specimen for piano (op. 35) was not one of his best efforts, being not even a very typical dumka and somewhat overloaded with elaborate detail; nevertheless the thematic material was attractive.

The *Theme with Variations* (op. 36) was a more substantial work. The Beethovenish theme with its characteristically Dvořákian hovering between two keys—A flat major and F flat major (= E major)—held out good promise, a promise which, however, was not altogether fulfilled. What the composer seems here to have had primarily in mind was to give the *pianist* a chance to display his technique: the fifth variation, for instance, was an 'octave' study: the seventh a 'running semiquaver' study. Judged solely as music, the most satisfying variation was the sixth, in which Dvořák quietly recapitulated the theme's most attractive features in the key of C flat major (= B major); he slipped back to A flat major, however, for the last dozen bars or so.

In January 1877 Dvořák, still absorbed with Moravia, set eight folk-verses from that province for male-voice choir; this was merely an attempt to keep the Moravian pot a-boiling. During the rest of the year he completed two works of supreme importance—a new operetta and a set of symphonic variations for orchestra, both of which we shall come to presently—and several others of less importance, among them four more Moravian duets and a handful of piano pieces. Of the new Moravian duets (op. 38) only no. 1, *Možnost* (*The False Hope*), with its continually shifting rhythmic accentuations, was anything but a pale reflection of the earlier ones. Of the piano pieces the *Scottish Dances* (op. 41) were no nearer to being Scottish than Dvořák was to being Bonnie Prince Charlie (and indeed it has been suggested that they were actually written many years previously, perhaps even during his student days), but two furiants in D major and F major (op. 42) deserve a word of commendation.

A furiant is a typically vigorous Bohemian dance measure

in quick 3/4 (or 6/4) time which often but not by obligation incorporates a cross-rhythm in 3/2, thus providing *three* strong accents to clash with a *pair* of strong accents. The two furiants of Dvořák's op. 42—both of which, by the way, demand considerable virtuosity on the part of the the the pianist—are excellent specimens of the genre, although neither exploits its rhythmic possibilities to the fullest extent; the first, in D major, has a particularly effective coda in a markedly slower *tempo*.

'ŠELMA SEDLÁK' ('THE PEASANT A ROGUE')

Early in 1877 the Dvořáks had moved into a larger flat just round the corner in Žitná ulice (Korngasse), and between February and August of that year Antonín devoted most of his energies to another operetta. This time his collaborator was the young and short-lived Josef Otakar Veselý (1853–1879), a more accomplished librettist than Bernhard Lobeský of *King and Collier* although perhaps lagging slightly behind Josef Štolba of *The Pigheaded Peasants*. The milieu of *The Peasant a Rogue*, like that of Dvořák's two previous operettas, was the Bohemian country-side. In the main plot boy loves girl, but there are difficulties because boy is penniless; boy and girl (aided and abetted by boy's father) indulge in a spot of blackmail on a wealthy prince whose moral attributes are open to question and wealthy prince has to throw his influence and riches on the side of true love. There are various complications involving other characters but in the end, of course, boy *gets* girl.

The music of *The Peasant a Rogue* is throughout fresh and spontaneous; once again there is no dialogue and recitative is reduced to a bare minimum. From the opening chorus onwards there are occasional recollections of *The Bartered Bride* (and why not?), but *The Peasant a Rogue* is by no means just second-hand Smetana. Dvořák displayed considerable individuality in the arias allotted to the principal characters and furthermore demonstrated, in the frequent ensembles, a flair for characterization which surpassed that of Smetana and rivalled that of Verdi. This is particularly noticeable in a quartet from Act I, 'Nedej ty se, má panenko' ('Never mind, my little darling'). Equally effective, in a different way, is the galloping first-act finale, 'Az skončí dnes' ('Until today').

The Peasant a Rogue is still staged in Prague and one only wishes that Sadler's Wells would risk a production. As it is one has to be content with an occasional broadcast performance of the excellent overture; let us be thankful for that small mercy.

SYMPHONIC VARIATIONS

At this stage of his career Dvořák could not be accounted a truly accomplished *symphonic* composer in the proper sense of the term; although he was presently to prove himself one, an addiction to melodic phrases rather than melodic sentences—and an allied tendency to develop them episodically rather than 'symphonically'—preclude even his later works in this particular field of creative musical endeavour, with a few noteworthy exceptions, from being ranked alongside the mightiest. By the same token (although the slow movement of his piano quartet op. 23 had provided no proof of it) his talents were peculiarly well-fitted to the 'variation' form, where the underlying potentialities of a single theme are exploited not over a wide canvas such as the 'development section' of a movement in sonata form but in a series of separate and self-contained 'variations'—which however may be interconnected and are normally played without a break in continuity.

The basic theme of Dvořák's *Symphonic Variations for*

Large Orchestra (unlike that of the 'Saint Anthony' variations, Brahms's best-known work in that form) came out of
the composer's own head; indeed he had used it earlier the
same year for one of his Moravian part-songs: *Já jsem
huslař* (*I am a fiddler*). It is in 2/4 time and comprises
three sections: first a seven-bar phrase, perhaps a wee bit
too austere to make an immediate appeal on its own account
and helped out only by persistently held bass-notes; then
a six-bar phrase, more grateful to the ear but just as parsi-
moniously accompanied; finally a repetition of the opening
seven-bar phrase, which now is accorded harmonic support
that gives one an inkling of ideas that may be lurking at the
back of the composer's mind.

In the first three variations, however, he merely repeats
the theme (all twenty bars of it) three times over, adding
some elaborate contrapuntal trimmings. Then the real fun
starts: during the course of the next thirteen variations (4 to
16) he plays with it much as a dog might play with its puppy,
turning it on its back and rolling it all over the place, licking
it affectionately when it submits uncomplainingly, and ad-
ministering punitive slaps when it becomes too obstreperous.

Variation 17, an abbreviated scherzo, brings the first
change of time-signature. Variation 18 brings the first
change of key—C major to D major—and along with it an
ingenious transformation of the theme's *harmonic* inflexions.
In Variation 19 Dvořák unexpectedly introduces a graceful
waltz-tune in B flat major, only very distantly related to
anything that has gone before. (Compare the 'Dorabella'
variation of Elgar's *Enigma*.) He is so much enamoured
of its seductive strains that he uses it as the basis of what
almost amounts to a set of seven subsidiary variations (20 to
26), some lively, some tranquil, and for the most part in
B flat minor. Not until Variation 27 is there a return to
reality and C major with pawkily rhythmical reiterations of
the component figures of the opening seven-bar phrase,
which in the next and final variation achieves apotheosis as

the main subject of a fugue, a fugue not only technically impeccable but also extraordinarily invigorating.

Completed in September 1877, the *Symphonic Variations* (subsequently published as op. 78) had its first performance that same autumn, in Prague. As we shall see later, it did not reach Vienna (or anywhere else) until 1887, but in retrospect can be seen to have raised Dvořák to the level of a great composer by establishing the fact that he was endowed not merely with talent but also with genius.

REACTION AND RECOVERY

Dvořák's satisfaction over the *Symphonic Variations* was clouded by domestic tragedy—the death within a few weeks of one another of his son Otakar (aged three) and his surviving daughter Růžena (aged one). Having now lost all his three children, he fell forthwith into a mood of deep depression, but Anna Dvořáková—a sterling character if ever there was one and as good a wife as any composer could wish for—was still at his side; with the approach of Christmas he pulled himself together and began to take an interest in the rehearsals of *The Peasant a Rogue* (which was to have its first performance on 17 January 1878).

Early in the new year Dvořák paid his first visit to Vienna, where he was hoping to meet Brahms. Unfortunately the great man had just left for a concert tour of Germany and all Dvořák was able to do was to entrust a bundle of scores to his housekeeper, hoping that Brahms would peruse them on his return. He also called upon Hanslick, with whom he established a cordial personal relationship. About the same time, too, he was sufficiently recovered from his depression to resume composition, and produced two works both of which were typically good-humoured, a string quartet in D minor and a *Serenade* in the same key.

The string quartet (op. 34), dedicated to Brahms in

recognition of the interest he had shown in the *Moravian Duets*, is enjoyable without being in any way Brahmsy. The first movement might almost have been written by Schubert (and indeed bits of it had been), but the other three were all genuine Dvořák, the second being a polka with a contrasted and graceful middle section in 3/8 time, the third a sonorous *adagio* in 3/4, and the finale a *poco allegro* in 6/8, straightforward and lively and commendably brief. And furthermore the assured handling of the delicate balance between the four instruments reminds one that by this time Dvořák was well on his way to becoming a master of the string-quartet medium.

The *Serenade* (op. 44)—which although often referred to as the 'wind' serenade requires cellos and double-basses as well as two oboes, two clarinets, two bassoons, a double-bassoon and three horns—is a cheerful evocation of Bohemian peasant measures. Unfortunately one's appreciation of any distinction the piece may hold is to a certain extent vitiated by the domination of the thick and reedy woodwind tone. Perhaps here Dvořák was for once a shade *too* democratic: this work portrays plebeian clodhoppers as vividly as its string counterpart (op. 22) portrayed elegant aristocrats.

It was probably hereabouts, too, that Dvořák produced his op. 43—part-song settings of three Slovakian folk-verses for male voices with piano-duet accompaniment. These were musically unremarkable but attained some local popularity: they helped to prove once again that their Bohemian-born composer, despite earlier Teutonic tendencies, was none the less a true Slav.

SLAVONIC DANCES

Dvořák's first *Rhapsody*, op. 14 of 1874, has already been commented upon. It was apparently originally intended as the forerunner of several others, and in March 1878 he did indeed start work on three more, to be entitled *Slavonic Rhapsodies*. No sooner had the first of the new series been completed, however, than publisher Simrock persuaded him to turn aside to a set of Slavonic dances for piano duet which would serve as a counter-blast, so to speak, to Brahms's *Hungarian Dances*, which at the time were being diligently thumped out day and night by every discriminating pair of amateur pianists in Europe. Dvořák accepted the challenge and never regretted his decision. (He returned to his *Rhapsodies* later in the same year and all three of them will come up for discussion in due course.)

This first set of *Slavonic Dances* (op. 46, March/April 1878) typifies in music three of Dvořák's basic human attributes: the sense of proportion without which no one can hope to cultivate a sense of humour; the passionate love of a homeland; the determination to justify whatever talents God might have given him by using them for the benefit of humble people in his own walk of life, the majority of whom differed from him only in that they didn't become great composers. And it must be added that the spirit which inspired these unrestrained evocations of jollity was matched by the technical skill which went into the fashioning of every detail. The young and unsophisticated dance gaily, while their elders watch with delight and connoisseurs listen with admiration.

As we have already noted, this work was commissioned for piano duet, but Dvořák almost simultaneously provided an orchestral version, which before long was acclaimed both in Prague and Berlin, where Louis Ehlert (1825–1884), the music critic of the *Nationalzeitung*, wrote a 500-word eulogy. (In return, Dvořák dedicated to him the 'wind' serenade, op. 44, when it was published later the same year.) As piano duets, too, the *Slavonic Dances* achieved immediate success, but today, when domestic music-making is no longer a customary middle-class relaxation, one is

SLAVONIC DANCES (first set) op. 46

No.	Name of dance (and district of origin)	Key	Time signature	Characteristics
1	Furiant (Bohemia)	C major	3/4	Enthusiastically vigorous and deservedly well-known (but not always played with the terrific gusto that Dvořák intended)
2	? (Serbia)	E minor	2/4	The *tempo* is frequently varied and for the most part the mood is courtly rather than bucolic
3*	Polka (Bohemia)	A flat major	2/4	Restrained at the start, but a typical polka-rhythm soon bursts in with outstanding effect
4	Sousedská (Bohemia)	F major	3/4	Marked *tempo di menuetto* but incorporates stronger rhythmical accentuations than do most minuets
5	Skočná (Bohemia)	A major	2/4	A lively dance with intermixed four-bar and three-bar phrases
6*	Sousedská (Bohemia)	D major	3/4	Bears the same relation to a waltz that no. 4 bears to a minuet
7	Skočná (Bohemia)	C minor	2/4	Not such a typical skočná as no. 5 (there are no three-bar phrases) but nevertheless one of the most brilliantly contrived pieces of the whole set
8	Furiant (Bohemia)	G minor	3/4	Even more invigorating than no. 1; students should note in particular the alternations between G minor and G major

* In the piano-duet version (and in transcriptions for piano solo published subsequently) nos. 3 and 6 change places.

more likely to hear them played in a public concert-hall than in a private drawing-room. In some ways this is a pity, since Dvořák paid due regard to the probable capabilities and limitations of amateur pianists; in other ways it is a blessing, since his professional expertise in instrumentation enabled him to endow the orchestral version with a colourful panache which neither a Rawicz and Landauer nor even a Rubinstein and Ashkenazy could hammer out of the most noble Bechstein or Steinway.

It will be noticed in the table on page 78 that seven out of eight of these dances belonged unequivocally to Bohemia. Not until a second set was composed and published some eight years later was a cosmopolitan balance to some extent achieved: Dvořák was then to call not only upon Serbia once again but also upon Slovakia and Poland and Russia.

EIGHT EVENTFUL MONTHS

On page 66 I had occasion to refer to Josef Srb-Debrnov, a great friend of Smetana and also a friend of Dvořák. The Srb-Debrnov family comprised, so far as musical talent was concerned, two amateur violinists and one amateur cellist and one amateur exponent (believe it or not) of the harmonium, and for their private practice and delectation Dvořák in May 1878 composed a quartet in G minor for two violins and cello and harmonium, which he entitled *Maličkosti (Bagatelles)*. He accorded it the dignity of an opus number (47), of which it was quite worthy. *Bagatelles* may hold little retrospective significance, but it was melodious and carefully-written: of its five movements the first and third and last, all in something like polka-rhythm, were thematically connected.

No sooner had Dvořák completed a work for four amateurs than he got down to one for six professionals: a sextet in A major for two violins and two violas and two cellos (op. 48). Like *Bagatelles*, it was dated May 1878 and light-hearted in conception, but it required greater delicacy of execution. The manner often recalled the *Slavonic Dances*, and the third movement went so far as to incorporate an almost exact quotation from the first of the two furiants in op. 46. Some of the tunes in this sextet, although engaging, do indeed sound rather trite for chamber music, but that criticism does not apply to the slow movement, an excellent dumka where the keys of D minor and F sharp major are set in effective contrast and which (like the duet from *King and Collier* cited on pages 54–5) is largely constructed on five-bar phrases. The finale consists of unduly protracted variations on a not very promising theme, but Dvořák did his best to keep up the interest by introducing individual quirks of melody and rhythm and harmony.

In June 1878 Dvořák found new happiness when Anna gave birth to a daughter. She was christened Otilie and was the first of six children all of whom were to survive the mortal perils of infancy. During that summer he eased off somewhat in composition: in July he wrote only a short 'concert piece' for violin and piano, which remained in manuscript until in 1929 Günther Raphael revised and published it along with the cello concerto of 1865; in August a sacred song (in Latin) for voice and organ; in September three inartistically elaborate settings of modern-Greek verses translated into Czech (op. 50). When autumn came round, however, he buckled down to complete the remaining two of the three *Slavonic Rhapsodies* which had been planned earlier in the year.

Dvořák's *Slavonic Rhapsodies*, published in a bunch as op. 45 nos. 1, 2, 3, were Slav all right (and unlike the earlier op. 14 owed little to Liszt) but not one of them was truly rhapsodical. Indeed no. 1 (in D major), which had preceded the first set of *Slavonic Dances*, showed the composer, to coin a word, at his most *un*rhapsodical; this was a straightforward piece of work, mainly in march rhythm and for the most part rather lacking in inspiration; it neither rose to distinction nor descended to vulgarity, but the poetic appeal of its dying moments—when horns and trumpets softly echo the main theme against a background of drum-taps—is worth waiting for. No. 2 (in G minor) and no. 3 (in A flat major) were more characteristic. It may have been a coincidence that no. 2 was based on two tunes and no. 3 on three; in any case all five melodies were pleasant but unmemorable, and the rhapsody element, such as it was, depended largely upon frequent changes of both *tempo* and time-signature. For instance, before no. 2 is a minute and a half old we have been treated in succession to *allegro ma non troppo* in 3/4 time, *moderato* in 4/4, *tempo primo* in 3/4, *allegro* in 3/4—and so it goes on. The bulk of no. 3 is in quick 2/4 time, but there are also several extended and much slower passages in an ingratiating 9/8 and in 4/4 with a 12/8 flavour. Taken as a whole op. 45, although by no means a negligible opus, gives cause for modest congratulation rather than great enthusiasm.

On Dvořák's fifth wedding anniversary (17 November 1878), whether by accident or design I do not know, there was a concert in Prague of his own works, at which he himself conducted the 'wind' serenade and the first two *Slavonic Rhapsodies*; songs and piano pieces were also included in the programme. During the same month he went to Berlin, where he made personal contact with Simrock and the directors of another firm, Bote & Bock, who between them arranged to publish a number of his recent compositions including all three *Slavonic Rhapsodies*, although the third of these was not yet actually finished. In mid-December he set off in the opposite direction to pay his second visit to Vienna, having ascertained that this time Brahms would be in residence. On the way there he dashed off five male-voice choruses based on Lithuanian folk-poems, of which only the fifth—*Hostina* (literally *The Feast*, but sometimes called *The Sparrows' Party*)—showed any originality.

Dvořák stayed two days in the Austrian capital and fulfilled his main purpose, which was to meet Brahms, thank
him for all his kindness, and present him with the score of
the string quartet in D minor op. 34. No record of their
conversation survives, but they established a close relationship that was very friendly from the start and was later to
blossom into something like a mutual admiration society;
Brahms right away undertook to bring Dvořák's music to
the notice of the distinguished Hungarian-born conductor
Hans Richter (1843–1916). Dvořák called next at Brno
(Brunn), where he was enthusiastically welcomed by Leoš
Janáček (1854–1928), who at the age of twenty-four was
director of the local choral society. The two men were
already well acquainted (during the previous summer they
had been on a walking-tour together) and now, at a concert
arranged in Dvořák's honour, Janáček conducted four of the
Slavonic Dances and the three Slovakian male-voice choruses
of op. 43. Although Dvořák did not indulge in composition
on his way home, that is not to say that he dozed off in a
comfortable corner-seat. It was perhaps because he had
lodged for so many years with his uncle Václav Dušík, who
was a railwayman, that anything to do with trains always
interested him nearly as much as did music. He spent many
leisure moments in engine-spotting and was on Christian-
name terms with most of the drivers stationed at the Prague
main-line engine shed. Indeed, did one not have his own
word for it on the title-page of the manuscript, it would be
difficult to believe that he found it necessary to while away
the time on a train journey from Prague to Vienna by
writing indifferent Lithuanian part-songs. But he had
promised to provide something for the Vienna Slavonic
Choral Society and had apparently left this till the last
moment. Perhaps, too, he hoped to be able to impress
Brahms with his industrious devotion to the cause of music,
for Brahms, so far as one knows, was not particularly
interested in locomotives.

CHAPTER EIGHT

Consolidation

By 1879 Dvořák was sufficiently well-established in Prague to be asked to compose music for special occasions—an anniversary of the Hlahol Choral Society, for instance, or the celebration of Emperor Franz Josef's silver wedding—but none of these made-to-measure works added much to his reputation. They included an excessively loud setting of Psalm 149 for chorus and orchestra; for orchestra alone a perfunctory Festival March and a vigorous but undistinguished polonaise. Of slightly greater retrospective importance were a polonaise in A major for cello and piano and a mazurka in E minor for violin and small orchestra (op. 49), a gay little piece with a particularly attractive middle section in B major. Of *far* greater importance was a string quartet in E flat major (op. 51) dedicated to Jean Becker (1833–1884), leader of the Florentine Quartet for whom it was specially composed.

In the first movement of this quartet (March 1879) the rich sonority of the splendid main theme was characteristically lightened by a background touch of polka-rhythm that persisted almost throughout. The second movement was an example of dumka-form being developed to its logical and ultimate conclusion: here a single basic melody alternated between slow 2/4 time in G minor and quick 3/4 time in G major, so that the overall effect was that of elegy-cum-furiant, and indeed the movement successfully combined the functions of both. Consequently for the third movement Dvořák was able to indulge, most acceptably, in a disarmingly simple and pastoral 'romance' (B flat major, *andante con moto*, 6/8). The finale, not for the first or last time in his instrumental works, was a vigorous Slavonic dance. Although op. 51 deservedly ranks high among his fourteen surviving string quartets—possibly so high as to be runner-up for top place—and the music of all four movements is unquestionably finer than that of the quartet op. 34 or the sextet op. 48, there are moments which suggest doubt as to whether on this occasion the composer was altogether happy in his choice of medium: it would be interesting, sometime, to hear the work played, in defiance of all tradition, on a string orchestra. (Smetana's quartet *From my Life* benefits from such unorthodox treatment.)

PUBLICATION PROBLEMS

Towards the end of March 1879 Dvořák packed his suitcase once again and went off on another visit to Berlin, where Simrock, by this time coining money from the *Slavonic Dances* (which had proved as popular in Britain as in Austria and Germany), bought the new quartet, along with several earlier works which were still in manuscript, and inveigled Dvořák into granting him an option on future compositions. Whether or not Dvořák understood the legal obligations of such an agreement one cannot be sure; the fact remains that he had also promised to keep at least three other publishing firms well supplied, namely Bote & Bock and Schlesinger (both of Berlin) and Hofmeister (of Leipzig). As time went on he therefore had to resort to a certain amount of subterfuge in order to deter Simrock from taking action to protect his rights. For instance, when Schlesinger offered better terms than did Simrock for the *Czech Suite* (an orchestral work composed in April 1879) Dvořák headed it op. 39, so as to give the impression that he had written it before signing his contract with Simrock; presently, with the same nefarious purpose in mind, he allowed Hofmeister to publish twelve nondescript piano pieces as op. 8, while at the same time keeping Simrock quiet with a set of waltzes, op. 54. Meanwhile he entrusted two songs and one duet (all three with organ accompaniment) to a Prague firm, Stáry, which later published them as op. 19. Small wonder that the chronological confusion over Dvořák's opus numbers soon became worse than ever!

Whatever the circumstances of their publication these compositions, for one reason or another, all demand more than a bare mention. The *Czech Suite* was a fitting pendant to the *Slavonic Dances* of the previous year, comprising as it did a 'pastorale' in D major, a polka in D minor, a sousedská in B flat major, a 'romance' in G major and a furiant in D minor. The orchestration of the 'pastorale', like that of the *Serenade* op. 44, was somewhat thick and reedy, but no one could cavil at the remaining four items; perhaps the high spot was the sousedská—a sousedská which by the way belonged to the waltz-type rather than the minuet-type.

With his 'op. 8' Dvořák pulled a fast one not merely on Simrock from whom he held it back but also on Hofmeister to whom he sold it—and who entitled it *Silhouettes*—and indeed on the public at large. It was not really a new composition at all, being for practical purposes merely a re-hash for piano solo of snippets from his 1865 *Bells of Zlonice* symphony and *Cypresses* song-cycle. In several of these twelve little pieces one can detect a pleasant flavour of Schumann, but most of them are either trivial or shapeless: no. 4 in F sharp minor, for instance, starts off very promisingly as a quasi-furiant and then inexplicably comes to a dead stop half-way through what should have been the 'trio' (middle section). *Silhouettes* was not a work of which Dvořák can have been proud, but at least it enabled him to prove to himself that he could challenge music publishers (whom he always regarded as rapacious) on their home ground.

As it happened the eight waltzes (op. 54) with which Simrock was fobbed off on this occasion were far more representative than *Silhouettes* and indeed remain among the most attractive of Dvořák's piano pieces. Perhaps the best of them is no. 1 in A major, which is exceptionally elegant and graceful. No. 3 hovers characteristically between two different keys, C sharp minor and E major; no. 4 in D flat major has a splendid thumping rhythm which surely makes it a waltz-type sousedská rather than a waltz proper; nos. 5, 6 and 7 all owe something to Brahms—and are none the worse for it.

The three (vocal) items of Dvořák's op. 19, published by Stáry, were settings of Latin words and were intended to be sung in church; *O sanctissima* was a duet for contralto and baritone; *Ave Maria* and *Ave Maris Stella* were solos for contralto *or* baritone. Musically these pieces are of little importance, but it is interesting to note that Dvořák dedicated the two solos to his wife ('uxori carissimae') and the duet to his friend Alois Göbl (1841–1907). Anna Dvořáková, let us remember, had sufficiently good a voice to have been able to hold down a permanent job at the National Theatre; she did not give up singing after her marriage, and indeed for many years to come was to step into the breach to sustain the principal contralto rôle in local performances of some of her husband's big choral works. Göbl, too, had been a colleague of National Theatre days, but he had failed to make the grade as a singer and was now acting as secretary to the wealthy Prince Rohan-Rochefort (1801–1892) on his estate at Sychrov near Turnov (Turnau), in the centre of that district of northern Bohemia that some sixty years later was to achieve unenviable notoriety as the 'Sudetenland'.

VIOLIN CONCERTO IN A MINOR

An account of how Dvořák coped with competing publishers has led us slightly astray from strict chronology. The *Czech Suite* allocated to Schlesinger was dated April 1879, but Hofmeister's *Silhouettes* and Simrock's waltzes and Stáry's vocal pieces belonged to the summer and autumn of that year, and in the meantime the admirable Brahms had put Dvořák in touch with the great Hungarian-born violinist Josef Joachim (1831–1907), who during the early summer studied and played the first-violin parts of both the string sextet op. 48 and the string quartet op. 51. He was so much impressed with these works that he encouraged Dvořák to write a violin concerto; he himself would be prepared to collaborate to the extent of proposing emendations to the solo passages and possibly to the construction. (Besides being a virtuoso violinist, Joachim was an accomplished composer and all-round musician.) Dvořák jumped at the chance, and in July 1879 set to work on its composition—in Alois Göbl's country home at Sychrov.

Joachim proved himself a splendid accomplice, going so far as to make pertinent suggestions regarding the counterpoint and orchestration here and there, but being a busy man with many professional commitments he took a long time over the job, so that although Dvořák completed the draft of the concerto at Sychrov in September 1879 it did not have its first performance until October 1883, when it was played not by Joachim (to whom it had of course been dedicated) but by the Czech violinist František Ondříček (1859–1922).

The first movement of this concerto is not of itself particularly interesting, but nevertheless the co-operation between Dvořák and Joachim can here be seen to have been rewarding: the basic material is somewhat slender, but what is probably Joachim's contribution to the soloist's part helps to fill it out. A tranquil interlude marked *quasi moderato* then leads without a break to an *adagio ma non troppo* in F major, in which Joachim may have touched up the virtuoso passages but which is more significant for another reason.

Generally speaking, as already noted, Dvořák had a tendency, even in symphonic music, to rely upon comparatively short self-contained melodic phrases, but the solo violin's melody at the beginning of this movement lasts no less than thirty-eight bars. (Its opening, incidentally, must surely have been at the back of Brahms's mind when six years later he penned the glorious 'second subject' of the *andante moderato* in his fourth symphony.) This unwonted flight of extended lyricism enabled Dvořák to complete a movement which marked what was perhaps his first successful attempt to prove himself a truly individual romanticist by international rather than local standards.

By tradition the third and last movement of a violin concerto should at least be cheerful and if possible gay, but in this medium, for some reason or other, even the greatest of composers have sometimes found it difficult to be cheerful and gay without at the same time sagging towards triviality. The finale of Dvořák's sole essay in the genre is somewhat reminiscent of the finale of Beethoven's; if you wholeheartedly enjoy the one you should wholeheartedly enjoy the other. Let us leave it at that.

In October 1879 Dvořák went to Vienna again, in order to attend the first performance in that city of his *Slavonic Rhapsody* in A flat major op. 45 no. 3, over which Brahms and Richter both waxed enthusiastic: Richter, who was meeting the Czech composer for the first time, made a big fuss of him. In the following February Brahms himself visited Prague, and this was probably the only occasion on which he and Dvořák had a meeting outside Vienna.

'CIGÁNSKÉ MELODIE' ('GIPSY SONGS')

During the course of his life Dvořák wrote about eighty songs (leaving aside vocal duets), but as a song-writer he could in no way challenge Schubert—so many of whose *six hundred* deservedly rank as masterpieces—nor could it be said that his output in this field rivalled in quality that of Robert Schumann, Johannes Brahms, Gabriel Fauré, Hugo Wolf, Gustav Mahler or Richard Strauss. Some of his songs have already been referred to in this chronicle and others soon will be; the vast majority provided a pleasant excuse for domestic music-making without aiming at or attaining any higher level of artistic achievement. Exceptionally, in seven *Gipsy Songs* (op. 55), written early in 1880, he was on top form by any standard, except perhaps in no. 5, the rather commonplace *Struna naladěna* (*Tune thy strings*). All seven were settings of poems by Alfred Heyduk (1835–1923); they were dedicated to the Bohemian-born Gustav Walter (1834–1910), a leading tenor of the Vienna Court Opera, and although written to Czech verses were first published in a German translation. This time it was Simrock who was the lucky man.

There have always been plenty of gipsies in Bohemia (one notes that the French word for 'gipsy' is 'bohémien'), but Heyduk on this occasion drew inspiration from the gipsy-lore of Slovakia, a more mountainous (and more exotic) Slav land away to the east. Dvořák was a patriotic Czech, but in *Gipsy Songs* he once again made it clear that this did not deter him from wider racial loyalties, and Heyduk's quasi-Slovakian verses could have found no more faithful musical interpreter.

Far and away the best-known 'gipsy song'—and indeed the best-known of all Dvořák's songs—is no. 4, *Kydž mne stará matka* (*Songs my mother taught me*), which is certainly a little gem of its kind. Like all the rest, however, it should for preference be sung by a tenor or baritone rather than, as so often, by a wobbly contralto addicted to *portamento*. All these songs (bar no. 5) achieve melodic distinction, and if specially honourable mention be made of no. 1, *Má píseň zas mi láskou zní* (*My song of love rings through the dusk*), and no. 6, *Široké rukávy* (*Wide the sleeves*), it is for different reasons. The former has an exceptionally attractive and varied piano accompaniment; the latter, which is in slow polka-rhythm, is another example of Dvořák's fondness for key-ambiguity, the contenders for supremacy this time being F major and D major.

AN EASY-GOING SPRING AND SUMMER

During the first few months of 1880 Dvořák also completed a violin sonata and some more short piano pieces. Although Šourek and other Czech musicologists have tried to make out that the violin sonata in F major (op. 57) was an attempt to reproduce in a more intimate milieu the characteristics of the violin concerto (op. 53), one's immediate reaction on listening to it is that this work, rather than the string quartet op. 34, should by rights have been dedicated to Brahms. The first movement, from its very opening bars, is so typical of Brahms slightly below his best that only an expert connoisseur, when hearing it for the first time, would be likely to attribute it to anyone else. The second movement is just plain dull—with the plain dullness that neither composer was able to avoid in moments when inspiration was lacking. The finale? Well, Brahms himself, although German by birth, wrote Hungarian dances, and had he been so minded could just as easily have written this Slavonic dance—although he would not have allowed it to drag itself out so interminably as Dvořák did.

Dvořák's piano pieces of 1880 included mazurkas and impromptus and 'eclogues', more than half of which were published within a few months of completion. Simrock, who had been graciously accorded the violin sonata, did not seem to be particularly interested, but Hofmeister was so well pleased with one collection that as in the case of *Silhouettes*, he dug up a French title for it—*Six morceaux pour pianoforte* (op. 52). At least two of these morsels, no.1

in G minor (a dashing impromptu) and no. 3 in C minor (a *larghetto* entitled 'Intermezzo'), showed Dvořák, as a composer for the piano, at his best. Nor had Bote & Bock any reason to be dissatisfied with six mazurkas, op. 56: inevitably there were echoes of Chopin here and there, but Dvořák outdid even Chopin in harmonic initiative when by the fifteenth bar of no. 2—in C major—he firmly established the key of F sharp major; no. 6, although not superficially the most attractive, seemed to foreshadow Skriabin's miniatures in this field. Others of the 1880 piano pieces remained in manuscript until after the composer's death, among them three *Albumblätter*—and why these should eventually have been published with a German title I do not know.

April 1880 saw Dvořák haggling once again with publishers in Berlin, but that summer he took a long holiday from such preoccupations. First he went to a country estate at Vysoká near Příbram, some thirty-five miles south of Prague, where his host and hostess were Count Kounic and Countess Kounicová. He had not many close acquaintances among the aristocracy, but this particular countess was none other than his sister-in-law, the Josefa Čermáková with whom in 1865 he had been desperately in love; she had become a successful actress, and later (like other successful actresses) had married into the peerage. After relaxing for six weeks or so in the Bohemian countryside, Dvořák made his way in mid-August to Wiesbaden to visit Louis Ehlert, the German music critic who had praised the *Slavonic Dances* so highly. On all these journeyings he took careful note of anything likely to interest a railway enthusiast, and while at Wiesbaden enjoyed a *Rheindampfschiffsfahrt* (Rhine steamer-trip) to Cologne and back. On returning home he performed a small labour of love by arranging and conducting a concert at Zlonice on 26 September, in memory of his old friend and preceptor Antonín Liehmann, who had died the previous year; next day he was off again to Vysoká—

but this time it was not to indulge in country pursuits or even to watch trains go by. Greatly refreshed by his holiday he settled down in peace and quiet to composition, and in less than three weeks completed a large-scale orchestral work which he may have sketched out at Wiesbaden and which ranks among the top ten symphonic masterpieces of the late nineteenth century.

SYMPHONY NO. 6 IN D MAJOR
at one time called No. 1 (see page 60)

Dvořák's sixth symphony neither propounds philophical problems nor probes deeply into human emotions; on the contrary it is throughout characteristically carefree (though by no means frivolous) in mood. Moreover, it is commendably straightforward in construction and none could deny its tunefulness. In other words it is a virtually impeccable work of art—untrammelled and unadulterated *art*.

The first movement, the opening of which may well have been inspired by the opening of Brahms's symphony no. 2 in the same key, rises to grandeur without becoming sententious. One section of the 'second subject' provides a splendid forging-ahead melody with an almost waltz-like lilt (bars 108–117), and one is surprised that Dvořák did not make more use of this theme in the 'development section'. Nothing is taken too seriously for too long; there are some unorthodox but logical deviations from the strict tenets of sonata-form, and any trace of solemnity that may momentarily have blown up is effectively punctured by a final shaft of jollity.

The second movement comprises lyrical diversions on an expressive tune to which Schubert would not have been too proud to put his name; the third is a furious furiant, a Bohemian equivalent of the scherzo in Beethoven's *Eroica* symphony, with a contrasted 'trio' section in which the piccolo plays a prominent part. Yet perhaps the crowning glory of this remarkable work is its finale. With the possible exception of Brahms's no. 4 I can think of no other well-known symphony belonging to the nineteenth century in which the artistic merit of the last movement equals let alone transcends that of all three that have preceded it. Dvořák's main theme is neither more nor less four-square than those of the symphonic finales written in the same key by Brahms and Franck, but he escaped from rigidity far sooner than did either of his contemporaries (at bar 15 to be precise) and showed exceptional mastery by squeezing every ounce of interest from it in a movement whose stirring rhythm drives the music forward with ever-increasing vitality towards a paean of triumphant jubilation.

Little more than a month after completing this symphony Dvořák took the score to Vienna and showed it to Hans Richter, who promptly accepted the dedication. He was indeed profoundly impressed, and promised to play the work in the near future; he had in mind 26 December of that year (1880), but in the event let Dvořák down. He had already arranged to present at this Boxing Day concert the first performance of Brahms's *Academic Festival* overture, and he did not feel it would be fair to ask his orchestra to tackle another big new work at short notice. (He substituted Beethoven's symphony no. 8.) Richter made amends, however, by conducting Dvořák's new symphony in London eighteen months later (May 1882), but by then it had already had its British première under the baton of August Manns (1825–1907). The first performance of all, appropriately enough, took place in Prague (March 1881) and was conducted by Dvořák's old friend of student days, Adolf Čech.

SOMETHING FOR EVERYONE

On his return home from Vienna in November 1880, Dvořák, at Simrock's request, made an orchestral transcription of some of Brahms's *Hungarian Dances*, which up till then had been known only in the form of piano duets. This task inspired him to compose another set of piano duets himself—and also provide an orchestral version. These ten *Legends* of op. 59 (February/March 1881) were an obvious attempt to repeat the astonishing success of the eight Slavonic dances of op. 46; they never achieved the same popularity, although nos. 1, 3, 5 and 9 were Slavonic dances in all but name. Taken collectively, the *Legends* (dedicated to Eduard Hanslick) look better suited to two pianists than to an orchestra; it should be added, however, that no. 8 in F major (a charming piece in varied *tempi* but maintaining throughout a 6/8 rhythm, now lilting, now spirited), and no. 10 in D flat major (which rounds things off in an unexpectedly pastoral and tranquil mood), would be acceptable in any garb.

The year 1881 was the most momentous in Bohemia's history since 1860. Divisions between the two branches of political nationalists had recently become so marked that adherents of a moderate policy (as originally propagated by František Palacký) had become known as the 'old Czechs' and the extremists as the 'young Czechs', but Czechs both old and young benefited from the enlightened attitude of Austria's new Prime Minister Count Taaffe (1833–1895), under whose régime they were granted a higher share of parliamentary representation in Vienna than ever before, while their language was raised to semi-official status. Applications for administrative posts in the civil service, for instance, were no longer required to be couched, as heretofore, in German; in law courts witnesses were henceforth allowed to give evidence in Czech. One immediate consequence of this relaxation of age-old restrictions under the Habsburgs was the establishment of a Czech University in Prague, where one of the first professors was Tomáš Masaryk (1850–1937)—who thirty-seven years later was to become the first president of an independent Czechoslovakia. It was a coincidence that 1881 also saw the completion of the new National Theatre building in the centre of Prague, overlooking the river Vltava, which had been envisaged in 1862 and of which the foundation stone had been laid in 1868, when Smetana's *Dalibor* had had its first performance at the 'Provisional Theatre'.

The ceremonial opening was arranged for 11 September, but the new theatre actually came into use on 11 June when, most appropriately, the attraction was the first performance of Smetana's latest opera, *Libuše* (not one of his best efforts, it must be admitted). Disaster followed however, for in August the new theatre was partly destroyed by fire, and for more than two years to come National Theatre productions had therefore to be staged, as previously, at the 'Provisional Theatre'. Among them was Dvořák's *Pigheaded Peasants*, which although composed in 1874 only received managerial approval in 1881; its première took place on 2 October, but possibly owing to the disorganization after the fire this delightful little operetta was perfunctorily rehearsed and in consequence did not achieve the success which it richly deserved. (The part of Řeřicha was sung by Karel Čech, who seventeen years earlier had been one of the composer's fellow-lodgers in a somewhat dingy Prague suburb.)

In April 1881 Dvořák had begun work on a third heroic opera (of which more anon), but he laid it aside during the summer, and for the next six months or so devoted his time to an impromptu in D minor for piano, a last-time-for-all Moravian duet for soprano and contralto (to neither of which works did he think it worth while to attach an opus number), a string quartet in C major (op. 61), incidental music for a play entitled *Josef Kajetán Tyl* (op. 62) and five part-songs (op. 63).

The quartet in C major was written at the behest of the Austrian violinist and conductor Josef Hellmesberger (1828–1893) to whom Dvořák dedicated it before he put a note down on paper. When the time came for him to fulfil his obligation he for once deliberately set out to follow the Viennese tradition of string-quartet writing, and it was therefore hardly to be expected that this work would achieve the spontaneity of the E flat major quartet op. 51. But although not particularly characteristic it nevertheless contained some excellent music, and Hellmesberger was delighted. The thematic material of the first two movements was indeed not unworthy of a Beethoven, but in each case it was developed by a Dvořák at his most discursive. The scherzo might have been contrived by a Schubert not quite at his best, an unusual feature being that although the scherzo proper was in 3/4 time the 'trio' section was in 2/4. (Compare the scherzo of the string quartet in F minor composed in 1873.) In the finale Mozart and Beethoven and Schubert all looked in on a Slavonic dance, and since each added something it could hardly fail to be satisfying—if somewhat mixed in style.

In real life Josef Kajetán Tyl (1808–1856) was a playwright and versifier who did much to encourage Czech dramatic aspirations during the age of Metternich; his poem *Kde domov můj? (Where is my home?)*, set to music in 1834 by František Škroup, formed the basis of what later became the Czechoslovakian national anthem. Appropriately enough, František Ferdinand Šamberk (1838–1904), the author of a play about him, was himself an actor (specializing however in comedy parts). Dvořák's incidental music consisted of an overture, two entr'actes and some 'melodrama' (background-music), but everywhere except in the first entr'acte, a lively polka-like *allegretto scherzando* in

F major, the easily recognizable opening of Škroup's tune too frequently dominated the proceedings: in the overture, for instance, the melody sounded impressive in slow 3/4 time, but lost significance when forced unwillingly into a tripping 6/8. In view of the fact that Tyl himself was a patriotic Czech poet and dramatist, and *Josef Kajetán Tyl* a play by a patriotic Czech actor with incidental music by a patriotic Czech composer, it is ironical that the overture was published (by Simrock) under a German title, *Mein Heim*. Dvořák's comment at the time was probably unprintable, but he soon lost interest in *Josef Kajetán Tyl* and its overture, and I see no real reason why interest should be revived.

The part-songs of autumn 1881—collectively entitled *V přírodě (Amid Nature)*—were settings of verses by Vítězslav Hálek (to whom Dvořák had already had recourse for the *Hymnus* and *Evening Songs*). Very simple in style and character they must surely have been composed with an eye on school choirs and village choral societies. The only one of the five in which one can detect an individual approach is no. 5: *Dnes do skoku a do písničky (This is in truth a day of joy)*. The other four all belong to the same category as Sullivan's *Oh hush thee, my baby* and Elgar's *As torrents in summer*. (This need not be interpreted as adverse criticism: I am a great admirer of both Sullivan and Elgar, neither of whom necessarily let one down in moments of quiet relaxation.)

Meanwhile, during that same autumn, Dvořák had been to Berlin again, to carry on his interminable arguments over terms with Simrock. He broke his homeward journey both at Leipzig, where Joachim happened to be giving a recital, and at Sychrov, where he was able to tell his close friend Göbl all that had transpired since their last meeting. Back home, at the first opportunity, he got down to work again on his half-finished opera.

'DIMITRIJ'

We must now glance at a page of Russian history. Although officially known as Ivan IV, Ivan the Terrible is generally regarded as having been the first actual Czar of that country: he ruled over its vast territories from 1533 until 1584 (to put the matter in historical perspective for English readers, from half-way through the reign of King Henry VIII until half-way through the reign of Queen Elizabeth I). When he died he was succeeded by his son Feodor, who so far from being Terrible was somewhat of a nincompoop, but meanwhile there were two other claimants to the throne, each of whom had his supporters: one was another of Ivan's sons, Dmitri by name, who was only two years old at the time of his father's death; the other was Ivan's brother-in-law, Boris Godunov, an ambitious noble-man who hailed from Tartary. When poor little Dmitri was murdered in 1591, Boris was generally believed to have been responsible, and on Feodor's death in 1598 it was Boris who duly became Czar. Presently, however, there appeared on the scene a mysterious figure who was in truth Grischka Otropiev, a de-frocked monk, but who made out that he was none other than the Dmitri who had supposedly been put out of the way ten years before but (so his impersonator claimed) had eluded his assailants and had been in hiding ever since. In his guise as Dmitri, Otropiev married Marina, daughter of the Polish Count Mnischek, and when Boris died in 1605 he advanced on a divided and disorganized Moscow with a Polish army at his heels and succeeded in getting himself proclaimed Czar to the exclusion of Boris's young son and heir. Retribution followed within less than twelve months. When the false Dmitri, now Czar, made Boris's daughter Xenia his mistress, his wife Marina took umbrage and denounced him as the impostor that he was, whereupon

Prince Vassali Shuisky, who had been Boris's Prime Minister, promptly disposed of him in the time-honoured manner—assassination.

Most of these events were covered in Alexander Pushkin's historical drama *Boris Godunov*, produced in 1825. An opera with the same title composed by Modest Mussorgsky (1839–1881) and first performed in 1874, was based on Pushkin's play but proceeded no further than the death of Boris. Dvořák's opera *Dimitrij* took up the tale where Mussorgsky had left off. (Henceforth I shall adopt the published *Czech* spellings of characters in the story.) The librettist was Marie Červinková-Riegrová (1854–1895), who relied partly on Pushkin's *Boris Godunov* and partly on Friedrich Schiller's *Demetrius* (1805) and partly on Ferdinand Břetislav Mikovec's *Dimitr Ivanovič* (1855). She did her job well, and only purists will complain that she may have over-romanticized what was probably in historical fact a rather sordid love-affair between Dimitrij (Dmitri)—who was really Otropiev—and Boris Godunov's daughter Xenie (Xenia).

To summarize the plot very briefly: Act I portrays the arrival of Dimitrij at the gates of the Kremlin and his acclamation as Czar: in Act II, after expressing his devotion to his wife Marina, he falls in love with Xenie; in Act III Marina discovers his infidelity and announces her intention of exposing him; in Act IV she does so, whereupon Prince Šujský (Shuisky) administers the *coup de grâce*. It need hardly be added that Dvořák made Dimitrij, the nominal hero, a tenor, and Prince Šujský, the nominal villain, a bass; Marina was a dramatic soprano, Xenie a lyric soprano, and Ivan the Terrible's widow Marfa a contralto.

So far as one can judge without having seen a performance, *Dimitrij* was a good opera, not musically so remarkable as Mussorgsky's *Boris Godunov* but better constructed (all due credit to Marie Červinková); the only slight dramatic weakness one can detect is that most of the exciting events took place during the last half-hour or so, but this at least ensured that the interest did not, as in so many operas, tail off towards the end.

There is no formal overture, but each of the four acts is preceded by a short prelude, and half-way through the second an orchestral interlude headed 'Proměna' (literally 'Change') marks a break in the continuity of the stage action although there is no actual change of scene. Not all of these five pieces bear any specific relationship to what immediately follows: in some cases Dvořák was just killing time. For instance, the slow prelude to Act I, although presaging ultimate and momentous tragedy, is based on nothing more significant than the music which in Act IV scene 5 forms the background to Xenie's sorrowful withdrawal to a nunnery. In the opera itself, the choral scenes, although now and again rather four-square, are on the whole most impressive, especially those in which the division of the chorus into two conflicting sides—Russians versus Poles—gave the composer opportunity for effective group-contrapuntal writing. The music allotted to the opposing parties, however, was impartially Slavonic, and indeed much of it impartially Bohemian: at one moment there was even a note-for-note reproduction (in a different key) of eight familiar bars from the opening furiant of op. 46.

Several of the songs and concerted items would be easily detachable from their context, but not all are of equal merit. In Act I there is a short and attractive duet for Dimitrij and Marfa (whom he claims as his mother), 'Ó potěš ditě své' ('Give comfort to your child'); he himself has a forthright aria at the beginning of the second half of Act II, 'Z divokého žití víru' ('From the turbulence of life'), and an expressive one to set things going in Act III, 'Viděl jsem ji' ('Then I saw her'). But the long love duet between Xenie and Dimitrij which comprises scene 4 in the second half of Act II, 'Ó chránce můj' ('Oh, saviour mine'), is melodically uninspired: despite a well-contrived vocal climax in the Italian manner, it falls below one's expectations. A more satisfying piece of lyrical music is a quintet in the last scene of all (Act IV scene 5), 'Ó Bože, Bože moj' ('Oh, Lord, my own dear Lord'), but I am not the first to have descried therein a resemblance to the glorious quintet that concludes the first half of Act III in *The Mastersingers*. Generally speaking, however, there is little of Wagner in *Dimitrij*, although Xenie is accorded a frequently-recurring *Leitmotiv* (guiding theme) and now and again Dvořákian matter is used in a Wagnerian manner. At the beginning of Act II, for instance, Dimitrij, who has not yet fallen for Xenie, expresses his affection for his wife Marina in the words—'Jak velká slast mi odménou po tuhém krutém boji' ('Your love for me is my reward for perils I have undergone'). (Compare Shakespeare's *Othello*, Act I scene 3: 'She lov'd me for the dangers I had pass'd; And I lov'd her that she did pity them.') In Act III scene 4 the same theme is introduced anew, in slightly different colouring and with good 'Wagnerian' effect, to provide the background for a showdown in which Marina, driven desperate by her husband's infatuation for Xenie, announces her determination to expose him as an unscrupulous adventurer.

As has already been noted, Dvořák worked at *Dimitrij*, off and on, for about eighteen months, and when first played in Prague (on 8 October 1882) it was well received by the public. Professional critics, however, were less enthusiastic. 'We would rather have Wagnerian music-drama', they said in effect, 'than French opera *à la* Meyerbeer.' Poor Dvořák! Although there may have been an echo here and there of Wagner in *Dimitrij*, and perhaps even a tiny echo of Verdi or Gounod, I cannot see where Meyerbeer (an admirable practitioner in his own line of country) came into the picture. But being sensitive to criticism Dvořák was perturbed by the reaction: ever since his viola-playing days in the National Theatre orchestra he had been convinced that he would eventually make his mark as a composer of opera, but so far (leaving aside that excellent operetta-trifle *The Peasant a Rogue*) success had eluded him. He became worried and muddled: was he or was he not working on sound lines?

CHAPTER NINE

International Fame

Dvořák's mother died on 15 December 1882 at Kladno, where she had been her husband's faithful helper in a *Gasthaus-Metzgerei* for the past twenty-three years. Her son's trio in F minor for violin and cello and piano (op. 65), composed during the following February and March, provides perhaps the most outstanding exception to the generalization, propounded in chapter one, that Dvořák rarely allowed subjective considerations to affect his creative art. He had always been devoted to his mother, and throughout this trio one is aware of a sense of distress—coupled, however, with a sense of conflict; the latter may have been occasioned not so much by sorrow at his recent bereavement as by indecision over his future course of action, following the mixed reception given to *Dimitrij*.

The first movement of this F minor trio is turbulent, with alternations of questioning and answering almost in the manner of Beethoven's 'Muss es sein? es muss sein' in the last movement of his last string quartet, op. 135; the actual music, however, suggests Brahms rather than Beethoven—or even Dvořák. The second movement, usually described as a scherzo, is a rather characterless *allegretto grazioso* in 2/4 time and the unconventionally contrasted key of C sharp minor. The third (*poco adagio*, 4/4, A flat major) starts off unpromisingly with a doleful melody for the cello, but presently comes to life in a more vigorous section which is marred, unfortunately, by some perfunctory writing for the piano: rarely can so many purposeless demisemiquavers have been packed into so few bars. In the finale, despite the fact that the mood is still sombre, we are back with the Dvořák whom we all know and whom most of us admire. Although constructed in a 'classical' manner, this movement is throughout in furiant rhythm, and one receives the impression that after a period of emotional *Sturm und Drang* Dvořák was once again something like his old self. Another point worth noting is that (leaving aside the passages in the slow movement just referred to) this piano trio maintained an admirable balance between the three instruments involved.

(About this time there was sad news of Bedřich Smetana: his terrible deafness had driven him more or less insane, and early in 1883 he was admitted to an asylum, where he lingered on for a year or so until his death in April 1884.)

'SCHERZO CAPRICCIOSO'

I would not presume to challenge Otakar Šourek and other biographers when they record that after his mother's death Dvořák remained in a state of depression for two years or more. With all respect, however, I challenge their assertion or assumption that this frame of mind was reflected in his compositions of those two years—apart from the first of them, the piano trio op. 65. Of the *Scherzo capriccioso* (op. 66), begun in March 1883 and completed in May, the Viennese-born conductor Hans Swarowsky has written that it was 'a forcible attempt to regain lost happiness after the death of his mother'; Šourek referred to its 'gloomy minor harmonies'. Neither of these two comments sound very encouraging, but fortunately for all of us Šourek was for once wide of the mark (there is hardly a 'minor harmony' from start to finish), and if the *Scherzo capriccioso* was a forcible attempt to regain lost happiness it was also a very successful one: this is perhaps the most light-hearted and certainly one of the most masterly of Dvořák's orchestral works.

In the eighteenth century every composer worthy of the name instinctively established the main key of a piece of music at its outset; in the nineteenth every pedagogue worthy of the name insisted that the practice should be maintained, and neither Wagner nor Brahms ever deviated from this principle by more than a hair's breadth. Consequently Tchaikovsky caused academic eyebrows to flutter when in 1875 he began his B flat minor piano concerto with a thumping tune in D flat major, and eight years afterwards Dvořák, with the finales of his own string quartet op. 16 and symphony in F major as precedents, became equally venturesome. The *Scherzo capriccioso* starts with a jolly horn-call, four bars long and unequivocally in the key of B flat major; not until forty bars later is it taken up by the whole orchestra in what ultimately proves to be the main key, D flat major. More surprises follow, for the violins soon introduce a lilting waltz-like strain in far-away G major—and it stays *there*, even, for only six bars. When it eventually subsides (and it is typical of this work that it should subside into F sharp major) there is some lively tossing to-and-fro of a variant of the opening horn-call. Then everything that has gone before is repeated, but this time there are modifications and expansions and the orchestration is enriched throughout.

In the 'trio' (D major, another unexpected key) the cor anglais has a hummable melody (taken up presently by the flute), and the subsequent cross-rhythmic accentuations are in the best Bohemian tradition. Next comes a 'development section' (a rare feature in a scherzo) in which the main themes of the scherzo proper become infected with the cross-rhythm bug of the second half of the trio. An admirably concise recapitulation of the scherzo proper leads to some further 'development' in a slower *tempo*, largely entrusted to flutes and horns and a harp, which has the virtue of straightforward simplicity. Finally, as though there wasn't already plenty to be thankful for, there is a brilliant *strepitoso* coda that would have warmed Rossini's heart-cockles. No symptoms of depression here!

BOHEMIA-VIENNA

In 1883 the Czech dramatist František Adolf Šubert (1849–1915), who was later to become artistic director of the National Theatre, planned a trilogy on the life and times of the great religious reformer Jan Hus; he asked Dvořák to provide incidental music, a request to which the composer gladly acceded. (All Bohemians, be they Catholics, Protestants, Jews or agnostics, have always rightly revered Hus as an outstanding figure in the history of their homeland; staunch Catholics like Dvořák overlooked his heretical tendencies and regarded him mainly as symbolizing a centuries-long struggle for freedom.) In the event Šubert's ambitious project got no further than the first act in the first of three projected plays, and Dvořák's contribution was limited to an overture, subsequently known as the *Husitzká* (*Hussite*) overture.

Like the D major symphony, this work was composed while Dvořák enjoyed the hospitality of his brother-in-law Vàclav Kounic at Vysokà; but it took a month to complete: he began it on 9 August 1883 and finished it on 9 September. His primary intention was to contrast and develop side by side an age-old Catholic hymn (which lauded the spiritual qualities of Saint Wenceslas) and a Hussite marching-song of the fifteenth century entitled *Kdož jste Boži bojovníci?* (*Who are the warriors of God?*). But it didn't work out like that: Dvořák, while trying to fill things in, conceived two better tunes on his own account and used them as the basis of an *allegro con brio* section which excelled in attractiveness the perfunctory treatment accorded to the Wenceslas melody and the somewhat heavy treatment accorded to the Hus melody. Consequently the *Hussite* overture remains a curious mixture of genuine artistry, patriotic sentiment and grandiose pomposity. Where Dvořák relied upon his own inspiration it is excellent; where he relied upon traditional tunes associated with either Wenceslas or Hus it sounds machine-made, and at the climax the ultimate triumph of the Hus chorale is ear-shattering.

In October 1883 Dvořák paid another visit to Brahms in Vienna—and they continued where they had previously left off. He took with him the final version of his violin concerto as amended by Joachim, and was able to report that on its first performance in Prague earlier that month it had been extremely well received. Brahms congratulated him, and after perusing the score passed it on to Hans Richter. Not to be outdone in the civilities, Dvořák expressed himself delighted—and how could he fail to have been?—when Brahms played through for him on the piano the first and last movements of his latest symphony (no. 3 in F major). These two firm friends, as they now were, both had good reason to be satisfied when at a Philharmonic concert on 2 December Richter conducted not only the first performance anywhere of Brahms's third symphony but also the first performance in Vienna of Dvořák's violin concerto; as in Prague, the soloist was František Ondříček.

When he returned from Vienna to Prague at the end of October 1883, the next excitement for Dvořák was the reopening on 18 November of the Czech National Theatre after the disastrous fire that had so nearly destroyed it some two years previously; the occasion was marked by the first performance of the *Hussite* overture. Thereafter he settled down to another group of piano duets, collectively entitled *Ze Šumavy*. Šumava is the Czech name for a range of mountains better known to the outside world as the Böhmerwald (see map on page 10) and while the German rendering of *Ze Šumavy* as *Aus dem Böhmerwald* is therefore most appropriate the English *From the Bohemian Woods* is misleading, since it suggests any old Bohemian woods, of which there are plenty, rather than *the* 'Bohemian Forest'. Of these comparatively short pieces no. 1, *Na přástjách* (*In the*

Spinning-room), is perhaps the best: here the bass-player does most of the spinning while his partner introduces some typically Bohemian melodies up above. No. 5, *Klid* (*Silent Woods*), is almost equally attractive, but its syncopated theme suggests Schumann rather than Dvořák. (The composer afterwards arranged this item both for cello and piano and for cello and orchestra.) No. 6, *Z bouřlivých dob* (*In Troublous Times*), is more characteristic, but the persistence of a 'dotted rhythm' becomes rather monotonous.

At the end of January 1884 Dvořák went to Berlin again, and after the usual financial haggling sold Simrock the *Hussite* overture and *From the Bohemian Woods*. A month later he was preparing himself for his longest trip abroad yet—a trip to England sponsored by the Philharmonic Society of London.

BOHEMIA–LONDON

In 1884 the most direct rail-and-sea link between Prague and London was the same as it is today; that is to say via Nuremberg, Frankfurt, Cologne, Brussels, Ostend and Dover. Dvořák found a fellow-traveller in the pianist Jindřich Kàan z Albestu (1852–1926), and on the evening of Monday 5 March 1884 they together boarded a train at what was then known as the 'Franz Josef' station, between the wars as the 'Wilson' station (in honour of that President of the United States who at the Treaty of Versailles insisted on the principle of national self-determination in Europe), and today simply as the 'hlavni' (main) station. They took the journey in fairly easy stages. After spending Monday night in the train they stopped off on Tuesday at Cologne, and on Wednesday proceeded no farther than Brussels. On Thursday Dvořák saw the sea for the first time, and since it was dead calm his impression was favourable. No record survives as to by which route he and Kàan travelled from

Dover to London, where they arrived at six in the evening. At the time there was a choice of two boat-trains: that of the South Eastern Railway would have landed them at Charing Cross, that of the London Chatham and Dover at Victoria, and lovers of Dvořák's music who share his interest in railways would be glad to know whether he made his first approach to London by way of Ashford and Tonbridge or by way of Canterbury and Chatham. Regrettably, his biographers have not enlightened us on this point; all they tell us is that he was met on arrival by the German-born pianist Oskar Beringer (1844–1922), whose flat in Hinde Street was to be Dvořák's home for the next three weeks, and Henry Littleton (1823–1888), senior partner in the influential firm of music publishers, Novello & Co.

Much of Dvořák's music had already made an impact on London concert-goers during the past five years or so. The *Slavonic Dances* (op. 46) had stirred great interest; the string sextet (op. 48) and the string quartet in E flat major (op. 51) had established his reputation; the symphony in D major (op. 60), which as already recorded had been conducted there by both Manns and Richter, had consolidated it: Oskar Beringer himself had played the piano concerto (op. 33); Joseph Barnby (1838–1896) had conducted a performance of the *Stabat Mater* (which however seems to have been an inadequate one). When the composer appeared in person, enthusiasm knew no bounds. At the Royal Albert Hall he conducted the *Stabat Mater*; at St. James's Hall the *Hussite* overture, the symphony in D major and the *Slavonic Rhapsody* in G minor op. 45 no. 2; at the Crystal Palace the *Scherzo capriccioso* and the *Nocturne* for string orchestra op. 40. None of these works, apart from the *Stabat Mater* and the symphony, had previously been heard in Britain; all were rapturously received by press and public alike.

Nor was social entertainment neglected. On Tuesday 13 March Henry Littleton—whom Dvořák described with charming naïveté as 'a very nice man and immensely wealthy'

—gave a dinner party at which the composer, feeling rather shy, was introduced to a hundred and fifty guests, among them almost every prominent musical personality in London. Dinner was followed by an informal concert, which began and ended with choruses from the *Stabat Mater*. (There had been a choral rehearsal of this work three days earlier, but the actual performance did not take place until two days later.) In between the choruses came the piano trio in G minor op. 26, an aria from *The Pigheaded Peasants* perhaps never heard in this country before or since, and a dozen or so other vocal items, including four of the *Gipsy Songs* and a bunch of Moravian duets. (Dvořák recorded that the duets 'were rendered by Mr Hutchinson and Mrs Monck-Mason', so presumably they were taken from op. 20 for soprano and tenor and not from the better-known op. 32 for soprano and contralto.) All in all, it must have been an exhausting evening, and Dvořák did not get to bed until three in the morning.

On 21 March, the Philharmonic Society provided a banquet in his honour at the Café Royal, and the chair was taken by Julius Benedict (1804–1885), the eighty-year-old composer of *The Lily of Killarney*. Dvořák himself made a short speech in halting English, in which he described the past fortnight as the happiest in his life. (Three months later the Philharmonic Society elected him an honorary member.)

There is no doubt that London, and his reception there, made a profound impression upon Dvořák. He wrote to his father, still living at Kladno, to point out that if the entire population of that town were to attend a concert at the Albert Hall there would still be plenty of room for more. He wrote to Velebín Urbánek (1853–1892), editor of the Prague musical journal *Dalibor*, that 'the English are a fine people, enthusiastic about music, and it is well known that they remain loyal to those whose art they have enjoyed'. This fulsome compliment may have been partly inspired by the comforting knowledge that Novello & Co. had just offered him £2,000, a huge sum of money in those days, to write an oratorio.

BOHEMIA-WORCESTER

It will not have escaped the notice of my readers that for several years now Dvořák had found the countryside more congenial than the town: when he wanted to settle to composition in earnest he was wont to leave Prague to stay either with his friend Alois Göbl at Sychrov or on the estate of his Kounic in-laws at Vysoká, where he worked in what was little more than a hut attached to some stable buildings. Early in 1884, with the money he had just been paid by Simrock for the *Hussite* overture and *From the Bohemian Woods*, he bought a small plot of land from Václav Kounic, and arranged for a house to be built there that would accommodate himself and his wife and their rapidly growing family. (There were now four children: Otilie, aged five and a half; Anna, four; Magda, two and a half; Antonín one. It was not long before another was on the way—it turned out to be a boy and was christened Otakar—and three years later the sextet was completed by the arrival of another daughter, Aloisie.) The village of Vysoká lay within easy reach of the fairly important railway line connecting Prague with Příbram, Březnice, Pisek and Budějovice (Budweis), and furthermore Dvořák could here indulge to heart's content his other great hobby—pigeon-breeding. One learns with mixed feelings that his interest in ornithology also led him to imprison thrushes and other songbirds in a private aviary.

When he got back from London at the end of March 1884 his new family home was not yet ready for occupation, so that he had to start earning Novello's £2,000 in the same outhouse where he had composed the D major symphony

and the *Hussite* overture. Since at the time he could find no
subject that appealed to him for an oratorio, he decided on
the next best thing—a cantata; he eventually chose as his
text *Svatební košile*, a poem by Karel Jaromír Erben (1811–
1870), a specialist in Czech legend and folklore. Dvořák
used to render 'Svatební košile' into English as 'The wedding gown', but literally it means 'the bridal nightgown';
Rev. John Troutbeck (1832–1899), who provided the
English version (as he had for the *Hymnus* of 1872),
evidently did not think that nightgowns should be referred
to in public, and so he christened it *The Spectre's Bride*. With
all respect to Erben and giving full credit to Troutbeck,
this was in fact a more appropriate title than the original:
the ballad concerns a young lady whose dead sweetheart
rises from the grave to carry her by night, in scanty attire,
from her 'humble dwelling' to his 'lordly castle'—which
proves to be a tomb in the local cemetery.

But although by the time September 1884 came round
Dvořák had been able to move from his brother-in-law's
shed to his own new house, he then had to break off work
on his cantata because he was due to pay another visit to
England. This time the sponsors were not the Philharmonic
Society but the promoters of the Three Choirs Festival—
held annually in the cathedrals and town halls of Worcester,
Gloucester or Hereford. In 1884 it was the turn of Worcester, and it was there that Dvořák went to conduct what
were as nearly as I can calculate the third performance in
Britain of his *Stabat Mater* and the fourth of his symphony
in D major. On his journey thither he spent one night in
the train, one in Brussels and one with Henry Littleton at
the latter's luxurious home, Wentworth House, Sydenham.
At Worcester he was entertained by the Mayor and
Mayoress and introduced to a host of local celebrities. When
writing home to his wife Anna he referred to the 'beautiful
ladies' whom he had met at a 'magnificent reception', but
stressed that what pleased him most of all about Worcester

was that ordinary people recognized him in the street and
came up to ask for his autograph: having thus attained in
English eyes a status comparable with that of a county
cricketer, he obviously felt that he had achieved democratic
success in a democratic country.

Barely a month after his return home from Worcester
Dvořák went to Berlin to conduct the first performance in
that city of his D major symphony and to make a round of
calls on publishers—without daring to tell Simrock, however, of his Novello enterprise. Nevertheless he managed
to complete the score of *The Spectre's Bride* well before
Christmas, when he always made a point of giving up
composition for a few days to join with his family in the
usual festivities. The first performance took place the
following March at Plzen (Pilsen), and a fortnight later
the work was repeated by the Hlahol Choral Society in
Prague.

Whatever may have been the literary merits of Erben's
grisly ballad, they were not apparent in Troutbeck's English
translation which, while religiously eschewing any suggestion of indelicacy that there may have been in the original,
was pretty feeble. And truth to tell, by the standards on
which the Dvořák of 1884 must be judged, the music came
within measurable distance of matching it. The construction
was in the conventional nineteenth-century oratorio/cantata
tradition. A baritone, backed by a chorus, relates the narra-
tive; between-whiles a soprano (the bride) and a tenor (the
spectre) occasionally burst into song, either separately or
together. Dvořák provided some pleasant music here and
there, notably a duet for the soprano and tenor, 'Hoj má
panenko' ('Ah, dearest child'), which concludes the first
section, set in the bride's 'humble dwelling'. But the wild
night-journey *à la* Erl King, incorporating such dramatic
incidents as the forcible seizure by the spectre of the bride's
prayer-book, is repetitive and fails to horrify one as it
should; the final graveyard scene, where the 'erring' bride,

out of consideration for her earthly misfortunes, is granted heavenly salvation, fails to move one as it should. It should be added that there are some very effective touches of descriptive orchestration, such as those which illustrate the line 'Psi houfem ve vsi zavyli' ('The dogs, awakened, howled and cried'). We shall soon be meeting *The Spectre's Bride* again—in an English midland town where the hard-headed population does not normally take much account of ghostly spectres.

Meanwhile Dvořák had thrown off a few more piano pieces, including a dumka and a furiant (published as op. 12 !), but he had promised the Philharmonic Society in London that at the first opportunity he would provide it with a new symphony. He had had one in mind ever since Brahms had played over to him part of *his* symphony in F major, and as soon as he got *The Spectre's Bride* off his chest he set to work on it.

SYMPHONY NO. 7 IN D MINOR
at one time called No. 2 (see page 60)

Dvořák's sixth and seventh symphonies were both masterpieces, complementary in the sense that they illustrated to perfection the contrasted characteristics of their respective keys: D major bright-hued and cheerful and suitable for jubilation; D minor sombre or stormy and better fitted for the expression of deep feeling. Although one would hestitate to assert that no. 7 (op. 70) is a greater work of art than no. 6 (op. 60), it is undoubtedly a more profound one. Nevertheless, and at the risk of being accused of irreverence, I shall use a zoological tag as a means of enabling listeners to recognize for themselves the significance of the phrase introduced at the start of the first movement by violas and cellos—in little more than a whisper but with rapidly increasing urgency.

> In a moment or two you may meet a big bear—
> Have a care . . . have a care . . .
> HAVE A CARE . . . HAVE A CARE!

Presently (after a charming but perhaps slightly inconsequent episode in which a horn and an oboe exchange graceful compliments in the friendly but remote key of E flat major) the whole orchestra reiterates the bear-warning in thunderous tones, leading the way to a quiet-flowing 'second subject' of Brahms-like affability. It is not long, however, before the bear emerges from his hiding-place; thereafter he rampages dangerously and almost uninterruptedly—although he retires discreetly into the background on the few occasions when the Brahmsy tune reappears. Eventually Bruin is persuaded to lie down quietly: when two dulcet horns softly echo the original warning there is no longer any need to have a care; everything then dissolves into silence.

The slow movement, which conventionally enough is in the key of F major, alternates between serenity and agitation; it is one of its composer's finest achievements, whether regarded as a component part of a great symphony or as a piece of music great in its own right. At the outset and close the mood is one of tranquillity, almost of spiritual resignation, but between-whiles there are many passionate outbursts of human entreaty. Those who know their *Tristan and Isolde* will prick up ears at a near-quotation from that opera; those who appreciate the art of instrumentation will discover a wide range of orchestral colouring; those who love Dvořák's music for its own sake will realize that for once in a way he was here appealing to the emotions through the intellect rather than vice versa.

In accordance with classical tradition there is a return to the main key of D minor for the third movement, which is entitled 'Scherzo' but is in reality a superb furiant based on two good tunes played simultaneously; since one of them is in 6/4 time it need hardly be added that the other is in 3/2. The same cross-rhythm persists throughout the singularly beautiful 'trio' section (which is in the unconventionally contrasted key of G major), but here the thematic material confines itself mainly to 6/4, leaving it to orchestral figuration to provide the 3/2 touch.

The structure of the finale reminds one, almost for the first time in this work, that Dvořák had a tendency to allow his themes to dictate a course of events to him rather than take charge himself and drill them ship-shape. But here an instinct to let things keep going regardless of academic considerations hardly seems to matter: the gloomy opening is extraordinarily impressive: when storm-clouds clear away for the time being, a stirring tune first announced by the cellos (one cannot help thinking of the corresponding moment in the finale of Brahms's no. 3) causes one to sit up and take notice; the heart-rending climaxes that follow are not unduly protracted, and finally all inhibitions are resolved in an emphatic assertion not of D minor but of D *major*—which leads one to think that perhaps symphony no. 6 has the last laugh over no. 7 after all.

Hardly had Dvořák completed this magnificent work—March 1885—than he stuffed the score in a suitcase, took it off with him to London (once again breaking his journey at Cologne and Brussels) and conducted its first performance at St. James's Hall on 22 April. This time Henry Littleton was his host for a full month. On 6 May Dvořák conducted his piano concerto with Franz Rummel (1853–1901) as soloist and on 13 May the first performance in Britain of the *Hymnus*. Meanwhile he indulged in some extensive sight-seeing (he was particularly delighted with such large open spaces as Hyde Park and Regent's Park) and visited many theatres. (Perhaps one of them may have been the Savoy, where the current attraction was *The Mikado*.) He was introduced to the Scottish composer Alexander Mackenzie (1847–1935), with whom he got on well (Czechs, like

Scots, are by tradition canny and dour), and to the American composer Dudley Buck (1839–1909), who was the first to put it into his head that he should some day visit the United States. He returned home by the same route as usual, with which he must have become familiar by now, but this time travelled straight through without a break.

BOHEMIA-BIRMINGHAM

While in London in May 1885, despite other preoccupations, Dvořák wrote two charming little songs with German words, *Schlaf mein Kind in Ruh'* and *Gott wird dir zur Seite liegen*, but on returning home to Vysoká he relaxed for the next two months with his family and his pigeons and his thrushes, as often as not spending his evenings at the 'local' over a glass or two of beer in the company of congenial neighbours—most of whom worked in nearby silver mines. During that summer he composed only an unimportant 'ballade' for violin and piano and *Hymna českého rolnictva* (*Hymn of the Czech Peasants*), a work no longer than an ordinary hymn in which the only feature of interest was the unexpected interpolation, every few bars, of a very un-hymn-like patter-rhythm. In mid-August he was off to England once again, for the Birmingham Festival at which *The Spectre's Bride* was to have its first performance outside Bohemia.

On his original journey to London seventeen months previously Dvořák had been accompanied by Jindřich Kàan; on the second his companion had been the writer Václav Juda Novotný (1849–1922); on the third the distinguished scholar Doctor Josef Zubatý (1855–1931). This time, however, he travelled on his own, and it seems that his interest in railways may have led him to choose a more devious route than usual; at any rate he ended up by crossing the straits of Dover at night and did not reach

London until six o'clock a.m. on Monday 17 August. He had to go straight on to Birmingham, where that very evening there was a chorus rehearsal of *The Spectre's Bride*. Next morning he returned to London for an orchestral rehearsal. (There was no City of Birmingham Orchestra in those days.) On Wednesday Henry Littleton (who rented a flat in Victoria Mansions, Hove) took him to Brighton, where he was intrigued to notice that ladies and gentlemen were allowed to bathe together in the sea. On Thursday he was back in London and on Friday set forth from Euston again —to undergo the ordeal of an English provincial Music Festival.

It astonished Dvořák then, as it astonishes most of us now, that the 1885 music lovers of Birmingham (which he described with fair accuracy as 'a vast industrial town where they make excellent trinkets of all sorts and the Lord knows what else') had either the time or the inclination to sit through eight concerts, each nearly five hours long, packed into the space of four days. Among the items presented on this occasion were Handel's *Messiah* and Mendelssohn's *Elijah* (almost needless to say); Gounod's oratorio *Mors et Vita* and Charles Villiers Stanford's *Three Holy Children*; a cantata by Frederic Cowen (1852–1935) entitled *The Sleeping Beauty*; Beethoven's *Leonora No. 3* overture and symphony no. 9; a symphony in F major by Ebenezer Prout (1835–1909); a familiar violin concerto by Mendelssohn and a less familiar one by Alexander Mackenzie; and excerpts from Wagner's *Tannhäuser* and *The Valkyrie*. Dvořák's turn came on the third day, Thursday, 27 August 1885, and on that date, whatever the judgment of 1966 may be, *The Spectre's Bride*, with Emma Albani (1852–1930) and Joseph Maas (1847–1886) and Charles Santley (1834–1922) as soloists, took the audience and music critics by storm.

Since Dvořák had meanwhile been invited to provide an oratorio for the Leeds Festival of the following year, it was a very contented composer who two days later started on the long trek back to Vysoká. As it happened it was a very trying journey: for reasons we can make a guess at, he had decided to travel for a change via Calais rather than Ostend; unfortunately the sea was so rough that the steamer was badly delayed and he missed the direct forward connection. Thereafter it became a matter of proceeding across Europe by slow stages, and even Dvořák had for the moment had all he wanted of trains by the time he eventually got home, very late and very tired, on the evening of 31 August.

BOHEMIA-LEEDS

Before leaving England Dvořák had confided to Henry Littleton his intention that the oratorio for Leeds would be based on an episode in Bohemian history which had taken place so long ago that it was almost legendary: the conversion to Christianity in the year 870 or thereabouts of Ludmila and Bořivoj, the grandparents of Saint Wenceslas. Littleton doubted whether this subject would appeal to the British public, and promised to send him, within the course of the next few days, a few alternative suggestions. But Dvořák was inclined to stick to his guns: here is an exact reproduction of a letter he wrote from Vysoká to Littleton in London. It was dated 10 September 1885 and proves, incidentally, that during the past eighteen months he had attained a tolerable command of the English language.

My dear Friend,
I am arrived quite well to my home. The verry merry days of Birmingham ar over and naw stay I agin quiet alone as before. Daily I am walking in the beautyful forsts and reflecting about Ludmila. Many thanks for reviewing Coppys of the Oratoris and Cantatas.
The Editor of the Graphic in London has asked me for my Portrait, but I am sorry not to have one. Please

will you be so kind and send him an photgraphy from
Birmingham, supposed they are ready.

Another time something more.

My best compliments fo your family.

God bye, yours sincerely,

Antonín Dvořák.

He was 'reflecting about Ludmila', and not all Littleton's
'Coppys' could turn his thoughts away from her. Indeed he
had already been in touch with the Czech poet Jaroslav
Vrchlický (1853–1912) whom he presently prevailed upon
to provide a suitable text. By November 1885, therefore,
Dvořák was ready to settle down to what proved to be six
months of almost uninterrupted composition.

Svatá Ludmila (Saint Ludmila) was dedicated to the
Žerotín Music and Choral Society of Olomouc, and an
English version was once again provided by the persevering
but inadequate Troutbeck. The work is divided into three
parts. In Part I priests and people, among whom is Ludmila
(soprano), gather together to pay homage to their goddess
Bába, but proceedings are interrupted by Ivan (bass), a
hermit, who shatters Bába's statue with a blow of his staff
and calls upon all present to worship instead the one true
God whose Son died upon the Cross; thereupon confusion
reigns. In Part II Ludmila is wandering in a gloomy forest
with her faithful attendant Svatava (contralto), but presently
Ivan reappears, and in a remarkably short space of time
converts her to Christianity. Meanwhile Bořivoj (tenor), who
is out on a hunting expedition, is taken aback when a deer
he has shot dead with an arrow is miraculously brought back
to life by Ivan; a couple of minutes later he catches sight of
Ludmila and promptly falls in love with her, whereupon the
holy man has no difficulty in adding him to his list of
converts. Part III is concerned with the ecclesiastical ceremonies surrounding the joint baptism and marriage of
Ludmila and Bořivoj.

Vrchlický, as a matter of fact, did a better job than this brief summary of his text might suggest: judged by nineteenth-century oratorio standards the only constructional weakness in his libretto was that the principal tenor had no opportunity to open his mouth until half-way through Part II, but this was to some extent mitigated by the incorporation in Part I (probably at the composer's suggestion) of solo items for two 'small-part' tenors who portrayed a Husbandman and a Peasant. But an oratorio stands or falls by its music, and although *Saint Ludmila* remains a more satisfying work of art than *The Spectre's Bride*, it cannot be reckoned as one of Dvořák's most outstanding achievements.

Much of the best music comes during the first half-hour or so, when pagan rites are performed in an extremely decorous and altogether charming manner, suggesting not so much the worship of a heathen idol as the worship of beneficent Nature. In this first half of Part I Dvořák continually reminds us of Handel in his most pastoral mood, and indeed Ludmila's song 'Od dětství ku oltáři' ('I long with childlike longing') is not unworthy of comparison with 'Love in her eyes sits playing'. As soon as Ivan the unwashed hermit appears on the scene, however, the composer seems to become as puzzled and frustrated as do the characters in the drama; for once in a way godliness makes a lesser appeal than cleanliness. The music only comes to life again when Bořivoj's long-delayed appearance is heralded by a trio for three of his attendants, 'Vesele hvozdem' ('Gaily through forest'). Part III both begins and ends with Dvořák's effective interpretation of a traditional Czech chorale, 'Hospidine, pomiluj ny' ('Mighty Lord, to us be gracious'), and includes some splendidly straightforward choruses as diatonic as those in Handel's *Messiah* but incorporating sufficient contrapuntal interest to keep things going; there is even a touch of *fugato* here and there. Dvořák did his best to endow *Saint Ludmila* with a measure of musical unity by introducing, at appropriate moments, emphatic orchestral declamations which he hoped would be regarded as representing 'the Cross of Christ' and so forth, but the only real *Leitmotiv* was that associated with Ludmila herself, which achieved apotheosis in Bořivoj's lyrical outburst when he first catches sight of her: 'Ó jaká sličná mlada divka' ('Oh, what a lovely youthful maiden').

Dvořák completed the score before the end of May 1886 and sent it straight off to Leeds, and although the first performance was not due to take place until October those enthusiastic Yorkshire choirs began to rehearse it straight away. During that summer Dvořák himself, as we shall learn in the next chapter, carried on with composition, but meanwhile let us jump ahead a few months to round off the saga of *Saint Ludmila*.

On his fifth trip to England within little more than two and a half years Dvořák took his wife with him (for the time being she had given up child-bearing), and for that reason he was anxious to ensure that the journey would be a comfortable one. On 22 August he wrote in his best English to Henry Littleton: 'I liwe Prague on 2/10; can you send me a time-tabel?' In the event Anna and Antonín left Vysoká on 20 September 1886. They then spent ten days in Prague, presumably so that Anna could do some feminine shopping, and on 3 October Antonín introduced her to Littleton at Wentworth House, Sydenham, which was to be their *pied-à-terre* for the next five weeks. We do not know what were Anna's impressions of England, but we do know that during the whole of that October our weather was at its most wretched. She and her husband were continually on the go. For the first week there were rehearsals of *Saint Ludmila* in London, and then everyone went north for its first performance in Leeds on 15 October. Once again two of the soloists were Albani and Santley; the contralto was Janet Patey (1842–1894) and the tenor Edward Lloyd (1845–1927). At this Festival, incidentally, two other distinguished composers each conducted the first performance of his most recently-completed choral work, Sullivan (*The Golden Legend*) and Stanford (*The Revenge*).

The audience at Leeds, which came from all over the country, was as enthusiastic as ever, but one or two critics (surprisingly, it seems in retrospect) compared *Saint Ludmila* unfavourably with *The Spectre's Bride*. Dvořák was not unduly perturbed. When the Leeds Festival was over he and Anna went to Birmingham, where he had been engaged to conduct yet another performance of his D major symphony, and on a day free from rehearsals they paid a duty-bound visit to Shakespeare's birthplace at Stratford-on-Avon. Next it was back to London for two more performances of *Saint Ludmila*, the first at St. James's Hall on 29 October and the second at the Crystal Palace on 6 November; a revival of *The Spectre's Bride* was sandwiched in between. Dvořák was pressed to stay on in England to conduct a concert of his own compositions that had been arranged to take place in Nottingham, but by now he was beginning to feel rather exhausted (and perhaps Anna was not enamoured of the British climate), so that he was glad to be able to hand over that responsibility to his friend Hans Richter. His fifth visit to Britain had resulted in further triumphs for which he was duly grateful, but as soon as obligations had been fulfilled Antonín Dvořák and Anna Dvořáková made their way back to Bohemia as fast as railway 'time-tabels' would allow.

CHAPTER TEN

Further Consolidation

After the great D minor symphony had been acclaimed in London in April 1885, Simrock had offered to publish it on terms which Dvořák regarded as totally inadequate: he wanted about twice as much for it as Simrock was prepared pay. Eventually a compromise had been reached: Simrock had doubled his offer on the understanding that Dvořák would throw in as make-weights another set of Slavonic dances for piano duet and a few more songs. It was these with which he occupied himself during the comparatively restful summer of 1886 that followed the completion of *Saint Ludmila* in May and preceded the October visit to England.

It has already been mentioned that individual items in Dvořák's second set of Slavonic dances (see table on page 125) crossed the frontiers of his native Bohemia more frequently than did those of the first set. This may be the reason why op. 72 of 1886, taken as a whole, seems to lack the homogeneity of op. 46 of 1878. Considered separately, however, each dance is an admirable composition providing yet further evidence of the steady growth of Dvořák's artistic sensitivity and perception. (He did not complete the *orchestration* of op. 72 until the following year.)

The four songs of *V národním tónu* (*In Folk-song Style*), op. 73, the other work with which Dvořák provided Simrock in accordance with their recent agreement, were settings of folk-poems, one Czech and three Slovakian. Musically they were very nearly, if not quite, up to the level of the *Gipsy Songs*: no. 2, *Žalo dievča* (*The Mower*), captured a particularly delightful open-air atmosphere; no. 3, *Ach, není tu* (*The Maiden's Lament*), was splendidly laid out for both singer and accompanist and achieved an intensity of feeling almost out of place in a simple 'folk' song. No one will be

SLAVONIC DANCES (second set) op. 72

No.	Name of dance (and district of origin)	Key	Time signature	Characteristics
9	Odzmek (Slovakia)	B major	3/4	A spirited affair with a rather jerky rhythm that persists even in the (slightly slower) middle section
10	Mazurka (Poland)	E minor	3/8	Perhaps the best-known item in this set and undeniably a gem
11	Skočná (Bohemia)	F major	2/4	More varied in both rhythm and *tempo* than either skočná from the first set
12	Dumka (Ukraine)	E flat minor/ D flat major	3/8	An effective dance-evocation of dumka characteristics; cannot make up its mind to which of two keys it properly belongs
13	Špasírka (Bohemia)	B flat minor	4/8	Starts in a stately manner but soon develops into something that a non-Slav might be forgiven for thinking was a polka
14	Polonaise (Poland)	B flat major	3/4	The middle section, where a perky melody is set against a background of smooth-flowing semiquavers, is particularly attractive
15	Kolo (Serbia)	C major	2/4	In character bears some relation to the Odzmek (no. 9) but preserves greater uniformity
16	Sousedská (Bohemia)	A flat major	3/4	For practical purposes an informal waltz (like no. 6 of the first set), alternating most effectively between moods of graciousness and vigour and ending up with graciousness

surprised to learn that Simrock published these songs only in a German translation—as *Im Volkston*.

CHAMBER MUSIC AND A MASS

When in November 1886 Dvořák got home from England, where he had just conducted *Saint Ludmila* with a chorus and orchestra nearly five-hundred strong, he composed, by contrast, something on a very much smaller scale. This unassuming little work, a trio in C major for two violins and viola (op. 74 and commonly known as the *Terzetto*) is charming from start to finish, and for once each of the four movements is commendably brief. First comes a very graceful 'introduzione' (*allegro ma non troppo* in 4/4 time), which leads without a break to a romantic *larghetto* (6/8, E major). The main section of the miniature scherzo (*vivace*, 3/4, A minor) is in furiant rhythm, the 'trio' (*poco meno mosso*, A major) being more of a *Ländler*; if this is the least interesting of the four movements, the finale, a theme with variations, makes up for it. The theme itself, in 2/4 time and marked *adagio*, is yet another instance of Dvořák's love of tantalizing us in the matter of key-structure; it starts in F major and modulates emphatically to D flat major before finding its 'right' key—C major. The five variations are all in quicker *tempo*; perhaps the first is a shade spun out, but the others are finished and done with almost before one realizes that they have started.

Dvořák was so well pleased with this string trio (as indeed he might be) that he promptly sketched out four *drobnosti* (trifles) for the same modest combination of instruments, but presently he changed his mind and completed them as *Čtyři romantické kusy* (*Four Romantic Pieces*, op. 75) for violin and piano, based on the same thematic material. He followed up by rearranging twelve of his old *Cypresses* songs of 1865 in the form of a suite for string quartet—placing them, however, in a different order. It cannot be said that they carried much more conviction as songs without words than as songs *with* words. The first violin was allotted the lion's share of what had been the voice part, and the viola only got a satisfactory look-in in no. 5, *de hledím na tvůj drahý list* (*The old letter in my book*.) But since Dvořák was by this time a technical master of the medium there was some excellent string-quartet writing here and there, and no. 6, *Ó, zlatá růže spanilá* (*You are my glorious rose*), is a model of simple yet effective chamber-music technique.

Dvořák next made two more attempts to bring the past back to life. First, he persuaded the writer Václav Novotný (who had accompanied him on one of his trips to England) to revise the libretto of the operetta *King and Collier*, which had lain neglected for twelve years; most of Novotný's alterations concerned the third act, for which Dvořák provided some new music. This included a fine lyrical aria for the tenor, 'Ó jak toužím' ('Oh, what longing'), and some ensembles markedly better contrived than anything of the sort in Acts I and II, which had been composed in 1874 and remained virtually unchanged. This latest and final version of *King and Collier* had a few performances at the National Theatre during June and July 1887, but then dropped out of the running until after Dvořák's death, when Oskar Nedbal and later Otakar Šourek and Günther Raphael started their slow but steady labour of reviving interest in compositions long forgotten.

It was of more real consequence that in March 1887 Dvořák asked Hans Richter to look through the score of his *Symphonic Variations* of 1877, which had not yet been played outside Bohemia. (In retrospect it seems surprising that Dvořák had not taken it with him on one of his visits to England, where he had conducted a few comparatively second-rate works.) Richter was profoundly impressed with the *Symphonic Variations*: in May of that year he introduced it to Vienna audiences, who received it so enthusiastically that thereafter he lost few opportunities of including it in concert programmes wherever he went. One performance per year was almost *de rigueur* at the Free Trade Hall in Manchester between 1900 and 1911, when Richter was conductor of the Hallé Orchestra.

(It is interesting to note that the correspondence that passed in 1887 between Richter and Dvořák was written in *English*. Richter spoke English fluently in a dialect peculiarly his own and with a marked accent; he good-naturedly played up to Dvořák in *his* attempts to secure a mastery of the language.)

Dvořák spent most of the summer of 1887 on the composition of a Mass in D major (a title which that sturdy Protestant the Reverend Troutbeck insisted on rendering as Communion Service in D major); it was written at the request of Josef Hlávka (1831–1908), founder of the Czech Academy of Sciences and Arts. In this work the choral writing throughout was more fluent than any that Dvořák had yet produced except in parts of *Saint Ludmila*: there were some effective *fugato* passages and he made occasional use of solo voices or a small choir to provide contrast with the full choir. One point must be made clear, however. In Bohemia, singing in church had always been as spontaneous an affair as dancing on the village green, and indeed Czech church music often held features in common with Czech dance music. Why shouldn't it? ordinary folk did not find piety incompatible with cheerfulness, nor did they automatically assume expressions of deep solemnity when passing through church portals. Consequently it was not unnatural that Dvořák should set the opening lines of the 'Credo' to a melody that would have served equally well for a graceful waltz, and having thereafter treated the references to Christ's crucifixion and death in a mood of deep seriousness he saw nothing incongruous in bursting once again into a somewhat perfunctory jog-trot at the words 'et resurrexit'. His Mass in D major therefore remains a typically Slav achievement which one is inclined to dub, irreverently perhaps, as charming rather than impressive.

Dvořák's other compositions of 1887 comprised a few piano pieces and songs and a piano quintet. Of the piano pieces *Dědeček tančí babičko* (*Grandpapa dances with grand-mama*) was a good deal better than its off-putting title might lead one to expect; of the songs, published collectively as op. 82, *Při vyšívání* (*Over her embroidery*) had an attractive melody and illustrated yet once again the composer's flair for key-magic: it started in E flat major and ended in D major. Magic of a different sort came to light in the piano quintet.

PIANO QUINTET IN A MAJOR, OP. 81

In theory the term piano quintet can be applied to a work written for any five instruments provided that one of them is a piano; in practice (although Schubert in his 'Trout' quintet employed a double-bass) the other four are nearly always the two violins and viola and cello that comprise a normal string quartet. Dvořák and Fauré each wrote two such works (that is to say twice as many as any other great composer) and curiously enough both of Dvořák's were in the same key, A major. The first, dated 1872, was briefly reviewed on page 49. The second was composed between mid-August and mid-October 1887, and with all due respect to Schubert, Schumann, Brahms, Franck, Saint-Saëns, Fauré, Elgar and Dohnányi it remains, to my mind, the best piano quintet ever written, demonstrating as it does from start to finish some of the most lovable characteristics of a lovable composer.

Only in the slow movement (and even there not to any great extent) does one come across questioning introspection: for the most part the mood is that of symphony no. 6 —cheerfulness tempered with mild sentiment. Furthermore, throughout this quintet the technical problems involved in combining the piano with other instruments (which have baffled so many composers—including Schubert), did not appear to trouble Dvořák at all: he had progressed a long way since that somewhat regrettable piano concerto of eleven years ago.

The main theme of the first movement, announced by the cello after two 'till ready' bars for the piano, is a smooth-flowing melody setting off confidently in A major but soon slipping, most effectively, into A minor; the 'second subject' is a slightly more perky affair, first introduced by the viola. Both were so well fitted for the 'episodic development' that was one of Dvořák's specialities that here he was able to complete a sonata-form movement which only the most hide-bound pedant would feel called upon to criticize from the constructional point of view and which is one hundred per cent aesthetically satisfying as well.

The second movement, a dumka, is also based on two themes, each such a splendid inspiration that one would have thought it capable of standing on its own. Dvořák had other ideas: he intertwined them, from the start, in a set of typically dumka-like variations—and in so doing produced a truly lovely piece of chamber music.

The third movement, although somewhat equivocally headed 'Scherzo (Furiant)' is in reality more like a very quick waltz, ear-tickling enough to be a firm favourite in establishments which see fit to provide 'light classical' music as an accompaniment to afternoon tea. An unusual feature is that the middle section, although in a contrasted key and slightly slower *tempo*, introduces hardly any fresh thematic material: there is already plenty to be going on with.

The finale takes us in one bound from the Strand Corner House to the heart of the Czech countryside, where this time we find ourselves present at a scene of village revelry. High jinks? yes. And moreover, thanks to Dvořák's brilliantly skilful and delicate handling of the lively tunes and spirited rhythms, no less perfect a work of national art than the dumka itself.

Within a month or so of completing this quintet, Dvořák himself took it to Berlin along with several earlier works, including the 'double-bass' quintet and F major symphony of 1875 and the *Symphonic Variations* of 1877, and sold the lot to Simrock for a lump sum which was evidently mutually agreed as being reasonable; for once the encounter between composer and publisher was comparatively cordial. Unfortunately Simrock went on to blot his copy-book in Dvořák's estimation—and ours—by messing up the opus numbers (see page 61).

'JAKOBÍN' ('THE JACOBIN')

Dvořák's only composition of importance dated 1888 was another opera, on which he was at work from January until November. The libretto, like that of *Dimitrij*, was by Marie Červinková, and once again she proved herself an efficient collaborator. This time the setting was neither the England of *Alfred* nor the Poland of *Vanda* nor the Russia of *Dimitrij* but the Bohemia of *King and Collier* and *The Pigheaded Peasants* and *The Peasant a Rogue*. *The Jacobin* however, while ending happily, had an amplitude and a seriousness of intent that raised its status from that of operetta to that of opera.

Let us first briefly sketch the background and the plot. The action takes place during that period of European history which immediately followed the French Revolution of 1789, when in circles which disapproved of the revolutionaries anyone who expressed a word of sympathy with them was automatically dubbed a 'Jacobin' (an opprobrious term of which modern equivalents have been 'Bolshie', 'Red' and 'Commie'.)

Bohuš, son and heir to Count Vilem of Harasov, has spent several years in Paris; when he returns home, unrecognized, and accompanied by his French wife Julie, he is just in time to learn that his father, believing him to be a 'Jacobin', has disinherited him; the title and estates are to go instead to the count's scheming nephew Adolf. Julie makes common cause with the broadminded local schoolmaster Benda to plead with the count for her husband's reinstatement—ultimately, of course, with success. There is a sub-plot in which Benda's pretty daughter Terinka is wooed both by a handsome young man named Jiři and by the count's steward Filip, a somewhat scurvy fellow; no prizes are offered for forecasting who wins her in the end.

Act I is set in the village square: the church is on one side and the inn (surely a *Gasthaus-Metzgerei*) on the other, while Count Vilem's castle towers in the background. (In the opera the village is called Harasov, but there is no doubt that Dvořák had in mind his own birthplace, Nelahozeves.) Mass is drawing to a close, but there is just time for Bohuš (baritone) and Julie (soprano), who have *not* attended the service, to introduce themselves to the audience before the populace streams out into the sunshine. Prominent in the crowd are schoolmaster Benda (tenor) and his daughter Terinka (soprano), with Jiři (tenor) and Filip (bass) both in close attendance. Presently each has a separate opportunity to press his suit upon her, and we are left in no doubt as to which of the two is better favoured by the young lady herself; her father has opposing ideas. Such domestic trivialities fade into the background, however, when Count Vilem (bass) emerges from the castle to cause surprise to all and consternation to some by announcing that he has decided to transfer the inheritance of his renegade son Bohuš to his nephew Adolf (baritone), whom he introduces to the assembled multitude as their new liege-lord.

There is no overture to the opera, but the opening sets a sprightly orchestral waltz side by side with the off-stage singing of the chorus inside the church—thereby providing, like the Mass in D major, a good example of the close relationship between the secular and the sacred in Bohemian music. Thereafter there are fewer 'detachable' items than in *Dimitrij*: this is genuinely *durchkomponiert* ('through-composed') music, which is lyrical or dramatic in turn according to the demands of the stage situation; even the introductory duet for Julie and Bohuš and a later one for Terinka and Jiři are not so much formal pieces as conversation put to music, and in the finale, although the prevailing march-tune is comparatively undistinguished, the big ensemble which follows the count's dramatic announcement is excellently contrived. So much for Act I.

Act II takes place in the schoolhouse. When the curtain rises Benda, who almost needless to say is the village choir-master as well as schoolmaster, is conducting a rehearsal of one of his own compositions. Benda (a name which incidentally is the Czech equivalent of Bach) was a character modelled on Antonín Liehmann, Dvořák's teacher at Zlonice, and Dvořák was brilliantly successful in crediting him in retrospect with a piece of music basically simple enough to have been conceived by a composer of Liehmann's modest capabilities and therefore entirely appropriate in the context, while at the same time endowing it with extraneous touches of subtle embellishment that a Liehmann would never have dreamt of. Benda's daughter Terinka and her devoted Jiři are both members of the choir, and Benda, although he hopes that Terinka will marry the count's steward Filip, is so much absorbed in the music that for a time he fails to notice that she and Jiři are taking advantage of his preoccupation to indulge in a spot of flirtation that causes great delight to both of them. Handled by a competent stage-director, this scene could be entrancing.

When the rehearsal is over, Bohuš enters, still incognito, and prevails upon Benda to provide temporary accommodation for his wife Julie and himself, but presently the usurping Adolf, egged on by Filip (who suspects that the hitherto unrecognized stranger is indeed none other than Bohuš), orders Bohuš's arrest and imprisonment as a revolutionary. Musically speaking, this second half of Act II is slightly disappointing : a somewhat similar dramatic situation has already been exploited in the finale of Act I, and when Dvořák tries to repeat the process in Act II he is less successful than before.

The composer comes into his own again in Act III, however. The scene is Count Vilem's castle, where Benda, hoping to secure the release of Bohuš, persuades the housekeeper Lotinka (contralto) to admit Julie in secret to an antechamber. Meanwhile Vilem grants Benda an audience, and admits to him that he has always held deep affection for his son, whatever his political views, but in his absence has been over-ridden by the persistent Adolf. This scene, 'Já vždycky snival ty slasti času dávného' ('I listen very gladly when you talk to me of long ago'), is genuinely moving, and the 'long ago' is audibly brought back to Vilem when Julie's voice is heard from the adjoining room, where by pre-arrangement with Benda she is singing a lullaby which Vilem's long-dead wife used to croon over their infant son Bohuš in his cradle. Vilem is so much affected by this 'coincidence' that he is ready to listen to Julie's appeal on behalf of Bohuš, to whom he promptly restores his inheritance. Benda, not to be outdone in generosity to the younger generation, agrees that after all Terinka may marry her Jiři.

That everyone except the rascally Adolf and the ill-favoured Filip would live happily ever after might of course have been foreseen from the first rise of the curtain, but to Dvořák's credit the jubilant finale of Act III is by no means a perfunctory reprise; it forms a fitting round-off to a fine lively opera which is still played in Prague but has rarely, alas, crossed the boundaries of Bohemia. It owed even less to Wagner than *Dimitrij* had; Dvořák was here his uninhibited self almost throughout. Once again he introduced only a single *Leitmotiv*, associated with Bohuš : this was not a particularly distinctive phrase, but Dvořák developed is so effectively that to complain on that score would be ungracious.

CHAPTER ELEVEN

Honours at Home and Abroad

During the nine or ten months that followed the completion of *The Jacobin* in November 1888 (it had its first performance on 12 February 1889 under the baton of Adolf Čech) Dvořák suffered from some ill-health, and it may have been partly for that reason that his few compositions of this period were not up to the standard which might have been expected from a great composer who by then had reached the summit of his powers.

First came a set of thirteen piano pieces (op. 85) entitled *Poetické nálady* (*Poetic Tone-pictures*), which showed up unfavourably beside the waltzes of op. 54 and the mazurkas of op. 56. (Straightforward dance-evocations were much more in Dvořák's line of country than allegedly descriptive tone-pictures.) A good deal of the piano writing in op. 85 was disfigured by tasteless decorations suggesting Liszt at his most vapid, and it is the comparatively unpretentious items that make the most appeal: nos. 2, 6 and 11, *Žertem* (*Toying*), *Vzpomínání* (*Sorrowful Reverie*) and *Ná táčkách* (*Tittle-tattle*). No. 13 of the set, *Na Svaté Hoře* (*On the Holy Mount*), is unique among Dvořák's compositions, I believe, in being in 5/4 time.

Even more disappointing (because here one might have hoped for a work comparable with the splendid piano quintet op. 81) is the piano quartet in E flat major (op. 87) composed during July and August 1889. Not that melodic inspiration is lacking : there are some good tunes, notably in the first movement (*allegro con fuoco*, 4/4) and in the third (*allegro moderato grazioso*, 3/4). What perturbs one is that in this quartet Dvořák seems temporarily to have lost his grip of the chamber-music medium. The 'second subject' of the first movement, for instance, is thumped out *fortissimo* and *marcato* by the pianist (in octaves) against a background of trivial arpeggio figuration on the violin and viola and apparently pointless 'shakes' on the bottom strings of the cello; presently all three string-players find themselves reduced to ineffective *tremolando*. The slow movement (G flat major, *lento*, 4/4 time) starts pleasantly enough, but pleasure is soon marred (as in so many of the *Poetic Tone-pictures*) by unnecessarily 'flashy' piano passages. The finale (*allegro ma non tanto*, 2/2) displays a similar lack of sensitivity to problems of balance: its energetic rhythms demand a far larger combination of instruments.

SYMPHONY NO. 8 IN G MAJOR
at one time called No. 4 (see page 60)

Dvořák's eighth symphony is a tantalizer; musicians and music-loving laymen alike have long been at loggerheads about it. The opinions expressed here must be regarded as purely subjective, and I have thought it only right to incorporate a few conflicting comments from two distinguished British musicologists, both of them acknowledged experts on Dvořák, to whose judgments I feel bound to pay respect even when I cannot find it in my heart to concur.

This symphony was composed during the late summer and early autumn of 1889. It is certainly not the least meritorious in the run-of-the-mill repertory of the late nineteenth century, but to my ears it remains unsatisfying by the standards which Brahms had by then set in all his four symphonies and Dvořák himself in his nos. 6 and 7. Each of the four movements contains some excellent music, but when the whole affair has run its course a listener is apt to come away feeling much as a sturdy trencher-man might feel after a meal consisting of clear soup, a small slice of smoked salmon, a light egg soufflé and a water-ice. [H. C. Colles: 'The symphony in G, because of its freedom from precedent of any kind, may be said to be the crown of Dvořák's work.']

The first movement is reasonably concise and by no means ineffective, but the solemnly impressive G *minor* opening—reappearing from time to time without being subjected to 'development'—is not matched in quality by the rest of the thematic material, which in due course is submitted to grandiose and not always well-timed development and has hardly sufficient strength of character to bear the strain. Perhaps in this instance Dvořák would have been better advised to adhere as closely in a symphony as he had in his piano quintet, dated two years previously, to the basic tenets of sonata form.

In the slow movement there is only one melody; it inaugurates proceedings agreeably in E flat major and acquires individuality when tilted into C major and unexpectedly tinted with a colourful touch of chromatic harmony. Presently it instigates a big build-up of arpeggios and scale-passages, almost unrelievedly in C major, which tend to outstay their welcome and distract one's interest. [Alec Robertson: 'This movement, which derives its material entirely from the opening phrases, I take to be one of the considerable achievements of symphonic literature.']

The third movement, so far from resembling the vigorous furiants of nos. 6 and 7, is marked *allegretto grazioso*. Alec Robertson finds it 'amiable rather than striking'; as a soufflé, I find it very tasty. The main section (G minor, 3/8 time) recalls Mendelssohn in his most gracious mood and the 'trio' (G major) is a piece of gentle Bohemian merry-making, later revived as a piece of enthusiastic Bohemian merry-making when called upon to round things off *molto vivace* (in 2/4).

The finale, too, is redolent of the countryside. Dvořák may have started off with the idea of writing a set of variations on one of the themes from the first movement (Otakar Šourek made out that that was just what he *succeeded* in doing), but I do not believe that either Alec Robertson or H. C. Colles (were he still alive) would pick a serious quarrel with me if I ventured to describe it as a lively pot-pourri of typically Czech tunes that chase one another round in circles: it is all very skilfully contrived of course, but not quite what a sophisticated listener expects from the finale of a symphony.

OUT AND ABOUT

During the three years that had elapsed since his fifth visit to England in the autumn of 1886, Dvořák had rarely journeyed far afield. He had been once to Berlin and now and again to Olomouc or Plzen or Dresden or some other comparatively nearby town to conduct his own compositions, but in general he had divided his time between Prague (in the winter) and Vysoká (in the summer). No sooner had he completed his G major symphony, however, than another round of foreign travel was set in motion.

First it was Berlin again (at the end of October 1889); this time not to haggle with Simrock but to attend two performances of the D minor symphony (op. 70) given by the Berlin Philharmonic Orchestra under the baton of Hans von Bülow (1830–1894). Next it was Vienna, where he and his wife were received in audience by Emperor Franz Josef himself, who bestowed upon the composer the coveted award of the Iron Crown (third class). This must have been a noteworthy and happy occasion for the Dvořáks: during their visit (the second week of December) the Emperor also received a deputation of distinguished Prague artists and musicians among whom were many old friends, including those colleagues of earlier days Karel Bendl and Mořic Anger, the music critic Velebín Urbánek (see page 110) and the unassuming but talented Czech composer Zdeněk Fibich (1850–1900). A few months later Dvořák was accorded another signal honour, when he was elected a member of the Czech Academy of Sciences and Arts.

While Dvořák had been at work on *The Jacobin* early in 1888, Peter Ilyitch Tchaikovsky (1840–1893) had paid a visit to Prague, and the two composers, although very different in temperament and outlook, had become friendly; about a year later Tchaikovsky wrote to invite Dvořák to Russia. Dvořák was delighted at the prospect, but the trip had to be postponed until after the first performance of his G major symphony in Prague on 2 February 1890. By the end of that month, however, he and his devoted wife were on their way to the land of the Czars, where they spent three weeks all told; for most of the time they were Tchaikovsky's guests in Moscow, and thereafter stayed for a few days at the Hotel Constant in St. Petersburg (now Leningrad) before returning home. While in Moscow Dvořák conducted performances of his F major symphony, the *Symphonic Variations*, the three *Slavonic Rhapsodies* and the *Scherzo capriccioso*. In St. Petersburg it was the turn of the D major symphony—and the Dvořáks were guests of honour at a banquet given by Anton Rubinstein (1829–1894), founder of the St. Petersburg Conservatoire.

Hardly was Dvořák back from this excursion eastwards than he was off on another excursion westwards—for the first performance in London of his G major symphony, which took place at St. James's Hall on 24 April 1890. This time he was in London for only a few days, but that was long enough in which to sell the score to Novello & Co.; Henry Littleton had died in 1888 but his son Alfred (1845–1914), who had succeeded him as director, paid a considerably larger sum than Simrock had been prepared to offer. When Simrock heard of this treachery he was naturally furious, and wrote to remind Dvořák that he was still under contract to *him*; Dvořák never replied to the letter and went his own sweet way, whereupon Simrock, who over the years had found him a very profitable investment, took no further action.

(Perhaps because it was published by Novello, the G major symphony became known as the 'English'; I can find no other convincing explanation for a singularly inappropriate nickname, which in any case has not stuck. Admittedly the distinguished British musicologist Donald Tovey—who by no means shared H. C. Colles's and Alec Robertson's enthusiasm for the work—suggested that it was 'an effort to meet what the composer took to be the English taste'; so far as the overall merit of this symphony is concerned I am more in accord with Tovey than with Colles or Robertson, but I cannot agree with his theory that its shortcomings were due to an attempt to catch a particular export market.)

A REQUIEM MASS

Several years previously Dvořák had promised to provide a new choral work for the Birmingham Festival of 1891. Few will regret that he went no further than to toy with the idea of setting John Henry Newman's poem *The Dream of Gerontius*, and that therefore that field was left open for a composer who not only shared Newman's religious views but was also his compatriot. Dvořák decided instead upon a Requiem Mass; he began it in January 1890 but broke off work in order to visit first Moscow and St. Petersburg and then London, and the score was not finished until the end of October.

This Requiem (for four soloists, chorus and orchestra) is unquestionably the finest of Dvořák's choral works. It opens *pianissimo* with a syncopated little phrase which thereafter reappears with great frequency—in many varied forms but more often than not in the original key of B flat minor. B flat minor is indeed the predominant key all the way through, and this fact, coupled with the use of the persistently prevailing *Leitmotiv*, helps to endow the whole with a large measure of artistic unity. It must be admitted, however, that we have had rather more than our fill of B flat minor by the time we are half-way through Part I—notably in the 'Dies Irae' (no. 3), which is in any case a comparatively ineffective and four-square setting in 6/4 march-rhythm, reminding one of the would-be dramatic scenes in *The Spectre's Bride*. The only other somewhat unsatisfying items in the work are the naïvely descriptive 'Confutatis maledictus' (no. 7) and the 'Offertorium' (no. 9). The latter is largely based on an old Slav hymn tune, and as in the case of the *Hussite* overture one wishes that Dvořák had been content to rely upon his own inspiration, which elsewhere in the Requiem shows few signs of flagging. The lovely quartet 'Recordare, Jesu pie' (no. 6), for instance, is virtually beyond criticism.

The four soloists, although only one of them—the soprano —is granted an aria or something like it, play a very important part throughout the work: of its thirteen numbers only two are allotted to the chorus on its own, and it may be significant that these are two of the weakest, the 'Dies Irae' and 'Confutatis maledictus'. A striking feature is Dvořák's very original treatment of the solo voices (whether singly or in pairs) to provide contrast with the various sections of the chorus, notably in the slightly Verdian 'Quid sum miser' (no. 5) and the extremely impressive 'Sanctus' (no. 11). All in all, despite musical lapses here and there, this Requiem Mass remains a deeply moving expression of faith on the part of a composer whose religious convictions never wavered.

Yet for all its splendid qualities most musicians would have to agree that Dvořák's Requiem must yield pride of place to Verdi's; one is bound to ask why. Although Dvořák did not live long enough to produce an *Otello* or a

Falstaff, it would be fair to say that these two composers not only worked on the same musical wave-length but were also of comparable calibre, and I hope that someone better qualified than myself to discuss such matters will presently step forward and explain why the Requiem which the devoted Catholic Antonín Dvořák completed at the age of forty-nine should, despite its great beauties, carry less conviction than that which the earnest freethinker Giuseppe Verdi completed at the age of fifty-nine. (Brahms's 'German' Requiem hardly enters into the comparison: it was not a Requiem *Mass*, being based on biblical and not liturgical texts.)

PROFESSOR AND DOCTOR

In 1889 the Prague Organ School (which Dvořák had attended during his youth) had been amalgamated with the Prague Conservatoire under the directorship of Doctor Josef Tragy (1830–1915), who immediately offered Dvořák the post of professor of composition. At first Dvořák, then hard at work on his G major symphony, had declined the appointment, but once he had completed both that work and the Requiem he reconsidered his decision and eventually took up the duties of professor from 1 January 1891. He was allowed to select his own pupils from among third-year students who showed exceptional talent, and was allocated a classroom in which he himself had spent many hours during his student days; he recognized the same musty smell that had been there thirty-two years before.

Dvořák proved himself to be as unconventional and successful a pedagogue as he was an unconventional and successful composer. He was ruthless (and perhaps heartless) in promptly dismissing from his class any students who did not come up to his expectations, but for those in whom he could detect real promise he went to endless trouble,

often extending lessons long past the prescribed hours (to
the despair of colleagues on the staff who were awaiting
their turn to teach); furthermore, he was always ready to
listen to tales of grievances and personal problems and if
necessary give fatherly advice. His favourite pupils respected
and adored him. The rejects may have regarded him with
respect but perhaps not with adoration. Of the dozen or
so that stayed the course throughout 1891, several have
recalled their teacher's aphorisms ('there is no merit in
conceiving a beautiful idea; merit is acquired only in the
difficult struggle to transform that idea into a work of art')
and his occasional pertinent comments on other composers
('Schubert's piano accompaniments are often simple but
never trivial'). The greatest treat of all came when study-
time was over and Dvořák entertained his enthralled young
listeners by playing to them on the piano the works of the
great masters—including, perhaps, a few of his own.

In March of this year (1891) Dvořák was installed as an
honorary Doctor of Philosophy at the Czech University in
Prague, and in June he went to Cambridge to be installed
(more appropriately) as an honorary Doctor of Music. On
the eve of the Cambridge ceremony he conducted a performance of his *Stabat Mater*, and subsequently confessed to a
sense of shame when he couldn't understand a word of the
Vice-Chancellor's customary welcoming and witty speech,
which like the *Stabat Mater* was couched, by long tradition,
in Latin; this is how it ended. 'Qua da re non aliorum egetis
testimonio: vos de matre dolorosa juxta crucem lacrimosa
carmen hesterno die egregrie recitatum audivistis. Vestro
igitur testimonio plus quam defensus, vestro indicio est
omnibus numeris absolutus, musicae doctor, Antoninius
Dvořák.' Dvořák comforted himself (and perhaps most of
my readers will be content to do likewise) with the reflection
that his *Stabat Mater* held not only literary merit but also
musical merit—which required no translation.

It has been recorded that on this occasion Dvořák

surprised and somewhat disconcerted Charles Villiers Stanford (Cambridge Professor of Music at the time) by speaking in slightly disparaging terms of Brahms, of all people. There would seem to be only two alternative explanations of this apparent temporary change in Dvořák's attitude towards his contemporary. Possibly Brahms had not been so enthusiastic as the touchy Dvořák would have liked him to be over the G major symphony, which had been played in Vienna five months previously under the baton of Hans Richter. Or it might be that Stanford—who while yielding to none in admiration for Dvořák regarded Brahms as a demi-god—unwittingly nettled his guest (always sensitive to criticism whether direct or implied) by expecting him to concur as a matter of course with the assumption that Brahms was the greatest of all living composers *bar none*.

Preoccupation with professorships and doctorships did not deter Dvořák from composition. Early in 1891 he completed his op. 90 and later the same year his ops. 91, 92 and 93—and for once a series of opus numbers was in strict chronological sequence.

Dvořák's op. 90 was a composition for violin and cello and piano, his fifth and last for that combination of instruments and commonly known as the *Dumky* trio. 'Dumky', however, is no arbitrary nickname, being merely the plural (in Czech) of 'dumka', and op. 90 does indeed consist of six detached dumkas, each in a different key. Nothing could be further removed from the traditional notion of a piano trio as conceived by Haydn and Mozart, and the work needs to be heard and judged as a set of dumkas, by analogy with a set of Slavonic dances, rather than as a piano trio in six movements. Indeed there is no logical reason why its individual movements should not be detached from their context and played independently; in practice this rarely happens, and in any case the melodic and rhythmic interest that Dvořák squeezes into each self-contained item is so skilfully varied that even purists are unlikely to be troubled by the inevitable overall lack of aesthetic balance (in the classical sense of the term). Anyone acquainted with this remarkable work will probably cherish his own favourite dumka out of the six. Mine is no. 2 in C sharp minor, where the main theme hovers continually on the verge of C sharp *major*.

It remains to be added that in the *Dumky* trio Dvořák recaptured the same mastery in combining the piano with stringed instruments that he had displayed in his piano quintet op. 81 but had temporarily lost in his piano quartet op. 87.

CONCERT-OVERTURES

During 1891 Dvořák also composed three concert-overtures, to which in the first instance he accorded the composite title *Příroda, Život a láska* (*Nature, Life and Love*); later he re-christened them independently as *V přírodě* (*In Nature's Realm* or alternatively *In the Countryside*), *Karneval* (*Carnival*) and *Othello*, giving each its own opus number (91, 92, 93). They were musically linked only to the extent that a theme from the first was briefly referred to in both the second and third, and nowadays they rarely make a public appearance in one another's company.

In Nature's Realm is lovely to listen to but unduly protracted. The mood is pastoral and mainly tranquil; if there are echoes of Siegfried's bird-friends or Peer Gynt's dawn-awakening, this merely serves as a reminder that nature, like art, knows no man-made frontiers. In the middle section (bar 130 onwards) there are passages of Gallic-like delicacy, something of a rarity in Dvořák's symphonic music.

Carnival, the most frequently played of these three overtures, is a straightforward no-nonsense work which hardly deserves the nasty things sometimes said about it. I for one am not ashamed to say that I enjoy it—especially the unblushing reference to Tannhäuser's carnal carnival on the Venusberg—although I must admit that the coda is not only noisy but also rather vulgar.

Whatever may be the faults of the *Othello* overture, vulgarity is not one of them. If one were to hear it immediately following *Carnival* (which, as already explained, is unlikely) one would receive the impression of having been instantaneously transported from a seat on the merry-go-rounds to a pew in some stately Gothic cathedral. Not that the ecclesiastical atmosphere prevails for long: once the two participants in the drama have been introduced to us in slow and solemn *tempo*, the work resolves itself into an alternating succession of rantings on the part of Othello and tender appeals on the part of Desdemona, interrupted only by what might be called an orchestral love duet; this is extremely beautiful but somewhat unrealistic, where it stands, from the 'programmatic' point of view. The descriptive handling of the final tragic dénouement, however, is masterly in every respect.

Othello marked Dvořák's first important venture in the field of serious 'programme music', a field in which he was never so successful as Smetana had been; nevertheless this overture compels one's admiration, being commendably concise and in places very moving. One remains unhappy about both the alternative titles: the original *Love* would be considered appropriate only by the most misanthropic of cynics, and *Othello* is not much better. This Othello is not specifically the Shakespearean character whom we all know: he might be *any* passionately jealous husband, as likely a Moravian as a Moor, an attorney-general as an army general. One is therefore inclined to regret that the composer did not settle for some such compromise as *Love and Jealousy*; in that case the work would hardly qualify as 'programme music' at all—and might be all the better for it.

Dvořák showed great faith in the musicianship of two of his most promising pupils at the Prague Conservatoire— Oskar Nedbal (see page 45) and Josef Suk (1874–1935), each only seventeen years old at the time—when he entrusted them with the task of making piano-duet arrangements of these three concert-overtures. About a year later the same two enterprising young men founded the Czech String Quartet, in which Suk played second violin and Nedbal viola. Among others of Dvořák's pupils who were eventually to make a mark in some field or other of composition were the extrovert Franz Lehár (1870–1948), whose father was of Czech origin although he himself was born in Hungary, and the introvert Vítězslav Novák (1870–1949), who in due course became Dvořák's next-but-one successor as professor of composition at the Prague Conservatoire.

INVITATION TO NEW YORK

We must now jump back seven years or so—and across the Atlantic Ocean.

Early in 1884 Jeanette M. Thurber (1852–1946), who was the wife of a millionaire grocery-tycoon in New York and was determined to blossom as a patroness of the arts, had inaugurated the American Opera Company—a name shortly afterwards changed to the National Opera Company—which she hoped would provide effective competition with the Metropolitan Opera House, founded in 1883; at the 'Met' performances were given in Italian or French or German as the case might be, whereas Mrs Thurber's watchword was 'opera in English'. After a couple of years or so this venture had cost her one-and-a-half-million dollars (at that time the equivalent of £300,000), and although such a sum of money was a mere drop in the Thurber bucket she decided to abandon opera in favour of keeping her name to the forefront in artistic circles by establishing a 'National

Conservatory of Music'. For its first director she chose a famous singer, the Belgian baritone Jacques Bouhy (1848–1929), who ten years previously had played the part of the toreador Escamillo at the première of Bizet's *Carmen* at the Opéra Comique in Paris. The National Conservatory, thanks to the bottomless Thurber purse, was able to operate on philanthropic rather than commercial lines: students were charged only such fees as they or their parents could afford, and indeed there were many who received free tuition; furthermore, and greatly to Mrs Thurber's credit, Negroes and red Indians, when they cared to apply, were admitted on the same terms as the white races.

When Bouhy returned to Europe in 1889, Mrs Thurber conceived the idea of replacing him as director with a *composer* of international renown; consultations with members of her teaching staff and with prominent musicians abroad were prolonged, and it was not until April 1891 that she sent a cablegram to Vysoká offering Dvořák the job. Dvořák, who had taken up his professorship at the Prague Conservatoire only four months previously, replied that for the time being he could not consider the suggestion.

Mrs Thurber, who by now had set her heart on securing Dvořák, was undeterred. In June she returned to the attack, giving further details of the terms which she proposed. The appointment would date from 28 September of the following year (1892), and in the first instance would be for two years only. For eight months in each year Dvořák would attend to his duties as director of her National Conservatory, the remaining four months being vacation. He would also be expected, during those two years, to continue with composition and conduct concerts of his own works. His yearly salary would be the fabulous sum of $15,000, the equivalent of £3,000. Dvořák, without committing himself, weighed the pros and cons, discussed the proposition with Alois Göbl and other friends, and went so far as to ascertain that Josef Tragy, if pressed, would be prepared to release him temporarily from his obligations at the Prague Conservatoire. The indefatigable Mrs Thurber, who must have sensed his indecision, followed up with more cajoling cables and eventually, by a master-stroke of diplomacy, sent a contract—unaccompanied by a covering letter—that required nothing more than a signature on the dotted line; by the autumn of 1891 her big fish was well and truly hooked, and a great European composer was committed to spend at least two years in America.

PREPARATIONS AND FAREWELLS

Dvořák's fiftieth birthday, 8 September 1891, was marked by celebrations in Prague which included a gala performance of his opera *Dimitrij* at the National Theatre. On this occasion the composer himself preferred to remain at his country hide-out in Vysoká. He explained to the authorities that while deeply appreciative of the honour bestowed upon him he always made a point, whenever possible, of spending such anniversaries where he always made a point of spending Christmas: with his family.

A few weeks later Dvořák was in England again—to conduct the first performance of his Requiem Mass at the Birmingham Festival on 9 October 1891. He was acclaimed as vociferously as ever by the public, but perhaps because the singers were not quite up to standard (Albani had to withdraw at the last moment owing to illness) the critics did not take so kindly to the Requiem as they had to *The Spectre's Bride* or even *Saint Ludmila*. (Posterity has reversed their judgment.) Dvořák may have been short-term irritated but he had no reason to be long-term worried: his expectations for the future were by now focused on a city even farther afield from Bohemia than Birmingham was—and he had nearly a year in which to make his preparations.

From late autumn 1891 until the following June Dvořák

devoted himself mainly to his professorial duties, except that between 3 January and 6 March 1892 he joined forces with the violinist Ferdinand Lachner (1856–1910) and the cellist Hanuš Wihan (1855–1920) to give concerts of his own compositions in what might be described as a farewell tour of Bohemia and Moravia: among the towns visited were Kladno (where his father was still living), Smetana's birthplace Litomyšl, and Mahler's home town Jihlava (Iglau). The repertory, although it may have varied slightly from place to place, always included the piano trios op. 26 and op. 90 (the *Dumky*), the *Four Romantic Pieces* for violin and piano op. 75, and a jolly *Rondo* in G minor for cello and piano (op. 94) which Dvořák provided especially to enable Wihan to display his virtuosity. (He thought so highly of his colleague that for once he broke a family tradition: he began work on this rondo on Christmas Day 1891—and finished it on Boxing Day.)

In April 1892 there was a somewhat surprising event when Dvořák's comparatively early symphony in D minor (op. 13) had its first complete performance at the little town of Klatový in the Böhmerwald, which lies only about thirty miles from Vysoká. At the end of May there was a very sad event even closer at hand: a serious accident in the nearby silver mines of Březové hory, which resulted in death or serious injury to many of those miners with whom Dvořák regularly fraternized of an evening in the local pub. He was greatly distressed, and it may have been for this reason that he excused himself from attending the International Exhibition in Vienna, at which, during June, the Czech National Theatre Company gave performances of Smetana's *Bartered Bride* and his own *Dimitrij*.

Meanwhile, Mrs Thurber was on the war-path again, bombarding Dvořák with cablegrams. She reminded him that the fourth centenary of Christopher Columbus's first landing in America would fall on 12 October 1892, just a fortnight after Dvořák himself was due to make *his* first landing there. Would he please put forth all his powers in a choral work that would fittingly mark the occasion? She would shortly be sending him a copy of a poem by Joseph Rodman Drake (1795–1820) entitled *The American Flag*, which glorified the achievements of the United States army in the war against Britain of 1812; she hoped that this would provide him with the necessary inspiration. Dvořák was very ready to oblige, but when by the end of June the promised poem had not yet reached him he decided to take things into his own hands and embarked instead upon a *Te Deum*, which he hoped would serve equally well to introduce him to the inhabitants of the continent Columbus had reached four hundred years before.

This *Te Deum* is not, of course, a long choral work (it lasts less than twenty minutes) nor perhaps a very important one when ranked alongside the Requiem; nevertheless it contains some splendid music. It opens with a choral setting of the words 'Te Deum laudamus' to strains of sturdy Handelian optimism, interrupted only by a soprano solo ('Sanctus') most attractively decorated with pastoral wood-wind interpolations that recall Haydn's philosophy: 'I hope that God will not be angry if I am irrepressibly cheerful in my worship of Him.' Thus far the music has hardly strayed from the predominating key of G major, but when the bass soloist comes into the limelight with 'Tu Rex gloriae, Christe', nominally in E flat major, we are whisked in quick succession through almost every key in the register; the effect is somewhat confusing, not to say overpowering. It was movements such as this that must have prompted W. H. Hadow, a great admirer, to the somewhat extravagant assertion that Dvořák was the first European composer to put into practice the idea of a *genre omnitonique* (polytonality). Next follows 'Aeterna fac sum Sanctis tuis'; this is exclusively choral, exclusively in the key of B minor except for one remarkable passage to which I shall refer again in a moment, and exclusively vigorous except when at its conclusion the music subsides into a mood of poetic tranquillity which serves to introduce another expressive solo for the soprano ('Dignare domine'). The work is rounded off, most appropriately, by a return to the opening; in recapturing the Handelian atmosphere Dvořák may here be said to have provided his own excellent 'Hallelujah Chorus'.

There are many points of semi-technical interest to be found in Dvořák's *Te Deum*: for instance the sopranos and altos of the chorus, as in the Requiem, are often detached from the tenors and basses; in 'Tu Rex gloriae' students will notice not only the slightly extravagant modulations mentioned above but also the 'mediant pedal' in bars 7–10 followed by an extended 'dominant pedal' in a different key, bars 11–20; they may discover, moreover, that in bars 59–70 of 'Aeterna fac cum Sanctis tuis' Dvořák anticipated Debussy by going 'whole-tone'.

Dvořák did not receive his copy of Drake's *American Flag* until after he had completed his substitute *Te Deum*. By then there was only a month to go before he was due to set sail for America and during those last few weeks at Vysoká he had only time to make a few sketches; as we shall see later, he did not complete the score until the Columbus celebrations were a thing of the past.

CHAPTER TWELVE

New York—and the Mid-West

When Dvořák set forth on his great adventure he took with him his wife Anna, their daughter Otilie (by now aged fourteen) and their son Antonín (nine); the other four children were left in the care of their grandmother, Klotilda Čermáková. The travelling party was made up to five by the inclusion of Josef Jan Kovařík (1870–1951), a young man who had been born in the United States shortly after his parents had emigrated there in 1869 and had been sent to the land of his fathers to study music at the Prague Conservatoire. Being a cellist, he was not one of Dvořák's own pupils, but Dvořák had made his acquaintance and formed such a favourable impression that he suggested he should accompany him to America in the capacity of personal secretary and general dogsbody. Kovařík, whose admiration for Dvořák was unbounded (he always referred to him reverently as 'the Master'), did not hesitate for a moment before accepting the offer.

The Dvořáks and Kovařík left Prague at three o'clock on the afternoon of Thursday, 15 September 1892, and after travelling overnight across Germany spent Friday and Friday night in Bremen before boarding the liner *Saale* on Saturday morning. On Sunday afternoon the *Saale* called at Southampton: Dvořák took advantage of the four-hours' halt to go ashore and cable his mother-in-law that all was well so far, and perhaps to give Otilie and Antonín a glimpse of England. Between Southampton and New York there were eight days on the ocean; although the voyage was for the most part uneventful and even enjoyable, storms were encountered in mid-Atlantic which for forty-eight hours caused nearly every passenger to feel very sorry for himself. Dvořák alone seemed to be immune from sea-sickness, and on several occasions he was the only one with the strength and stomach to reach the dining-room, where he enjoyed his meal in the sole company of the captain; all the other tables were deserted.

America was sighted on 26 September, but the *Saale* was held in quarantine at Staten Island for twenty-four hours (there had recently been an outbreak of cholera in Europe) and did not dock at Hoboken until next day. The Dvořáks were welcomed on the quayside by the secretary of the National Conservatory and a group of Czech immi-grants, who conducted them to the Clarendon Hotel on the corner of Fourth Avenue (Park Avenue) and East 18th Street, where accommodation had been reserved for them. The Conservatory itself was only a few hundred yards away, at 126/8 East 17th Street, and on 1 October the gratified Mrs Thurber was able to introduce her staff and students to their new director.

For the moment little work could be done, because preparations were in full swing for the Columbus celebra-tions of 12 October; consequently the Dvořáks had time to look round and get their domestic arrangements organized. Since they found their hotel both noisy and expensive, they moved to an apartment at 328 East 17th, five minutes' walk down the street from the Conservatory and facing Stuyvesant Park. In a letter to Josef Hlávka of the Czech Academy in Prague, Dvořák explained that the rent of $80 a month 'is for us a lot of money but here quite normal'; his thrifty soul was comforted when the firm of Steinway found it incumbent to instal a grand piano free of charge.

No sooner had Christopher Columbus been got rid of for another hundred years—without the aid of either Dvořák or *The American Flag*—than Mrs Thurber had an oppor-tunity to display her captive in public: in Carnegie Hall on 21 October he conducted the three concert-overtures *In*

Nature's Realm, Carnival and *Othello,* and the first performance anywhere of his recently-completed *Te Deum.* Everyone was delighted, not least the composer and his New York
guardian angel.

FIRST IMPRESSIONS OF AMERICA

It would be fair to say that during the three hundred years
that followed Columbus's first landing on the American
continent (roughly the sixteenth and seventeenth and
eighteenth centuries) the 'arts' had had a raw deal; immi-
grants from Europe were concerned almost solely with
establishing a *livelihood* in the New World—and who could
blame them? Eventually, however, travelling orchestras
and opera companies from Europe ventured upon tours
of the United States, and a realization of the benefits of
'culture' was soon awakened, at least among the wealthier
sections of the population that clustered round the eastern
seaboard. The West may have remained Wild, but after
the Civil War (1861–2) New York and Boston made a
determined attempt to challenge the hitherto-accepted
cultural superiority of Rome, Vienna, Berlin, Paris and
London.

The Metropolitan Opera House, as already recorded,
had been established nine years prior to Dvořák's arrival in
New York. In 1892 its current repertory included Mozart's
Don Giovanni; Beethoven's *Fidelio*; Bellini's *Sonnambula*
and *Norma*; Meyerbeer's *Huguenots, Le Prophète, Dinorah*
and *L'Africaine*; Thomas's *Mignon* and *Hamlet*; Flotow's
Marta; Wagner's *Lohengrin* and *The Mastersingers*; Verdi's
Rigoletto, Il trovatore, Aida and *Otello*; Gounod's *Faust* and
Romeo and Juliet; Delibes' *Lakmé*; Bizet's *Carmen.* This
was a feast to satisfy the hungriest opera-lover.

Meanwhile regular orchestral concerts were given in New
York both by the Philharmonic Society—director Anton

Seidl (1850–1898)—and by the Symphony Society—director Walter Damrosch (1862–1950). The Boston Symphony Orchestra was directed by Artur Nikisch (1855–1922); its leader, the violinist Franz Kneisel (1865–1926 and a compatriot of Dvořák), had also founded the Boston String Quartet, which frequently toured the larger towns in the eastern States giving concerts of chamber music. Nor was the appeal of piano virtuosity neglected: there had recently been recitals by such illustrious visitors from Europe as Ignaz Paderewski (1860–1941) and Eugen d'Albert (1864–1932). Add to this that there were several flourishing choral societies, and it will be realized that the New Yorkers of 1892 had plenty of opportunity to listen to good music. When it came to creating it, it was a different story: the only young American-born composers who had yet made much of a mark were Edward Macdowell (1861–1908) and (in the limited field of operetta) Reginald de Koven (1859–1920)—both of whom had been educated in Europe. The time was clearly ripe for Jeannette Thurber's National Conservatory, under the direction of Antonín Dvořák, to encourage a school of *American* music. There was a lot of spade-work to be done, however, before the soil could become fruitful.

So far as the actual teaching of composition was concerned Dvořák was reasonably well satisfied: most of the pupils were of a serious-minded type. He gave them a two-hour-long morning lesson (nine to eleven) each Monday, Wednesday and Friday, and was delighted to find that many of them, although inevitably imbued (as he himself once had been) with the spirit of Weber and Wagner, were also prepared to take notice of local—that is to say Negro and red-Indian—influences. He hoped that through the benefit of such impacts American composers of the future might do for their country what Chopin had done for Poland, Liszt for Hungary, Smetana and himself for Bohemia, Grieg for Norway. As a somewhat under-privileged inhabitant of the Habsburg

Empire, he had an inborn sympathy for anyone who might feel himself to be in a similar predicament, and therefore gave particular attention to 'coloured' students; later he even persuaded Mrs Thurber (not that that enlightened lady needed much persuasion) to insert in the press an announcement to the effect that all aspiring entrants to the National Conservatory of Music, whether white, red, yellow or black, would be judged solely on their achievements in the entrance examination—which Dvořák himself made a point of supervising.

So far, not so bad. It was the training of the Conservatory orchestra (Tuesday and Thursday afternoons, four to six) that caused Dvořák to tear his hair. Here he had to cope not with budding composers (the majority of whom, however untalented, were at least sincere in their aspirations) but with budding executants, many of whom, though of course not all, had been sent thither from luxurious homes on Long Island by parents who hoped to acquire greater social status if Junior could play the fiddle or tootle acceptably on the flute. Whereas at the Prague Conservatoire attendance at orchestral practices was compulsory, Dvořák found that in New York it was voluntary; driven nearly to distraction by the lackadaisical attitude of some of the participants, he had to revise the regulations and insist on stern disciplinary action when they were broken. Thereafter rumours were put about by the 'smart set' that this uncouth Bohemian was hardly a fit and proper person to be the head of a National Conservatory. Jeannette Thurber had the moral guts to back Dvořák, and her confidence in him was soon to be justified.

On the whole Dvořák got on well with the citizens of New York: as a democrat he particularly appreciated the fact that here there were neither Princes and Counts (as there were in his own country) nor Lords and Sirs (as there were in Britain): everyone, from the President downwards, was just plain Mister. He was delighted, too, to discover an aviary in Central Park which housed pigeons, and although it was a long way away he visited them at least once a week. He was distressed to find, however, that since New York City had been built on an island (Manhattan) there was only one big railway station within easy reach—and even there, casual observers such as himself were not admitted to the main-line platforms; it involved an hour's journey on the 'El' (New York's one-time elevated railway network, dependent in those days upon steam traction) to reach a vantage-point from which to watch express trains rumble by, but he made a pilgrimage to this spot as often as his professional duties would allow, and because it took such a long time to get there and back he always tried to get value for money by staying till the last possible moment. Mrs Thurber had no sympathy with this extraordinary passion for pigeons and trains, but so long as it didn't interfere with Dvořák's work at the Conservatory she was unconcerned; one feels sorry, however, for poor Kovařík, who willy-nilly had to accompany him on most of these excursions—and was no doubt bored stiff.

Perhaps because his thoughts were often on far-away Europe, Dvořák also developed a new interest in big steamers: of an early morning he might often have been seen prowling round the docks, inquiring from captains and pursers about departure dates, so that he could write at the last moment to his proud father at Kladno, his kind mother-in-law in Prague, Alois Göbl at Sychrov or some other old friend elsewhere in his native Bohemia—and be sure that his letter would catch the next transatlantic post.

In New York the Dvořáks lived as nearly as possible the simple life to which they were accustomed. As a rule they took their midday meal at a café round the corner where the clientèle was cosmopolitan and which had the great advantage that customers were allowed to peruse fortnight-old newspapers published in Vienna or even in Prague; more often than not they were joined there by Otilie and

Antonín, who were attending a nearby school. Dvořák, who at the time was not enjoying particularly good health, seems to have been nervous of going out alone in the evenings; he always preferred to be accompanied either by his wife or by Josef Kovařík. Indeed, during his first eight months in New York he went only once to the 'Met' and attended only four concerts apart from those at which he himself appeared as conductor. The normal evening routine was a modest meal, a quiet game of cards, and then early to bed.

One pleasant piece of news which Dvořák received about this time was that he had been elected a member of the Berlin Academy of Fine Arts, the first official honour he had been accorded outside the Austrian Empire or Britain. Meanwhile he worked away, without much enthusiasm, on what had been Mrs Thurber's pet project—the cantata based on Drake's *American Flag* for which he had made a few preliminary sketches before leaving home. As has already been noted apropos the *Hussite* overture and *Josef Kajetán Tyl*, Dvořák was rarely successful when he tried to evoke conscious patriotism as distinct from spontaneous nationalism; the *Hymnus* of 1872 remains the most satisfying exception to this generality. Since he had failed to carry conviction in his portrayal of the Hussite warriors of 1412 it was not surprising that he could not cope convincingly with the Yankee warriors of 1812, and *The American Flag* was a very pale reflection of the excellent *Te Deum* which Mrs Thurber had accepted as a substitute. *The American Flag* is divided into four sections, of which the last is little more than a reprise of the opening of the first; representative Dvořák only peeps out in the third section (*allegro giusto, alla marcia*, 2/4 time), which soon settles to be a polka. (The work was not performed in New York, even, until after Dvořák had left there for ever; he himself never heard it—and perhaps never wanted to.)

This labour of obligation was completed round the turn

of the year, and in January 1893 Dvořák, as composer, was free to embark upon something more like a labour of love —his ninth symphony.

SYMPHONY NO. 9 IN E MINOR
at one time called No. 5 (see page 60)

So long as he remained in America Dvořák allowed it to be believed that his symphony 'From the New World' (op. 95) was influenced, to a certain extent at any rate, by Negro music; after his return to Europe he repudiated the suggestion. Both the original acknowledgement and the subsequent denial were half-truths. Folk-tunes often tended (one could put it no higher than that) to be based on a pentatonic scale—C, D, E, G, A (or the equivalent)— indigenous to Bohemia, Somerset, the Hebrides, Ireland and the Appalachians; furthermore the old 'plantation songs' of the 'deep south' of north America sometimes held rhythmic inflexions similar to those of Slav folk-music. Dvořák had the peasant sagacity to capitalize on these coincidences. The melodies of his ninth symphony, no less than of the three other important instrumental works which he was to complete whilst in America, were all of his own devising; in many cases, however, their nostalgic character- istics were sufficiently inter-racial to make an immediate appeal to audiences in the United States while at the same time appeasing his own national hankerings. For instance there was an obvious resemblance between a haunting tune in the first movement of the 'New World' symphony and 'Swing low, sweet chariot, coming for to carry me home', but surely Dvořák was here expressing a longing for a chariot (or a liner) to carry him home to his beloved Bohemia; the familiar cor anglais solo at the start of the second movement has been described as a typical Negro melody (and with even less excuse as a typical red-Indian melody), but in any other context it might with equal justification have been described as typically Czech.

Whatever its sources of impetus, this symphony is a fine one, but it is so popular that concert-promoters all too often regard it as a hackneyed standby, and it is seldom accorded the careful preparatory rehearsal which it deserves. Most of us, at some time or another, have heard it played competently by orchestra A under conductor X and perfunctorily by orchestra B under conductor Y. Those who have never had the good fortune to hear it played by the Czech Philharmonic Orchestra under Karel Ančerl have missed a musical treat: a rare opportunity of being enabled to appreciate to the full the many and varied beauties of its melodic, harmonic, contrapuntal and rhythmic felicities, and the consistent brilliance of the orchestration.

Judged strictly as a symphony, Dvořák's no. 9 does not rank alongside no. 6 and no. 7, although it must be said at once that the first movement is masterly in every respect. Here, while again side-stepping the strict dogma of sonata form, the composer gave greater heed to its underlying principles than he had in the first movement of no. 8. But he fell so much in love with its main theme that he could not resist the temptation to recall it to his aid (somewhat incongruously, one might feel) when inspiration began to flag towards the end of the second (slow) movement and the end of the third (a scherzo rather than a furiant). Nor did the closing stages of the finale gain appreciably in aesthetic stature through the incorporation of snippet-quotations from all three preceding movements. An attempt to 'unify' a symphony in this manner was by no means unprecedented, and indeed might have been praiseworthy had not Dvořák's *modus operandi* been too slap-dash to carry conviction.

The man-in-the-street who is also a lover of music does not bother his head unduly over such considerations. He enjoys good music as it comes to him: a symphony by any other name would sound as sweet, and it does not occur to him to speculate as to whether or not his enjoyment might have been even greater had the composer devoted more care to architectural details; argument of that sort is best left to highbrow critics. And in this instance most highbrow critics have been driven by afterthought to recognize what the man-in-the-street recognized by instinct: that taken as a whole the 'New World' symphony, despite structural weaknesses in three out of its four movements, is a piece of work both inspired and inspiring.

HOLIDAY PLANS

Ever since early in the nineteenth century there had been a continuous stream of immigrants from Bohemia and Moravia to the Mid-West of America; by 1893 there were at least 300,000 Czechs spread throughout the States of Illinois, Wisconsin, Minnesota, Iowa and Nebraska. Most of them lived and worked in Chicago or in other important though less vast industrial centres like Milwaukee, St Paul, Minneapolis, Des Moines and Omaha, but some had established themselves as farming smallholders in self-contained village communities. Dvořák knew very well that at one of these—Spillville in Winneshiek County, north-eastern Iowa—his secretary's father, Jan Josef Kovařík (1850–1939), was schoolmaster and choirmaster, in fact the local Antonín Liehmann. Being preoccupied, however, with his professional duties at the Conservatory and Carnegie Hall and his private duties in connection with pigeons and trains and steamers, he expressed little interest in the place until one day in February 1893 Kovařík proposed to him that instead of returning all the way to Vysoká for his summer holiday—as he had planned—he should spend it instead at Spillville. Dvořák thereupon catechized Kovařík closely regarding its situation and surroundings and inhabitants; when he learnt that it was apparently something not far short of Nelahozeves transplanted from Bohemia to Iowa he decided forthwith to adopt Kovařík's suggestion. One difficulty remained to be overcome: Anna and he were agreed that they could no longer bear to be separated from the four children left behind in Prague; they would now have to be brought to America to join them. So arrangements were made for young Anna, Magda, Otakar and Aloisie to travel out in charge of their mother's sister Terezie Koutecová (*née* Čermáková), who also brought a nursemaid in tow; they reached New York on 31 May (just one week after Dvořák had completed the 'New World' symphony).

Three days later, on Saturday 3 June, Kovařík, now acting as courier, drove everyone out of bed at an early hour and shepherded his flock across the Hudson river to what was then the Pennsylvania Railroad Harbor Terminal in New Jersey to catch the Chicago express leaving at 8.00 a.m. (Eastern Standard Time). There were eleven in the party all told: the Dvořák parents, their six children, aunt Terezie, the mother's-help, and Kovařík himself.

For Dvořák this was one of his most enjoyable days since arriving in America. Delighted to be at last reunited with the whole of his family, he also found plenty to interest him in the station workings at such points as Philadelphia and Harrisburg where locomotives were changed, while on the crossing of the main range of the Alleghany Mountains between Altoona and Johnstown the scenery reminded him of the Böhmerwald and the Erzgebirge. It was still daylight when the train called at Pittsburgh (another engine-changing spot) and if Dvořák went to sleep at all during that short summer night he was awake in plenty of time to savour the fast run across the level plains of northern Ohio and Indiana through Lima and Fort Wayne to Chicago (more than a thousand miles from New York), where he made special note of the fact that the train was dead punctual on arrival—11.00 a.m. (Central Standard Time).

The rest of that Sunday was spent in Chicago, perhaps strolling along the shore of Lake Michigan, until at 9.00 p.m. the itinerant Bohemians set out on the next leg of their long journey. This time the train was a less impressive one than the New York–Chicago express; it followed a second-ary main-line route (Chicago to Minneapolis via Dubuque) and took eleven hours to cover the two hundred and fifty miles or so to McGregor, a small town on the banks of the upper Mississippi. Here they had to change, but the hour-long wait from 8.00 a.m. to 9.00 a.m. was occupied with breakfast, and two hours later eleven weary travellers alighted from a branch-line train at the country station of Calmar (still eight miles short of their destination), where they were met by Kovařík senior, his wife Josefa, Tomáš Bílý (Spillville's Catholic priest) and František Vrba (priest of Protivin, another nearby Czech settlement). These four good people between them could provide sufficient pony-trap accommodation to convey ten of the party to Spillville in time for lunch. The indispensable Kovařík junior stayed behind at Calmar to organize transport for a considerable quantity of luggage, with which he followed on in mid-afternoon. By then Dvořák had approved the unattractive-looking but comfortable stone-and-brick-built dwelling belonging to a Mr. Schmidt (a German, curiously enough) where through the offices of the Kovařík family he had been able to obtain living accommodation for the whole party on reasonable terms; he was already exploring his new sur-roundings, delighted to be able to introduce himself, in his native language, to anyone whom he chanced to meet in the village.

SPILLVILLE

From Dvořák's point of view there were only three snags about his holiday hide-out. First: although plenty of richly-hued birds nested in the vicinity, there were no pigeons or thrushes. Secondly: the nearest railway station—the small one at Calmar—was eight miles away. Thirdly: the local river, the Turkey (a tributary of the upper Mississippi), was navigable only by the tiniest of craft. Debarred from the delights of pigeons and main-line locomotives and ocean-going steamers, he turned instead to the delights of musical composition in a milieu very different from that of East 17th Street. First came a string quartet in F major (op. 96), commonly known as the 'Nigger' quartet (although since that word has become taboo in the country of its origin the nickname has fallen somewhat into disuse).

Despite the popularity of this work it can hardly claim to rank among the greatest of Dvořák's achievements: in three out of the four movements one tends to become irritated by the frequent and almost nervy repetition of pentatonic melodic phrases and jerky little rhythmic figures (half Bohemian, half negroid) that seem to have been left over from the 'New World' symphony. On the credit side let it be said right away that the construction is admirably concise, that an impeccable chamber-music balance is maintained almost throughout, and that the truly superb second movement (*lento*, D minor, 6/8 time), regarded on its own, is a fine work of art. Taken as a whole, however, op. 96 sounds less skilfully adapted to the needs of the moment than the admittedly 'Viennese' op. 61 in C major. Nor is one inclined to agree with Šourek's contention that the work was directly inspired by the rural surroundings of Spillville: Dvořák sketched out all four movements before the end of his first week there; in so short a time he can hardly have got over his surprise at finding himself in this unfamiilar Czech corner of the Mid-West—where in any case there were no 'niggers'—let alone have absorbed its atmosphere.

Ten days later Dvořák completed the score, and since he was determined to *hear* it as soon as possible he prevailed upon somebody (almost certainly his devoted secretary) to copy out separate parts for four instrumentalists. Plenty of local family talent was available, and so this famous quartet had its first scratch performances ('scratch' might be *le mot juste*) towards the end of June 1893 in a private house at Spillville (Iowa). The executants were: first violin, Antonín Dvořák himself; second violin, schoolmaster Jan Kovařík; viola, Kovařík's daughter Cecilie; cello (need it be said?), his son Josef—who as we already know had often gone through far more trying experiences than this in order to give a few hours' pleasure to his beloved master. Josef Kovařík left it on record, however, that the work was by no means easy to sight-read: 'we just had to swim through to the end as best we could.'

Dvořák soon became a popular figure in Spillville (population about 300), where most of the older generation of inhabitants had originally come from Tábor, Budějovice or Pisek, three towns in southern Bohemia that all lay within less than sixty miles of Vysoká. Every morning he attended Tomáš Bílý's celebration of early Mass; he would either lead the choir or play the organ, and his wife often obliged with a solo anthem. Dvořák explored the dead-flat countryside on foot, and wrote to his friend Doctor Emil Kozánek (1856–1927)—a distinguished lawyer and keen amateur musician who was president of a flourishing Music Society at Kroměříž (Kremsier) in eastern Moravia—to explain how different it was from the rolling, wooded, and comparatively well-populated landscape of their native land. ('Here a farmer's nearest neighbour may be five miles away.') One day a group of red Indians, belonging to the Algonquin tribe, arrived at Spillville, peddling their 'herbal remedies' Dvořák, who since leaving New York had recovered his normal good health, was for the moment not interested in herbal remedies, but he was greatly intrigued to listen to these quaint characters singing and playing their own music in the village street of an evening. Indeed it is possible to detect (or at any rate to imagine) traces of Indian influence in his next composition, a string quintet in E flat major (op. 97) which he completed during July. This did not, like the earlier string quintet in G major of 1875, incorporate a double-bass; it comprised the more usual combination of two violins and two violas and one cello.

If Dvořák's quartet in F major is sometimes overpraised, this second Spillville composition tends to be underrated. Some critics have found the first movement (in 3/4 time) a shade trivial; if played *allegro vivace* it might be, but at the *tempo* the composer indicated—*allegro non tanto*—the contrast between the second viola's smooth opening phrase (most skilfully treated in later developments) and the subsequent lively red-Indian(?) rhythms sounds decidedly original. Algonquins—with quasi-percussion effects—take over to a greater extent in the scherzo (B major, *allegro vivo*, 2/2), but the most attractive feature of this movement is its charming and fragile 'trio' section (B minor, *poco meno mosso*). Next comes a theme with variations (initially A flat minor, *larghetto*, 3/8) which takes us straight back to Europe and indeed to the Europe of the early nineteenth century: at least one admirer of Dvořák's music has here continually to remind himself that he is not listening to Beethoven or Schubert. After this beautiful if slightly inconsequent Viennese interlude, the finale (*allegro giusto*, 2/2), overburdened with 'dotted rhythms', sounds disappointingly ordinary, but a redeeming feature is the graceful 'second subject' (which puts in its first appearance in the key of G flat major).

It was about this time that Dvořák had one of his periodical reconciliations with Simrock, with whom relations had been strained ever since he had sold his G major symphony to Novello. In a remarkably short space of time they settled between them by correspondence upon a mutually agreeable fee for a bundle of Dvořák's compositions of the interim, including the *Dumky* trio, the three concertovertures *In Nature's Realm*, *Carnival*, and *Othello*, the 'New

World' symphony and the two latest chamber works. The scores were safely conveyed by the postal authorities the not inconsiderable distance from Spillville to Berlin, and in Dvořák's absence in America Simrock in due course asked Brahms in Vienna to correct the proofs on his behalf. From the readiness with which this laborious task was undertaken and the fulsome terms in which Dvořák expressed his gratitude it is clear that any tiny rift that there may have been between the two composers at the time of Dvořák's visit to Cambridge in 1891 was by now completely healed.

In August Dvořák, leaving the rest of the family behind at Spillville, took his two eldest children, Otilie and Anna, on a week's jaunt to Chicago to visit the World Fair, where 'Czech Day' (12 August 1893) was celebrated in the Festival Hall by a concert dedicated to the works of Bohemian composers. Among them were Smetana (the overture to *The Bartered Bride*), Bendl (two short choral works) and Fibich (an aria from his opera *Nevěsty messinské, The Bride of Messina*); Dvořák himself was represented by his G major symphony, three *Slavonic Dances* from op. 72 and the overture to *Josef Kajetán Tyl*.

During the first week of September Dvořák made a round trip on his own of eight hundred miles or so—Omaha, Sioux City, Minneapolis, St. Paul and back—to visit and be lavishly entertained by the leaders of several large Czech communities in those areas. But duty was calling, and on 16 September the Dvořák entourage had to bid a reluctant farewell to the hospitable Mid-West. The return journey to New York was made by a somewhat circuitous route which involved the crossing of some two hundred miles of Canadian territory (between Detroit and Buffalo and lying to the north of Lake Erie); Dvořák was thus enabled to store up in his mind some novel railway experiences, and the whole party was enabled to visit the Niagara Falls, by which one and all were duly impressed.

The quiet corner of Iowa in which a great composer from

Bohemia had spent such a contented holiday paid tribute to his memory thirty-six years later: in 1929 a new motor-road, sixty miles long and running north-westwards from Calmar through the Czech settlements of Spillville and Protivin to Preston, just beyond the Minnesota State border-line, was officially named the 'Dvořák Highway'.

CHAPTER THIRTEEN

Back and Forth Across the Atlantic

In sleepy Spillville, relaxing in a Bohemian atmosphere somewhat akin to that of Vysoká, Dvořák had been very happy, and when in mid-September 1893 he found himself back in a bustling New York crowded with go-getters he became prey to nostalgia. But there were great material benefits to be gained so long as he stayed on there and did his job properly, and he countered his longing for his own people by plunging conscientiously and wholeheartedly into the performance of his duties at the National Conservatory; during that autumn he consequently found little time for serious composition. In October he made a few sketches for an orchestral suite in D minor, one of which incorporated a melody which he is said to have jotted down on his cuff when visiting the Minnehaha Falls near Minneapolis early the previous month, but the project never progressed beyond the embryo stage. Dvořák used this Minnehaha theme, however, as the basis of the slow movement of a sonatina for violin and piano, which he completed in November. This was an intentionally unassuming little work, specially designed to be played by his fifteen-year-old daughter Otilie and his ten-year-old son Antonín. It remains a touching tribute to family affection, being sympathetically contrived to meet the limited technical ability of juvenile executants, but fails to match the artistic excellence of the simpler items in Schumann's *Kinderscenen* or Tchaikovsky's *Album for the Young*, with which one might have expected it to merit comparison. At this stage of his career, however, Dvořák was at last trying to keep his opus numbers under control: as a fond parent he had worked out that with the violin sonatina composed for his young daughter and son he would achieve the 'century'—and therefore inscribed it as 'op. 100'. The works known as op. 98 and op. 99 were not completed until later, but they must have been planned and may even have been started before he got down to the sonatina.

On 15 December 1893 the first performance of the 'New World' symphony took place in Carnegie Hall, New York. Its enthusiastic reception was a cause of great gratification not only to the composer but also to Jeanette Thurber: she now felt entirely vindicated for her unconventional choice of a director for the National Conservatory, and being human as well as wealthy and ambitious she no doubt enjoyed saying 'I told you so' to those of her socialite acquaintances who had previously been Dvořák's detractors. All that worried her was whether or not she could persuade him to stay on after the expiration of his present contract, which was for two years only. Eventually it was agreed between them that Dvořák could have five months leave in which to go home to Bohemia for the summer of 1894, and that he would then return to New York until the spring of 1895. With that Mrs Thurber had to rest content.

Rehearsals of the 'New World' symphony had inevitably brought Dvořák into close contact with Anton Seidl, conductor of the New York Philharmonic Orchestra, and presently a curious friendship sprang up between this pair of opposites. Seidl, who though born in Budapest was of German parentage, had been one of Wagner's principal assistants at successive festivals at Bayreuth; like his late master he was both a social rebel and an agnostic. Dvořák, at first horrified at Seidl's religious beliefs (or lack of them), soon came to find his conversation stimulating as well as blasphemous, and the two men used to meet regularly at a German café on Broadway to discuss this and that over a mug or two of beer.

Perhaps it was Seidl who persuaded Dvořák to visit the Metropolitan Opera House more frequently than he had during the previous season; at any rate he consented to go and hear Rossini's *Semiramis* and Wagner's *Tannhäuser* and *Siegfried*. He didn't altogether enjoy the performances (he walked out after the first act of *Siegfried*), but his thoughts were being turned to opera again by Mrs Thurber, who wanted him to write one based on Longfellow's *Hiawatha*. For the time being Dvořák shrugged this idea aside, but while in the operatic mood he revised the music of several scenes in *Dimitrij*. Meanwhile Kneisel and his Boston String Quartet gave the 'Nigger' quartet its first two public performances—on New Year's Day 1894 in Boston and on 12 January in New York. In the same month Dvořák completed a suite in A major for piano solo (op. 98), sometimes called the 'American' suite, which he later orchestrated. This is a work of little character, which apart from a few 'Negro' touches in the finale might have been produced by almost any competent composer, whether hailing from Bohemia, Berlin or either of the two Bostons; of its five movements the fourth (*andante*, A minor, 4/4 time), based on a pleasant but somewhat undistinguished melody (first heard on the oboe in the orchestral version), is the most attractive.

On 23 January students of the National Conservatory gave a public concert under Dvořák's direction. The composers represented ranged from Mendelssohn—the *Midsummer Night's Dream* overture—to Stephen Foster (1826–1864)—*Old Folks at Home*. At Dvořák's suggestion, the entire proceeds were handed over to a charitable organization whose resources were devoted to improving the living conditions of New York's slum-dwellers.

'BIBLICKÉ PÍSNĚ' ('BIBLICAL SONGS')

Dvořák's best-known songs, apart from the *Gipsy Songs* of 1880, are those contained in the collection of ten entitled

Biblical Songs (op. 99), most of which were composed in New York during February and March 1894. They were settings (in Czech) of texts selected from the Psalms, and were originally written for voice and piano. (Several years later Dvořák orchestrated five of them.) According to Otakar Šourek (always on the look-out for subjective influences), Dvořák was at the time greatly affected by the recent deaths of Gounod (18 October 1893), Tchaikovsky (6 November 1893) and Hans von Bülow (12 February 1894), and one hesitates to question his authoritative statement. But although Dvořák may have admired Gounod's music and even his personality, they can hardly have met more than once—at the Birmingham Festival of 1885. He had been on very cordial terms both with Tchaikovsky and with von Bülow (who had conducted his symphonies almost as frequently as had Richter and to whom he had dedicated his no. 5 in F major), and would naturally regret the loss of these two good friends. But surely the term 'greatly affected' was somewhat of an exaggeration; Dvořák was probably much more distressed on receiving news that his seventy-nine-year-old father was lying dangerously ill in his home at Kladno. (He died on 28 March.)

However that may be, Šourek was prompted to a eulogy in which he described the *Biblical Songs* as belonging to 'the most magnificent fruits of Dvořák's inspiration'; other knowledgeable critics have praised them in terms almost as fulsome. As in the case of the G major symphony, I must voice my own personal opinion at the risk of finding myself in a small minority. The only two out of the ten which appear to me to be within measurable distance of justifying Šourek's encomium are nos. 1 and 3. No. 1, *Oblak a mrákota* (*Clouds and darkness*), is an effectively forthright piece of work, well laid out for the voice, and no. 3, *Slyš, ó Bože!* (*Hear my prayer!*), is deeply expressive. No. 7, *Při řekách babylonských* (*By the waters of Babylon*), and no. 10, *Zpívejte Hospidinu píseň novou* (*Sing ye a joyful song*), are for practical purposes imitation Negro spirituals and as such may pass muster. The remaining six, I am afraid, strike me as being either mawkish or merely dull.

SUMMER AT HOME

When on the morning of 30 May 1894 Dvořák and his large family, having set forth from New York on the steamship *Aller* eleven days previously and had a rather stormy crossing of the Atlantic Ocean, alighted on a platform at Prague's 'Staatsbahnhof' (today Praha-střed), they were welcomed by a deputation of enthusiastic Bohemian musicians; among them were Karel Bendl, Mořic Anger, Adolf Čech, Jindřich Kàan and Josef Suk (to all of whom my readers have already been introduced), along with Karel Weis (1862–1938), who at the time was principal conductor of the opera house at Brno and was later to become a composer of operas and operettas that followed the Dvořák tradition. Dvořák was urgently pressed to spend that night in Prague: there was to be a gala performance of *The Jacobin* at the National Theatre. He excused himself from attending on the grounds that he was very tired after his long journey, but the truth was that he couldn't bear to lose a moment before getting back to Vysoká after an absence of more than a year and a half. When the curtain rose that evening on *The Jacobin*, the composer was thirty-five miles away, happily communing with his pigeons and thrushes; while Act II was in progress he was probably being fêted in the nearby pub; by the time the singers and conductor were acknowledging the applause of the audience Anna would already have tucked him safely up in bed.

For the next few months, not surprisingly, Dvořák was content to laze. He was always up betimes, however, in order to attend early morning Mass, when he would often officiate at the organ. He went to Prague now and again to look up old acquaintances, but for the most part spent his days wandering through what he had described nine years before to Henry Littleton as the 'beautyful forsts'. (By now, however, he spoke and wrote English with at least the same facility that he spoke and wrote German.) After dinner he would as often as not go and hob-nob with his cronies at the 'local', chain-smoking cheap cigars and drinking good beer. Such a low-class evening diversion did not altogether meet with the approval of his wife and family, but by this time they had learnt to put up with it.

During that summer Dvořák composed only some short piano pieces, among them a set of eight humoresques (op. 101), one of which—no. 7 in G flat major—soon tripped its delicate way into every sitting-room in Europe and every 'parlor' in North America. It should be pointed out that several of the others, though less well known, are equally attractive, notably no. 4 in F major.

To mark his fifty-third birthday, 8 September 1894, Antonín Dvořák—who at one stage of his career had not been able to afford the hire of a piano—presented the church at Vysoká with a new organ. It cost him just about as much as he had earned during the whole of the three years 1874 to 1877, when he himself had been a full-time church-organist. Three matters alone were causing him some temporary concern. In a dispute between the recently-formed Czech Philharmonic Society and the longer-established Czech Society for Chamber Music, Dvořák and his old friends the conductor Adolf Čech and the cellist Hanuš Wihan and his young friend Karel Kovařovic (1862–1920), a talented conductor and composer who was later to become musical director of the Czech National Theatre, were all to a certain extent implicated, however involuntarily; fortunately Dvořák managed to steer clear of personal acrimony, and remained on cordial terms with the others. Besides this, his daughter Anna became seriously ill; in the end she fully recovered, but there had been a period of anxiety. Finally, Dvořák dreaded the prospect of having to return to New York.

There was one pleasant public occasion before the arrival of the deadline however, when on 22 October he conducted a concert of his own works in Prague, which included the first performance in that city of the 'New World' symphony. A week later Anna and he were on their way to Hamburg, where they were entertained by Josef Bohuslav Förster (1859–1951), son of the Josef Förster who thirty-five years ago had been a teacher at the Prague Organ School. (Förster the younger was then working in Hamburg as a free-lance music critic; in later life he became first a professor and subsequently the director of the Prague Conservatoire.)

Next day the Dvořáks embarked on the *Bismarck*, bound for New York. This time, since it was to be a comparatively short visit to America, they took with them only one of their children—nine-year-old Otakar: he and his brother Antonín (eleven) were evidently both high-spirited lads, who when in harness together might have proved too much of a handful for their grandmother—and in any case Dvořák wanted Otakar to improve his English.

NEW YORK AGAIN

During Dvořák's first eight months in New York (October 1892 to May 1893 inclusive) he had remained reasonably content: as already recounted he had been intensely interested in his new surroundings; he had been assured of the sympathetic patronage of Jeanette Thurber; he had known he was doing a good job of work at the

National Conservatory; he had been enthusiastically received by all except a few disgruntled entrants in the Social Register; he had joyfully discovered the Central Park pigeons and a railway bridge over the Harlem river where he could watch the expresses of the New York Central and the New York, New Haven & Hartford Railroad Companies buzzing to and from Albany and Boston. After an enjoyable holiday among his fellow-countrymen at Spillville however, he had found it less easy to settle down on his return (mid-September 1893 to mid-May 1894); and since a three and a half months' break in a Czech corner of the Mid-West had dampened his appreciation of New York's advantages it is not surprising that a four and a half months' break at Vysoká itself had engendered a feeling akin to distaste for that vast metropolis. Dvořák was much too sensible of the material advantages accruing from residence there to allow his inner feelings to leak out in public, but the fact remains that during his third spell in New York (November 1894 to mid-April 1895) he was terribly homesick; he may have been more gratified than comforted when he was elected an honorary member of the New York Philharmonic Society.

Being extremely conscientious, he carried on as before with his routine duties at the Conservatory, and even reconsidered Mrs Thurber's earlier suggestion for a *Hiawatha* opera; he went so far as to make a few sketches for it, but found himself dissatisfied with the garbled text provided for him and eventually abandoned the project. Instead, he devoted much of his time during the early months of 1895 to the composition of a cello concerto; he may have been inspired to this task either by Hanuš Wihan—to whom it was dedicated—or by the Irish-born Victor Herbert (1859–1924, principal cellist of the New York Philharmonic Orchestra and later a composer of successful operettas), with whom he had become friendly. Before ultimately leaving New York in April, Dvořák also began a string quartet in A flat major which he labelled op. 105, but after completing the first movement he put the work aside until the following December.

CELLO CONCERTO IN B MINOR

Dvořák's second cello concerto (for the previous one see page 36) was the best concerto he ever wrote for any instrument. Attentive listeners who know the 'New World' symphony will once again notice here and there, from the start, those ambiguous little tics of melody and rhythm that characterize the folk-music of both Bohemia and the deep south, but all national frontiers are overstepped by the 'second subject' of the first movement, a glorious tune fully capable of holding its own anywhere on the globe. Its initial announcement by a horn (bars 57–64), ranks as a classic example of expressive writing for that instrument and when the soloist takes over, although the 'racial' features of the 'first subject' are by no means pushed into the background, one becomes aware that the horn-tune is an equal mainspring of the subsequent outpouring. This movement is one of Dvořák's most inspired and best-constructed achievements in the symphonic field, and indeed may be said to be beyond criticism.

A similarly glowing tribute might be paid to the lovely second movement (G major) but for the fact that its closing stages are too long-drawn out. The G minor middle section is derived from one of Dvořák's songs—*Kéž duch můj sám* (*Leave me alone*), dated 1887; it has been described by one distinguished commentator as 'stormy' and by another as 'strident', but personally I think that 'restless' would be a more appropriate epithet; in any case its restlessness (or storminess or stridency) possesses a beauty all its own and provides an effective contrast to the sweet serenity of the

strains that precede it so admirably and follow it so interminably.

The first two movements of this concerto do indeed hold
one enthralled in a high stratosphere, and although it would
be going too far to say that the finale brings one down to
earth with a bump, one is left with the impression of having
made a gentle descent by parachute from Dvořák at supreme
heights to Dvořák at a more normal level. Several good
tunes, in alternating moods of vigour and comparative
tranquillity, are allowed to have things rather too much
their own way; they almost get out of hand before at last
(and not before one's patience is strained) a flash-back
to the opening of the first movement heralds a very brief and
satisfactory wind-up that sets tongue-in-cheek pomposity
alongside spontaneous sprightliness.

This was the last work that Dvořák completed while in
the United States: it was a worthy tribute to a great nation.
On 16 April 1895, along with Anna and young Otakar,
he embarked on the *Saale* (by coincidence the same ship
by which he had originally travelled out in September 1892)
and waved his final farewell to New York. Mrs. Thurber
tried hard to persuade him to return, but he was adamant.
The next two directors of her National Conservatory (each
of whom, like Dvořák, held the position for about three
years only) were at the same time conductors of the New
York Philharmonic Orchestra—Seidl's successor Emil Pauer
(1855–1932) and *his* successor Vassily Safonov (1852–
1918); between-whiles Mrs Thurber herself had to do the
best she could to control the curriculum, the staff, and the
students. In 1913 she at last prevailed once again upon
a distinguished European composer—Engelbert Humperdinck (1854–1921), whose delightful *Hänsel and Gretel*
(1893) still deservedly holds the stage—to accept the post,
but at the eleventh hour he had to cry off owing to commitments in Germany. Two years later the estimable Jeanette
Thurber reluctantly retired from the fray, and thereafter

the National Conservatory ceased to play any particularly significant part in the musical education of young New Yorkers; its founder, however, could always look back with satisfaction on its days of glory under the directorship of her pet lion.

CHAMBER-MUSIC CULMINATION

If the previous summer had been a lazy one for Dvořák, that of 1895 was lazier still. He did not put a note of music on paper, and although now and again he travelled to Prague and elsewhere to call on some of his many friends he again spent nearly all his time at Vysoká. A frequent visitor there was his ex-pupil Josef Suk, and it soon became clear that from Suk's point of view the main attraction in the Dvořák household was seventeen-year-old Otilie. On the occasion of these visits Suk had strict instructions from his host that he was to note down the number of the engine that headed the afternoon train from Prague to Příbram. Once, when he failed to so, Dvořák pretended to be furious and growled to his daughter 'how can you expect me to let you marry a young man with so little sense of responsibility?'

Nevertheless, despite Dvořák's leg-pullings and indeed with his barely-disguised approval, Otilie and Josef continued to hold hands on every possible occasion, and only one sad event marred the domestic tranquillity of this happy period: the death of Anna's sister Josefa Kounicová, with whom Dvořák himself had been in love thirty years ago and who for the last ten had been the family's nearest neighbour. (Brother-in-law Václav Kounic, the hereditary Count, survived his actress-wife by eighteen years.)

In September 1895 Dvořák transferred himself from

Vysoká to Prague to take up once again his duties as professor of composition at the Conservatoire; before the end of the year he also found time to compose a string quartet in G major and to complete that in A flat major upon which he had begun work in New York earlier in the year.

The string quartet in G major (op. 106) was the finest he ever wrote—which is saying plenty—and may be regarded as a hymn of thanksgiving for his safe return, alive and well, to his native land: except perhaps in the third movement (see below) the mood was appropriately and emphatically 'national'. Indeed in the first movement (joyous throughout) and again in the last (with contrasted moods of gaiety and nostalgia) the music at times suggests not so much Dvořák himself as Smetana at the height of his maturity, although it must be stressed that Dvořák always possessed a greater understanding than did his predecessor of the tricky *technical* problems of chamber music. (Students should take a close look at bars 109–114 in the first movement: this passage, with its simple but varied rhythmic figuration on the three instruments accompanying the first violin's melodic phrases, demonstrates to perfection the composer's understanding of the string-quartet medium.)

Yet one cannot help thinking that some of the typically Bohemian melodies in this quartet, had they been composed while Dvořák was in America, might have been acclaimed *there* as typically Negro, notably the tune that provides a basis for the deeply expressive second movement, in which a hovering of tonality between E flat minor and E flat major persists from start to finish. The third movement, however, provides a big surprise: so far from being reminiscent of Smetana it is on the contrary a genuine scherzo in B minor and the Viennese manner, and the occasional substitution of two crochets for three in quick 3/4 time, though engaging, perhaps hardly compensates for the lack of a stimulating *furiant* cross-rhythm which one might have thought that Dvořák, on this occasion above all others, would have been keen to reproduce. In the gay finale, excessive exuberance is admirably held in check by almost dumka-like alternations between *andante sostenuto* and *allegro con fuoco*.

Two other features deserve mention. Although it has often been pointed out that Brahms, in his first symphony, was unorthodox but logical when he stepped up the key of each movement in sequence by a 'major third'—C, E, A flat, C—so far as I know it has never yet been pointed out that Dvořák, both in his *Te Deum* and in this quartet, was equally logical when he reversed the process by stepping the keys of the movements *down* by the same interval—G, E flat, B, G. One notes, too, that when half-way through the finale he could not resist incorporating recollections from the first movement, but he did so with greater perception than he had shown in the finale of the 'New World' symphony, and this time an attempt to achieve artistic unity by such means was wholly successful.

The A flat major quartet (op. 105) holds many beauties, but on the whole is less consistent in quality. The first movement (composed in New York) is variable in mood and sounds less spontaneous than one might have hoped for, while in the finale, after an originally-contrived and surprisingly effective opening, the customary light-heartedness is not only unduly prolonged but also somewhat forced. No serious criticism, however, can be made of the two middle movements. A bouncing furiant in F minor (placed second) does duty as a scherzo, and is one of the best specimens in all Dvořák's chamber music. (The melodious middle section, although there is no change of key signature in the score, is actually in D flat major.) The truly lovely slow movement, taken on its own, is an even better achievement: here Dvořák recaptured (in the same key, F major) the appealingly romantic atmosphere of the slow movement of his violin concerto

—and applied greater resource to its development. This *lento e molto cantabile*, I feel, stands in the same relation to the rest of his work as does the *adagio molto espressivo* from the quartet in B flat major (op. 130) to the rest of Beethoven's—and that is high praise indeed.

CHAPTER FOURTEEN

Concentration on Bohemia

It is worth recalling that when the thirty-two-year-old Dvořák married Anna Čermáková in November 1873 he had so far given the world only one opera, one operetta, one choral work, three orchestral works, nine chamber works, two piano pieces and about twenty-five songs. The corresponding figures at the end of 1895 were: four operas; four operettas; nine large-scale choral works; about thirty orchestral works (not counting orchestral arrangements of piano duets and so forth); a like number of chamber works (again not counting arrangements); about one hundred and ten pieces for piano solo or piano duet; eighty songs; thirty vocal duets; twenty-five part-songs or short choruses. His rate of output over the last twenty-two years had in fact compared very favourably with that of other great composers whose most significant spells of creative activity were spread over a longer period and who are therefore commonly regarded as having been more prolific.

There is another point to remember. When Dvořák was thirty-two his name had been quite unknown except to a small circle of musical connoisseurs in Prague, and the only work he had managed to get published was one single song; by the time he reached the age of fifty-four he had produced works of the highest quality in every field of composition, was internationally famous, was able to dictate his own terms to would-be publishers. To gain some idea of the stature he had attained, let us tabulate in age order the names of fifteen of the most prominent composers who were practising their art to good advantage in 1895, ranging down the scale from three grand old men still giving of their best to five comparative youngsters who had already made their mark without necessarily having yet reached full maturity.

Verdi (eighty-two years old)
Bruckner (seventy-one)
Brahms (sixty-two)
Saint-Saëns (sixty)
Dvořák himself (fifty-four)
Massenet (fifty-three)
Sullivan (fifty-three)
Grieg (fifty-two)
Rimsky-Korsakov (fifty-one)
Fauré (fifty)
Puccini (thirty-six)
Wolf (thirty-five)
Mahler (thirty-five)
Debussy (thirty-three)
Strauss (thirty-one)

Not everyone would put Dvořák at the head of the 1895 championship table, but bearing in mind that several of the younger entrants had not yet really got going, few critics outside the ranks of partisans would grudge him a place in the first three. Furthermore, by 1895, Antonín Dvořák had put Bohemia well and truly on the musical map of Europe—not to mention America—and that ardent Czech nationalist Bedřich Smetana, had he still been alive, would have been the first to applaud this achievement.

SYMPHONIC POEMS

It is a moot point whether or not Smetana would have been the first to applaud Dvořák's change of direction in 1896, when he gave up the composition of 'absolute' music (symphonies, string quartets, songs, piano pieces and so forth) and for practical purposes devoted the remainder of his life to 'programme music' and music for the stage, nearly all of it with a strongly Bohemian slant.

It is an even mooter point whether or not this change of direction should be applauded, with the benefit of hindsight, by posterity. One need not quibble about the strongly Bohemian slant: after his long sojourn in America it was only natural that Dvořák should turn again, with delight, to the inspiration of the legends and folk-lore of his own country. What one is inclined to regret is that during the next couple of years or so he should have devoted so much of his time to attempts to express his devotion to his homeland in 'programme music', a branch of composition in which now and again Smetana had shown supremacy but for which Dovřák's great talents, many-sided though they were, were less well-fitted.

Be that as it may, Dvořák made his own decision, and his output during 1896 comprised four symphonic poems based on folk-ballads by Karel Jaromír Erben, all as lurid in character as the one which it will be remembered had served as a text for *The Spectre's Bride*. (My dictionary tells me that 'lurid' means 'ghastly and sensational', and I think that this makes it the right adjective to use.) In *Vodník* (*The Water-Goblin*) an evil-minded sprite marries an innocent and unsuspecting girl who has a child by him; when she pays a visit to her mother and fails to return by the hour her husband has appointed, he murders the baby and deposits its headless corpse on the threshold of their cottage. In *Polednice* (*The Noonday Witch*) a young mother tries to quieten a fractious child by saying that if it hasn't recovered its good temper by twelve o'clock the 'noonday witch' will come and administer punishment; this idle threat turns to reality when at noon a witch does appear on the scene and strikes dead both the child and its mother.

In some respects the fantastic and complicated plot of *Zlatý kolovrat* (*The Golden Spinning-wheel*) is even more ungracious: at one stage of the proceedings the heroine has her arms and legs cut off and her eyes gouged out, and after she has been miraculously put together again and recovered her former loveliness the perpetrators of the original crime are thrown to a pack of hungry wolves who tear them to shreds; it should be added that such uncouth happenings do not prevent the whole affair from concluding (to paraphrase Otakar Šourek) in a mood of happy rejoicing. The tale of *Holoubek* (*The Wood-Dove*) is by comparison almost ingratiating: a sprightly young widow who has poisoned her first husband readily consents to a second marriage, but then finds herself plagued night and day by a dove, a reincarnation of the dead man, whose persistent reproaches drive her first to distraction and eventually to suicide. (Dvořák, it seems, preferred not to illustrate in music this act of suicide: according to the recently-published translation of a comment by a Czech musicologist, it was typical of him 'that despite the literary original he did not allow the ballad to end with a warning reminder of damnation but rounded off the tragedy with a morally liberating catharsis'.)

Although Erben's legendary Bohemia was not on the face of it a very peaceful place in which to spend one's mortal existence, the composer took in his stride what would appear to non-Slavs to have been little more than horror-comics (but which have been acclaimed by students of Czech literature as near-masterpieces), and as often as not, particularly in the quieter and more contemplative passages, provided some admirably descriptive and beautifully orchestrated music. The melodic and rhythmic outline of many of the themes, however, was deliberately contrived to fit the scansion of the original lines in the ballads (there were even bits of quasi-recitative) and outsiders are not thereby helped to appreciate their intrinsic worth. (The attractive opening of *The Water Goblin*, which somewhat incongruously recalls the dance at the start of Act II of Bizet's *Carmen*, was most assuredly *not* a case in point.) One's main quarrel with Dvořák over these symphonic poems is that they are not truly symphonic: for those who are unacquainted with Erben's poems, the music is apt to sound as inconsequent as would the music of Dvořák's fellow-Slav Serge Prokofiev (1891–1953) were his *Peter and the Wolf* to be played without a spoken commentary; moreover, surely a listener to so-called symphonic poems has a right to expect here and there a spot of 'symphonic development'—or at least something more than mere musical illustration—but he will find hardly anything of the sort.

Let it be said right away, however, that some of Dvořák's musical illustration is first-rate; notably the tune associated with the *Water Goblin* himself and the (orchestral) dialogue between the harassed mother and the petulant child in *The Noonday Witch*. In *The Wood-Dove* there is plenty of enjoyment to be found, so long as one is content to forget the 'programme' and listen in succession to a funeral march, to an evocation of a wedding-breakfast, to a good deal of sinister dove-cooing, and finally to the epilogue so vividly described as 'a morally liberating catharsis'. *The Golden Spinning-wheel*, too, contains some pleasant music, and although this is nowadays the most frequently played of these four symphonic poems it is to my mind the least attractive among them: there are some exuberant horn tunes, but they recur so frequently, against a background which even if one does not take it too seriously nevertheless remains sadistic, that when allocated to the full orchestra they tend to outstay their welcome. In present-day performances, however, this work is usually cut to about two-thirds of its original length.

Meanwhile (or strictly speaking between November 1895 and March 1897), Dvořák went once again to London and no less than five times to Vienna. He took Otilie with him to London, and since there was no longer a Henry Littleton to extend kind hospitality they stayed at the Langham Hotel. Their purpose was to attend the first performance in Britain of Dvořák's cello concerto, which took place at

Queen's Hall on 19 March 1896 with Leo Stern (1862–1904) as soloist; other items in the same programme were the *Othello* overture, the G major symphony and several of the *Biblical Songs*; indeed the only intruder on the Dvořák preserve was Beethoven's 'Emperor' piano concerto. Although these works had a great reception from the audience and Otilie no doubt enjoyed basking in reflected glory, Dvořák himself, on this ninth and last visit to England, seems to have found London almost as uncongenial as he had come to find New York: Bohemia now meant everything to him.

And indeed, when about this time he was continually and urgently pressed to accept the lucrative position of professor of composition at the Vienna Conservatoire, he refused the tempting offer on the grounds that it would mean leaving home—although Brahms was prepared to put his own house (which was much larger than he needed for himself alone) at the entire disposal of the Dvořák family. Short visits to Vienna were always enjoyable, however; Dvořák went in February 1896 for the first performance there of the 'New World' symphony, conducted by Richter, and again about six weeks later. On this occasion he had a meeting with Anton Bruckner (1824–1896), who was regarded there as Brahms's main rival and had recently retired, owing to ill-health, from the post at the Conservatoire which it was hoped (vainly) that Dvořák would now consent to fill. All his life Bruckner had been as devoted a Catholic as Dvořák had been, and if the two men had had further opportunities to meet and exchange views they would probably have got on famously together. At the moment when Dvořák paid his call, however, the aging and ailing Bruckner, although receiving him in the kindliest fashion, appeared to be even more distrait than usual: he explained that he was spending all his time on the composition of his ninth symphony, and was therefore unable to accept Dvořák's invitation to accompany him to a concert. (Bruckner's ninth symphony was never finished: he died some six months later, before completing its last movement.)

In March 1897 Dvořák was elected an honorary member of the internationally-known Viennese Society of *Musik-freunde* (Friends of Music), but this particular visit to the Austrian capital must have remained more engraven on his memory for the reason that it marked the occasion of his last meeting with Brahms, who died on 3 April. The two composers, each born under his own star, had some affinities in common—but not many. Brahms, for one thing, was an out-and-out German, who by instinct and upbringing regarded Czechs, collectively, as an inferior race; Dvořák, by contrast, was an out-and-out Czech, who by instinct and upbringing regarded Germans, collectively, as an over-bearing would-be master-race. It is a tribute to the tolerance and artistic integrity of both men that on their first encounter they became close friends and that they thereafter remained mutual admirers. As a pious Catholic, Dvořák was deeply distressed and could not understand how it came about that Brahms, although not actually an agnostic, refused to accept the doctrines of any established Christian religion and indeed relied to a certain extent on the somewhat pessimistic philosophy of Arthur Schopenhauer (1788–1860); his puzzlement found expression in the words: 'such a great man, yet he believes in nothing'—possibly a rather over-simplified assessment of Brahms's viewpoint. None the less, there is little reason to doubt that Brahms's death meant more to Dvořák, personally, than had the death of his mother or the death of Tchaikovsky—the temporary effect of which upon his outlook was so much stressed by Otakar Šourek. During most of that summer of 1897 he remained in a state of despondency; it was not until August that he felt in a mood to compose—and re-wrote parts of Act III of *The Jacobin*. About the same time, Dvořák was extremely gratified and comforted to learn that he had been appointed to the vacant place (previously occupied by Brahms) on the

Austrian State Commission for Music, from which he himself, some twenty years ago, had received such welcome financial assistance.

On 20 September 1897 there came another blow—the death in Prague of Karel Bendl, who had been a very kind friend in earlier days and a faithful one ever since, but Dvořák was not deterred from starting work next month on a fifth symphonic poem, *Píseň bohatýrská* (*The Hero's Song*). Unlike the preceding four, this was not based on a ballad by Karel Erben or anyone else; indeed there was no satisfactory 'programme' enabling one to understand what it was really all about: the actual title is said to have been suggested to him by his ex-pupil Vitězslav Novák. Some commentators believe that the work was intended to be autobiographical, like Strauss's *Heldenleben* of 1899; others (and they are probably right) that Dvořák had in mind some legendary or symbolic Bohemian hero of the Middle Ages; not even those who regard him as a 'subjective' composer have ventured to suggest that it might have been based on the lives of one or other of his recently-deceased friends and heroes Johannes Brahms and Karel Bendl—which would have suited the contention but which on internal evidence would have been in either case an extremely implausible conjecture. Whatever its originating impetus, this work does not amount to much: the terse opening phrases recall the start of the finale of the string quartet in A flat major op. 105, but thereafter there is little to engage or hold one's attention except a modicum of noisy vulgarity. Let it be emphasized once again, however, that in all his five symphonic poems of 1896–7 Dvořák demonstrated anew, whatever their other shortcomings, his command of orchestral effect: their construction may have been disjointed and the music itself may sometimes have been uninspired (least noticeably so in *The Wood-Dove*), but the instrumentation was masterly. And incidentally, for almost the first time in his career, the opus-numbering of

Dvořák's works over an extended period, two years in this case, remained truly and acceptably chronological: these five symphonic poems are successively numbered ops. 107, 108, 109, 110 and 111.

PUBLIC AND PRIVATE AFFAIRS

In 1897 and the early part of 1898 there were considerable political disturbances in Austria (and notably in Bohemia)—the most serious internal political disturbances in the empire since 1848. The Prime Minister at the time, Count Kasimir Badeni (1846–1909), who was Polish by origin and therefore inclined to be favourably disposed towards Slav minorities, introduced a system of parliamentary reform which so far as Bohemia was concerned tended to favour Czechs at the expense of Germans, and which, when it came to an actual election, tended to favour the extremely nationalistic 'young Czechs' at the expense of the more moderate 'old Czechs'. Thereafter, by a new ordinance, the Czech language was raised to equal status with German: not only were Czech-speaking inhabitants allowed to use their own tongue in law courts and so on (as they had been since 1881), but all German-speaking inhabitants of the province were now instructed to learn Czech with the idea that they would ultimately become bilingual. This was more than traditional German culture could stand; there were demonstrations, and indeed serious riots accompanied by bloodshed, both in Prague and in many towns on the fringe of the Sudeten 'language-frontier'. Since these demonstrations and riots were organized by the German-speaking population, the wheel appeared to have turned through a half-circle over the half-century that had elapsed since 1848, but in the outcome, as in 1871, Emperor Franz Josef was overruled by Hungarian opposition to these emancipatory proposals and was forced to give way to the 'establishment': Badeni fell from power, the new laws were repealed—and the ambitious 'young Czechs' found themselves more or less back where they started from. The bitterness aroused by these events was never fully healed until 1919, when after the First World War all inhabitants of Bohemia, whatever their native language, were for the next twenty years or so united, for the most part amicably, in the new republic of Czechoslovakia under the presidency first of Tomáš Masaryk (see page 95) and later of Eduard Beneš (1884–1948).

It is right to note at this stage that although Dvořák, unlike Smetana, never played an active part in political affairs, there was no question as to where his allegiance lay. And as a one-time nominal colleague of Masaryk's at the Czech University, he may well have given that future world-statesman a few hints on the way of life in America, where Masaryk was later to spend much time in his endeavour to propagate Czech political aspirations. At any rate, both Masaryk and Beneš subsequently expressed their appreciation of the great part that Dvořák had played in furthering the cause of national culture in the hereditary 'Lands of the Crown of Saint Wenceslas'. It is interesting to learn, too, that Marie Červinková, the competent librettist of *Dimitrij* and *The Jacobin*, was the daughter of František Rieger, who had earlier been František Palacký's closest associate and was now the leader of the 'old Czech' party.

In 1898, however, being barely recovered from the double shock of the deaths of Brahms and Bendl, Dvořák was more concerned with private than with political affairs; although he had long since planned to attend that year's Bayreuth Festival in Richter's company, he gave up the idea because of Otilie's approaching marriage to Josef Suk, by now a very promising composer. They had been in love with one another for at least three years, but the ceremony was postponed so that it would coincide with the silver-wedding anniversary of the bride's mother and father on 17

November 1898. On that date there were celebrations on a
scale that would have done credit to the ambitious parents
of Britain's best-favoured débutante of the year: Dvořák
—bless his heart—was determined to keep up with
Prague's most status-seeking Joneses. This was appropriate
enough: during that same month he had learnt that on 2
December Emperor Franz Josef would mark the completion
of fifty years' reign over Austria (*inter alia*) by bestowing
upon him the high award of the Medal of Honour for Arts
and Sciences. Brahms was the only musician upon whom this
distinction had previously been conferred.

'ČERT A KAČA' ('THE DEVIL AND KATE')

During the summer of 1898, Dvořák, who though still
only in his fifties was by now very much the grand old man
of Czech music, had begun work on a new operetta, *The
Devil and Kate*; he finished it in February 1899. The
libretto by Adolf Wenig (1874–1940), a young schoolmaster, was based on a boisterous Bohemian farce by Josef
Kajetán Tyl, which most unusually, for a work in this
category, contained no love interest.

There are really two separate plots, somewhat disconnected and not neatly tied together until the third of the
three acts. In the main one (Devil and Kate) the titular
heroine (mezzo-soprano), who so far from being the
customary village beauty has been endowed by nature with
unattractive features and an outsize figure and a shrewish
disposition, not surprisingly fails to attract the admiring
attention of any local youngster; determined to find a partner
during feast-day celebrations she declares that she would
dance with the devil himself if given the chance. And it so
happens (as in the corresponding 'Kermesse' scene of
Gounod's *Faust*) that there *is* a devil—Marbuel (bass)—

mingling with the crowd; although subsequent events are to prove him a less resolute one than Mephistophiles, he does his stuff at the moment to such good purpose that Kate allows him to offer her first a drink and then a dance and eventually to carry her down through a trap-door in the stage to the nether regions. Once they arrive there all the devils in Hell, and not least Marbuel himself, find nagging Kate such a confounded nuisance that they seek the first opportunity to dispatch her upstairs again.

In the converging sub-plot (*čert a Jirka* or devil and George) the hero (tenor) is a shepherd in the employ of his country's hard-hearted Queen (a rôle for a soprano with an effective vocal range of more than two octaves). Having just been given the sack for being a few minutes late at work and told to go to the devil, poor George thinks he may as well do just that—and jumps down through the open trap-door in the wake of Marbuel and Kate. On landing below, he is cordially welcomed by Lucifer (bass), Prince of Hell, who tells him that he has long had his baleful eye on the cruel Queen and indeed has her in mind for permanent occupancy of a particularly uncomfortable corner of his own domain. In due course it is suggested that George should return home (and will he please take that intolerable Kate with him) so as to prepare the ground for Marbuel to remove the Queen to the underworld.

Safely back on earth—along with Kate—George double-crosses Lucifer by offering to save the Queen from the horrible fate in store for her, but only if she will first of all abolish serfdom throughout her dominions and appoint George himself as Prime Minister. She agrees to his conditions, and when Marbuel reappears on the scene to carry out Lucifer's instructions regarding her, George arranges for him to be warned that Kate is still determined to get her claws on him; on receipt of this information Marbuel decides that discretion is the better part of valour and promptly plunges back to the comparative quietude of Hell.

And so while Lucifer is robbed of his prey everyone else can settle down to live happily ever after; Kate herself is compensated for her troublesome adventure with money and a home of her own—two acquisitions which she is confident will further her matrimonial prospects.

All rather fantastic, but at least out of the ordinary! Dvořák's overture is out of the ordinary too, being largely although not exclusively based on two tunes (one of them definitely in folk-style) that are not heard in the operetta itself. This was his last composition in anything like classical sonata form, and although the key-relationships are typically unconventional the two main themes are intertwined with considerable skill; indeed there is more 'symphonic development' in this comparatively short overture than in all the five 'symphonic poems' put together. Dvořák was obviously taking everything very seriously.

The rest of the music of *The Devil and Kate* included some excellent waltzes and polkas and so forth for the villagers in Act I, and a no less excellent (and no less Slavonic) *pekelný tanec* (infernal dance) for the devils in Act II. Dvořák's devils, by the way, wouldn't frighten anybody: to quote Otakar Šourek, 'they are just good fellows'. Dvořák linked them with the peasants and everyone else in a completely assured manner which served to demonstrate how far he had matured since the days of *The Peasant a Rogue* (1877). Nevertheless, in a few passages perhaps slightly over-influenced by Wagner, one is aware of a lessening of spontaneity compared with the earlier work, and there are not many opportunities for lyricism. In Act I, however, George is granted a charming song, 'Já ubohej ovčáček' ('I'm just a poor shepherd-boy'), and Marbuel has a chance to show his vocal paces while pressing Kate to accompany him down below: 'Je sic to trochu deleko' ('It's not so very far away'). Perhaps the most satisfying detachable item is the Queen's big aria at the beginning of Act III (in which one notices something like an *obbligato* for the cor anglais) when, already in remorseful mood, she complains 'Jak smutno v zámka' ('How tragic fate is'). But none should overlook Kate's delightful and all-too-short little solo 'Však když mám ted'ka dum a penize', which immediately precedes the final chorus; 'Having now both home and money too', Kate here expresses the hope that as a comparatively well-tamed shrew she may presently catch her own Petruchio.

The Devil and Kate was first played on 23 November 1899, in Prague. It has rarely crossed the frontiers of Bohemia, but in 1932 I had the good fortune to attend one of several performances given by the enterprising Oxford University Opera Club. The production enabled those who took part to indulge in a certain amount of undergraduate horse-play—but this was by no means inappropriate: for instance, during ten minutes or so in the first half of Act II, Marbuel has to go on singing his part while at the same time staggering round the stage with fat Kate on his back. I hope, however, that some day soon we in Britain may meet Kate and George and their merry devils in a more sophisticated and more professional milieu.

That slapstick was part and parcel of *The Devil and Kate* reminds one that much the same could be said of *The Bartered Bride*, *The Pigheaded Peasants* and *The Peasant a Rogue*, and impels a brief digression on the subject of nomenclature. I was taken to task by one or two people for discussing these works in a book entitled *Composers of Operetta*, being told that they were not operettas but operas, and that I should not have referred to them at all in a book devoted to the lighter genre. I remain unrepentant. If *The Pigheaded Peasants* and *The Devil and Kate* are to be accounted operas rather than operettas then so must *Trial by Jury* and *Orpheus in the Underworld*—to my way of thinking an absurd proposition. Dvořák, during the course of his career, composed six real operas, four of which have so far been discussed in these pages, but I for one prefer to regard his *comic* evocations of Bohemian peasant-life as operettas; admittedly they do not incorporate spoken dialogue—but then neither does *Trial by Jury*.

'RUSALKA'

The twelve months that followed the completion of *The Devil and Kate* in February 1899 were comparatively uneventful, although in December of that year Dvořák paid his first and only visit to Budapest. (In 1882 he had had to cry off at the last moment from an engagement to conduct his D major symphony there.) In the Hungarian capital there was a 'Dvořák evening', when selections from his chamber music were played by the young violinist Jan Kubelik (1880–1940) and the Czech String Quartet founded by Oskar Nedbal and Josef Suk. Next day, he himself conducted performances of the *Carnival* overture, the cello concerto (with dedicatee Wihan as soloist) and *The Hero's Song*, scoring a great personal triumph. Not to be outdone in courtesy, he expressed himself delighted at the opportunity of listening for the first time to the famous *tzigane* bands in various restaurants of the city, where perhaps he was reminded of his own beer-garden days with Karel Komzák.

Dvořák's only composition during this period was a *Slavnostní zpěv* (*Festival Ode*) for mixed choir and orchestra, a *pièce d'occasion* written to mark the seventieth birthday of Josef Tragy, recently retired from the directorship of the Prague Conservatoire. It was based on a typically Slav theme, first sung and played in octaves, but cannot be regarded as presentative of Dvořák at his best. All along, however, he was on the look out for a possible subject for another opera (not an operetta this time) and at last he came across one.

Before being brought by chance to his own notice in April 1900, the libretto of *Rusalka*, by the Czech poet

Jaroslav Kvapil (1868–1950), had been turned down as unsuitable by two of Dvořák's ex-pupils, Nedbal and Suk, as well as by J. B. Förster (who by now had returned from Hamburg to his homeland). Dvořák himself was delighted with it, and completed the score by the end of the year. Although considerably less gruesome than most of Karel Erben's folk-ballads, it belonged to the same dim world of Bohemian fantasy and legend. For instance there was another *vodník* (water-goblin) and another witch (although not a specifically 'noonday' one); neither the water-goblin nor the witch, however, was so malevolently-inclined as were their Erben counterparts, and indeed the goblin, although he is of a rather interfering nature, emerges as the only principal character in the story who at one and the same time is both sane-minded and disinterested—by which I do *not* mean 'uninterested'.

It is he who tries to deter Rusalka, a water-nymph, from allowing her infatuation for a handsome prince to get the better of her good sense. His advice goes unheeded, and so do the warnings of the witch, who tells her that before she can marry a mortal she herself must become one, which will involve losing the power of speech. Furthermore, if Rusalka's lover should at any time prove unfaithful, then there will be dire tragedy for both of them. The determined Rusalka accepts the conditions; she allows the witch to transform her into a mortal—and so catches her prince. The latter, however, fails to derive much satisfaction from a dumb bride, and falls for the more loquacious charms of a 'foreign princess'. His own and Rusalka's doom being sealed by this act of perfidy, her voice is restored to her and she is able to tell the whole truth. The princess thereupon flounces out, and the remorseful prince, by now only too ready to return to Rusalka, sends emissaries to the water-goblin and the witch in the hope that they will intercede for them both. Goblin and witch are unable and unwilling to avert the outcome; after one final embrace the prince dies in Rusalka's arms, and she herself then slips into a watery grave. (Several British commentators, including at least one who should have known better, have been led into error by a piece of mistranslation in a summary of the plot written in something like English that is incorporated with the published vocal score. Here it is stated that Rusalka, when turned into a mortal, will become *deaf*; in the actual text, however, the witch's stipulation is clear enough: 'Chĕes být nĕma?'— 'Would you wish to be dumb, then?')

Kvapil's libretto, apart from certain unnecessary complications and slight faults of construction, was quite a competent piece of work and inspired Dvořák to compose some splendid music. As in parts of *Dimitrij* and *The Jacobin* the texture is here and there Wagnerian. (With such a plot how could it fail to be?) But many passages in *Rusalka*, particularly those which concern such semi-supernatural beings as Rusalka herself and the water-goblin, provided him with just the stimulus he needed to put forth everything he knew: there was no *reliance* on Wagner, but sensibly enough Dvořák adapted *Valkyrie* methods to his own purposes when it suited him to do so. (One only wishes that he had adopted something like the same approach to his symphonic poems.)

The scene of Act I is the shore of a lake in a forest clearing, with the witch's cottage in the background. After a comparatively short and evocative orchestral prelude, we are introduced in succession to a chorus of very Slavonic water-nymphs, to the slightly Wagnerian water-goblin (bass) and to Rusalka (soprano)—who is typified throughout the opera by one of the loveliest themes that Dvořák ever conceived. In a passage of surpassing beauty, 'Sem často přichazí' ('He comes here frequently'), she tells how she has fallen in love with a prince who often bathes in the limpid waters of the lake, and soon afterwards Dvořák provides her with a magnificent aria which is the most easily detachable and most frequently detached item from the work: 'Mĕsícku na nebi hlubokém' ('Silvery moon in the great dark sky'). Paying no heed to the goblin's kindly and urgent advice, Rusalka puts her future in the hands of the witch (contralto), who after warning her of the consequences puts upon her a spell which turns her into a mortal. (Musically speaking, this witch, with her *čury mury* or hocus-pocus incantations, bears a distinct family resemblance to her better-known cousin in Humperdinck's *Hänsel and Gretel*.) Presently the prince (tenor) appears; he is on a hunting expedition—and indeed throughout this scene one is continually reminded of Part II of *Saint Ludmila*. After indulging in a gloriously lyrical outburst on catching sight of Rusalka, 'Vidino divná' ('Vision entrancing'), the prince carries her off to be his bride.

At the start of Act II, set in the grounds of the prince's palace, an elderly gamekeeper (tenor) and a young kitchen-lad (soprano) are gossiping together about their master's odd choice of a mistress for them: they have also already noticed him in amorous dalliance with the foreign princess. This human scene is one of the most attractive in the whole opera, providing as it does a welcome measure of light relief, not untouched by earthy humour. Thereafter, however, this act is dramatically inconsequent and musically unsatisfying: the main point at issue—the transference of the prince's affections from Rusalka to the princess (another soprano)—is almost lost sight of in a dignified procession of wedding-guests followed by a formal operatic ballet on Parisian lines (a totally superfluous interpolation) and an equally unexpected and unexplained reappearance, from the prince's private swimming-pool, of the ineffable water-goblin. Dvořák does his best to bring some musical sense into this particular scene by allowing the goblin to continue his grumblings throughout a wedding guests' chorus, but a contrapuntal device of this nature, effective though it might have been in a work like *The Jacobin*, seems out of place and somewhat pointless against a more sombre background. Rusalka's subsequent attempted intervention 'Ó marnó' ('How futile') restores reality for a moment or two, but the finale, a duet for the prince and princess, although passionately tuneful, is uncharacteristic and perhaps hardly worthy of its composer.

For Act III we go back to the setting of Act I and are glad to do so: Dvořák was more at home in a forest clearing than at a royal court, and was once again able to give of his best. The opening scenes, in which Rusalka laments her cruel fate, first in soliloquy and then in conversation with the witch, are romantic and poignant. There is a change of atmosphere when the gamekeeper and the kitchen-boy, a curious pair of ambassadors, come to plead their employer's cause. They plead in vain: the goblin receives them with curses and the witch with mockery. Another entry of the golden-haired and daintily-tripping water-nymphs, enlivened this time by exceptionally charming solos for two 'small-part singers', fails to beguile the goblin's distress of mind: in a brief but moving passage he chides their light-heartedness and tells them the sad news about Rusalka, whereupon they vanish disconsolately into their lake. Next, the prince himself appears on the scene, crying out urgently for his lost bride; by now both realize that there can be no happy ending to their short romance, but at least they enjoy a few moments of ecstasy in an exquisite duet, 'Proč volal jsi mne v nařuc svou' ('When holding me in a close embrace'), before they have to yield up their lives. The goblin characteristically pops up again to point a moral, but Dvořák (always the perfect gentleman) allows Rusalka the last word: 'Bůh tě pomiluj!' ('God, be merciful!').

Ever since its première on 31 March 1901, conducted by Kovarovic, *Rusalka* has been Dvořák's most popular opera; it is still frequently given in Prague and has also been played in cities as far apart as Madrid and Kaunas (which at the time was the capital of the short-lived independent Slav republic of Lithuania). The outbreak of the Second World War put paid to a projected production at Covent Garden in 1939; there were a few performances at Sadler's Wells in 1959, but for some reason or other these failed to attract much attention. Meanwhile one can only go on hoping that the authorities who have had the enterprise to stage Janáček's *Kát'a Kobonová*, *Příhody lišky bystroušky* (*The cunning little vixen*), *Věc Makropulos* (*The Makropoulos Case*) and *Z mrthého domu* (*From the House of the Dead*) will not wait too long before again reviving the fine opera composed in 1900 by his illustrious compatriot. Janáček himself would have been the first to lend them support. He was a frequent and welcome guest in the Dvořák household, and Dvořák, on his visits to Brno, always stayed with Janáček, whose admiration for him was unbounded. It was at Dvořák's suggestion that Janáček made a comprehensive revision of his first opera, *Šárka* (1888), before allowing it to be performed; this was only one of several large-scale compositions which he dedicated to his predecessor in gratitude for help and encouragement.

CHAPTER FIFTEEN

The Closing Years

While *Rusalka* was in rehearsal Dvořák paid another
officially-sponsored visit to Vienna: he left home as a
commoner and returned as a Life Peer—for on 3 March
1901 he was elected a member of the Austrian Upper House
(the equivalent of the British House of Lords). Travelling
with him, and similarly honoured, was Emil Frída, the
Czech poet better known under his *nom-de-plume* of Jaromír
Vrchlický, who fifteen years previously had provided the text
of *Saint Ludmila* and more recently that of Janáček's
oratorio *Amarus*. Although each managed to preserve a
straight face during the solemn swearing-in ceremony, it
seems that the new Lord Dvořák and the new Lord Frída did
not treat the proceedings altogether as seriously as the
authorities might have hoped. It was not to be expected that
after taking the formal oath of allegiance they would open
their mouths again during the subsequent dull debate—nor
did they—but Dvořák, whose taciturnity was a byword,
afterwards made a big joke when he boasted to Anna, who
had been waiting downstairs, about the eloquence of his
'maiden speech'. This one and only attendance at the Upper
House was not wholly unrewarding however: Dvořák found
a large bundle of his favourite pencils (Hardmuth no. 2)
lying on the desk to which he had been allocated—and
promptly stuffed them into his pocket.

Four weeks later, on the morning after *Rusalka*'s successful première (was it by chance or by fate that this was the
morning of April-fool Day?), its composer had a meeting
with its librettist, Jaroslav Kvapil, who by now had secured
a permanent job as stage manager at the National Theatre.
Dvořák, not surprisingly, was in enthusiastic mood, and
demanded forthwith another libretto as good as that of

Rusalka—which would once again, of course, have to include a leading part for the fine soprano singer Růžena Maturová (1869–1938) who on the previous evening had greatly distinguished herself in the title rôle. Kvapil, still a comparative youngster, was baffled; he told Dvořák that he could not produce opera-texts out of his head at a moment's notice in the same way that a conjurer produced rabbits out of his hat. But Dvořák was not content to wait: realizing subconsciously, perhaps, that only a few years were left to him, he parted company with Kvapil and sought a libretto elsewhere. After their recent journey together it was only natural that his thoughts should turn to Vrchlický; at first his fellow-Peer was not too keen on the project, but eventually he agreed to do his best provided that a suitable and mutually agreeable subject could be decided upon in the meantime. Dvořák would probably have done better to stick to Kvapil, because 'preliminary' discussions with Vrchlický were almost endless, and it was not until the following spring (1902) that he was able to start work on his new opera. His only composition of 1901 was a single and final song in the true Bohemian tradition, *Zpev z Lešetínského kováře* (*The song of the blacksmith of Lešetín*).

While he was waiting impatiently for a libretto, Dvořák's life went on much as before.

On 15 April 1901 he renewed acquaintance with Artur Nikisch, who by now had returned from America (Boston) to Europe (Berlin) and visited Prague during the course of a concert tour with the Berlin Philharmonic Orchestra. (*The Wood-Dove* was included in the programme.)

On 6 July, having given up his post as professor, Dvořák was appointed *director* of the Prague Conservatoire. This was perhaps only a nominal directorship: at any rate he thereafter spent more time than ever at Vysoká with his wife, his family, his pigeons and his friends from the Břesové hory silver mines; he rarely went to Prague unless it was to interview an engine-driver and discuss important

railway matters with him, although on such jaunts he doubt-
less also called in at the Conservatoire to see how his colleagues were getting on without him.

On 20 August Fritz Simrock died. As we know, Dvořák's
professional association with him had not always been
smooth, yet the two men had all along regarded one another
with a certain amount of respect and perhaps with grudging
affection: even the most demanding letters from composer
to publisher had customarily begun with the words 'Mein
lieber Freund'. And whether he was regarded as friend or
foe, Simrock's death snapped another link with the past.

The main excitement of the year 1901, however, was the
round of celebrations in connection with Dvořák's sixtieth
birthday, which fell on 8 September. To mark this anniversary, the National Theatre that month staged successive
productions of *The Pigheaded Peasants*, *The Peasant a
Rogue*, *Dimitrij*, *The Jacobin*, *The Devil and Kate* and *Rusalka*,
with a dramatized version of *Saint Ludmila* thrown in for
good measure. Dvořák was delighted to think that he had at
last realized a life-long ambition to be acclaimed as a
successful operatic composer; for once he tore himself
away from Vysoká to partake in various public ceremonies
and even to make a short speech or two—including one at
Nehalozeves, his birthplace, where the rejoicings were as
loud as anywhere else.

By the time October came round it was back to normal—
and to continual prodding of Vrchlický to get a move on
with the new opera.

'ARMIDA'

It has never been convincingly explained why Dvořák,
who from 1896 until 1901 wrote hardly a bar of music that
did not owe its inception to Bohemian life or legend, should
in collaboration with Vrchlický in 1902 have decided to

venture by complete contrast on territory which although well-trodden in former days was full of snares and pitfalls for unwary strangers belonging to the late nineteenth century. Perhaps the triumph of *Rusalka* and the enthusiastic flurry of operatic revivals at the time of his sixtieth birthday had induced a temporary surfeit of self-confidence (although no composer was less addicted to swollen-headedness) and had encouraged Dvořák to believe that he would be equally successful in a non-Slav opera, which might stand a better chance of making an impact abroad than had *Dimitrij* or *The Jacobin* or *Rusalka*. Or perhaps he was over-influenced in his choice of subject by Vrchlický, but there is no evidence to suggest this and on the whole it seems an unlikely hypothesis. The fact remains that the *mise-en-scène* of Dvořák's last opera was Syria during the 'crusade' period of the twelfth century—a milieu as foreign to him as was that of his *first* opera, which it will be remembered was concerned with England's King Alfred of the ninth century.

Alfred Löwenberg's standard *Annals of Opera* lists no fewer than fourteen works based on the Italian poem *La Gerusalemma liberata* (*The liberation of Jerusalem*) by Torquato Tasso (1544–1595)—or on some portion of it. Eleven out of the fourteen, including those by Lully, Gluck, Haydn, Rossini and Dvořák, are entitled *Armida* (or *Armide*); Handel alone, among great composers, named his opera after the nominal hero, Rinaldo.

In the Vrchlický/Dvořák version of an episode in the poem, the crusaders come up against necromancy as well as force of arms: the Saracens are aided and abetted by a magician, who encourages them to use the lovely Armida as a decoy; she soon captivates Rinald (Rinaldo), who is perhaps a shade less fervent a Christian than most of his companions and certainly more susceptible to sex-appeal. But presently he is torn from Armida's embraces and has to rejoin his comrades; when Armida later appears on the opposite side of the battlefield in male armour it is Rinald who, not having recognized her, stabs her nearly to death. ('Nearly' because there must be a concluding love duet with Armida expiring on the last note.) The involved farrago cooked up by Vrchlický was quite unworthy of the reasonably efficient librettist of Dvořák's *Saint Ludmila* and Janáček's *Amarus*, and it must regretfully be recorded that only here and there did the music do much to enliven the dramatic shoddiness.

What the composer here seems to have had primarily in mind was a 'singers' opera': in *Armida* there are more detachable items even than in *Dimitrij*—let alone than in *The Jacobin* and *Rusalka*—and in the arias and ensembles alike one notices a tendency to exploit *bel canto*, often with considerable success. The extraordinary thing is that there are at the most no more than two or three passages of any length in the whole work which are unmistakably recognizable as being characteristic of Dvořák. There is plenty of second-hand Wagner, the early four-square Wagner of *The Flying Dutchman* and *Tannhäuser* and *Lohengrin*; there is a fair share of second-hand Verdi, the Verdi of the *Don Carlos/Aida* period rather than either the early Verdi of *Nabucco* or the late Verdi of *Falstaff*; Dvořák even has recourse to pseudo-orientalism, in the form of 'tonic pedals' on drone-basses, and to short stretches of *recitativo secco* which might have been contrived by any competent imitator of that routine Italian practice of the eighteenth century. There is hardly a trace of the 'through-composing' that was such a pleasing feature of *The Jacobin* and *Rusalka*, but in some of the more attractive lyrical passages one catches a surprising echo or two of Hugo Wolf. Surprising, and perhaps ironical, because of all the distinguished music-maker's in Dvořák's circle Wolf was the only one who appeared to cherish a personal grudge against him and belittled his achievements continually and venomously. (It must be remembered, however, that Wolf, a fine composer in his own small field, was the angriest and most unstable of angry and unstable young men and never attempted to maintain a cordial personal relationship with *any* musician: he made it clear that he was at daggers drawn not only with Dvořák and Brahms but also with younger contemporaries.)

Dvořák's *Armida*, then, remains a hotchpotch, but since it was his final fling and was based on a text provided by a reputable Czech poet I shall attempt an act-by-act summary which I hope will be found intelligible and in which I shall in any case do my best to minimize the absurdities of the plot. (Absurdities which if truth be told were no more chaotic than those in Schikaneder's libretto for *The Magic Flute*, but Dvořák, great composer though he was, was no Mozart.)

The overture is based partly on the tune of Armida's 'gazelle' aria (see below) and partly on two rhythmically well-contrasted but unremarkable themes subsequently associated with the crusaders.

Act I, set in the royal gardens at Damascus, opens with the Saracen king, Hydraot (bass), being entertained by the choral singing of his euphemistically-termed 'ladies-in-waiting' and attendant courtiers. After a call to prayer by the *muezzin* (baritone), he is reminded of more serious matters by the magician Ismen (another baritone), who brings news that there are crusaders in the vicinity. The impetuous Hydraot wants to engage them in battle right away, but the shrewd Ismen suggests that he should stay his hand. 'Lstí zvítězíš' ('Guile for victory') is the advice he gives in forthright strains that might almost have been lifted from *Lohengrin*. There should be no need for Hydraot to risk bloodshed, he maintains, so long as he can exploit his beautiful daughter Armida (upon whom Ismen himself is already casting a roving eye); let *her* be sent to the Christian camp, where none will be able to resist her charms and there will consequently be a sapping of morale. Hydraot agrees to his proposition, and off they go to leave the stage clear for the entrance of Armida herself (soprano). To an ingratiating melody in slow 3/8 time which one afterwards comes to realize should be regarded as her *Leitmotiv*, 'Za štíhlou gazelou' ('With a slender gazelle'), she relates how in her dreams she has seen a handsome young knight with whom she has fallen in love. Hydraot and Ismen return, but when Armida is told to run along and do her stuff with the Christians she refuses indignantly and thereby earns a father's curse; she changes her mind, however, when Ismen conjures up for her a magic vision of the Christian camp, in which she recognizes the knight of her dreams in the midst of a group of crusaders.

At the start of Act II the encamped Christian warriors sing a tub-thumping chorus interspersed with conventional fanfares for horns and trumpets, but it soon becomes clear that one of them, Rinald (tenor), is less enthusiastic about the Cause than are most of his colleagues. Presently a herald (bass) summons everyone to a council of war with the leaders, Bohumír (baritone) and Petr (bass). Meanwhile Armida has made her way to the camp, and her next aria, 'Ó srdce, ztiš svůj tlukot smělý' ('Be still, my wildly beating heart'), brings one closer to genuine Dvořák, in romantic mood, than anything else in the opera. When she is found by Petr and Rinald, the former, who holds strong views on the subject of women, is profoundly shocked to encounter a female intruder and wants to have her turned off the premises, but Rinald, having caught Armida's eye, intercedes on her behalf with Bohumír, who consents to hear what she has to say. Thereupon Armida spins a cock-and-bull yarn: 'Slyš, hlutim bídy svoji' ('Listen to my doleful story') she sings, and goes on to explain that she is relying upon the crusaders to rescue her from the clutches of a wicked uncle. Bohumír (a more trusting fellow than Petr) is taken in by her apparent sincerity and agrees to help, but insists that lots must be drawn to decide who is to lead the expedition. Rinald, who has already fallen heavily for

Armida, becomes impatient, and after an impassioned but musically uninspired duet, 'Mně nelze čekat dél' ('We cannot longer wait'), the pair try to escape together, only to find the way blocked by the firm-minded Petr. In the nick of time, however, Ismen the magician appears from nowhere (in a chariot of fire drawn by a dragon, according to the stage directions) and himself carries them both away.

The setting of Act III is reminiscent of Klingsor's magic garden in *Parsifal*. Backed by a chorus not of flower-maidens but of nymphs and sirens Armida and Rinald sing a lyrical duet, 'Jen níž' ('Speak low'), which is very beautiful but by no means everywhere characteristic of Dvořák; some of the soaring vocal phrases remind one, rather, of Wolf at his best. In a laudable attempt to restore the balance of style, the nymphs and sirens then make their exit to the strains of a graceful waltz that would not have been out of place in *The Peasant a Rogue*. Meanwhile Ismen, who himself has designs on Armida's person, has been considerably perturbed to observe her obvious infatuation with Rinald, and he now tries to stake his own claim in an effective Verdian monologue, 'Na práhu děsných pouští' ('On thresholds of the desert'), but Armida will have none of him. And apparently her love for Rinald is even strong enough to overcome Ismen's magical powers: at any rate he cannot prevent her from leading her lover into an 'enchanted palace' that stands conveniently close at hand. Almost immediately, however, two of Rinald's bosom-companions, Sven (tenor) and Ubald (bass), arrive on the scene, their mission being to try and rescue Rinald from the seductive Armida and return with him to the Christian fold. Ismen, by now only too ready to help them, provides a 'magic shield of Michael the Archangel' which he assures them will do the trick. And so it does: Sven and Ubald, magic shield in hand, surprise the guilty couple *in flagranti delicto* and convey Rinald away; Armida is left in tears, Ismen in triumph, the enchanted palace in ruins.

At the beginning of Act IV, set in an oasis near the crusaders' camp, the remorseful Rinald is tossing to and fro in fitful slumber. In a monologue, 'Sám, v poušto, sám' ('Alone in distant lands'), where the music is as restless as the singer and which occupies sixteen pages of vocal score, he goes over in his mind his recent experiences. Petr, who although stern-minded where women are concerned is essentially good at heart, comforts him in his distress with the solace of the Christian faith. Rinald thereupon repents of his sin and recovers sufficient vigour to rejoin his comrades, who are about to prove their mettle in a foray against the Saracens. In the battle which ensues Rinald engages Ismen in single-handed combat and kills him. In his moment of triumph he lets out a curse on the name of Armida, but his next challenger is a black-visored knight who (believe it or not) is Armida herself in disguise; when she hears the curse from Rinald's lips she drops her own weapon and allows him to stab her. In their final love-and-death duet, 'Ó vládce nebes' ('Oh, bluest heaven'), Dvořák seems to have been trying to recapture (in the same key, G flat major) the atmosphere of the closing scene of *Aida*. It was the last piece of music he ever wrote, but it must be admitted that it was hardly a worthy swan-song.

Many admirers of Dvořák would understandably prefer to disregard *Armida* altogether, but as an honest chronicler I am bound to take note of the fact that his last opera represented the culmination of a life-long weakness—a weakness which I shall do my best to explain and partially condone in my next (and final) chapter. Meanwhile let me round off the biographical details.

ILLNESS AND DEATH

It took Dvořák the best part of a year and a half, from April 1902 until August 1903, to complete *Armida*, and the opera did not go into rehearsal at the National Theatre until February 1904. During the latter part of this period he often complained of feeling unwell (which may possibly help to excuse the perfunctoriness of much of the music.) Nevertheless there were plenty of happenings in which he was able to take pleasure. For instance, in March 1903 Edvard Grieg (1843–1907) paid a visit to Prague to conduct a concert of his own works; at the time he too was somewhat under the weather, but Dvořák, who had long been an admirer of his Norwegian contemporary, did everything he could to ensure that his stay in the Bohemian capital was a happy one. In the domestic field Dvořák was delighted when Otilie presented him with a grandson, and he thoroughly enjoyed the wedding celebrations of his second daughter, Anna, who on 20 October 1903 married a respectable lawyer named Josef Sobotka. And all along he took great interest in the progress of his third daughter, Magda, who at twenty-two was already beginning to make a name for herself as a professional soprano and indeed had taken part in Grieg's concert in March.

During his youth Dvořák had suprisingly been excused military service on medical grounds, but only twice in his whole career had he experienced prolonged periods of even slight ill-health, neither of which had been sufficiently serious to incapacitate him in any way; one had occurred during the Prague winter of 1888/9 and the other during the New York winter of 1892/3. But although he himself did not realize it (his doctors never told him) he was by now suffering from premature arterio-sclerosis, hardening of the arteries, which in this instance impaired the proper functioning of the kidneys. No wonder that he sometimes felt below par.

There was an unfortunate incident in January 1904. At the time Dvořák was staying in the Prague flat of which he had taken occupation twenty-seven years ago. (Plans were afoot, of which he did not approve, for a family transference to a larger one.) On entering a café one morning he came face to face with a group of old friends, and when the customary greetings were exchanged he complained of a pain in his back: 'lumbago, the doctors tell me'. Whereupon one of the circle, the composer Jan Malát (1843–1915), recalled, innocently enough but rather tactlessly under the circumstances, how his brother-in-law had been *told* just that, whereas in truth he had a virulent kidney disease—and was dead within a month. This story did not go down at all well with Dvořák, who was in one of his gruffer moods: he may not have suspected that the tale would prove to be only too prophetic of his own case, but disliked having the possibility brought so crudely to his attention.

He still retained great faith in his operas—and above all a pathetic faith in *Armida*; indeed, on 1 March 1904, just before its production, he granted a rare interview to the press.

'As long as God gives me health', he was reported as saying, 'I want to devote all my powers to the creation of opera. I do not write opera from a desire for glory but because I consider it the most beneficial for the people. This music is listened to by the broad masses, whereas when I compose a symphony I might have to wait years to get it performed. I get frequent requests from my publishers for chamber works, which I always refuse; by now they should know that I shall no longer write anything just for *them*. Yet they bombard me with questions: why do I not write this or that? They still look upon me as a symphonic composer, and do not seem to realize that symphonies and string quartets no longer hold any attraction for me; I have proved time and again that my main bias is towards *opera*.' He went on to add that he already had two or three more in mind.

Alas for his 'main bias'! *Armida* was at that very moment running into rehearsal-trouble. Vrchlický was dissatisfied with the scenery; Dvořák with the conductor (Kovařovic's deputy); both of them with the stage director. Everything kept going wrong, tempers were frayed—and eventually the première had to be postponed from 11 to 25 March. When it did take place, Dvořák had an attack of giddiness after the first act and had to be taken home (so that he never heard his last opera complete); it was perhaps fortunate that he escaped the embarrassment of a reception from the audience which at best could be regarded as respectful and was certainly far from enthusiastic.

Although Dvořák was soon up and about again, he caught a chill while paying his customary visit to the main-line engine-sheds in some unseasonably wintry weather, and when he got home that evening Anna had to put him straight to bed. Thereafter his illness took a turn for the worse, and to his great disappointment he was unable to attend a big Czech Music Festival that was being held in Prague at the time. Nevertheless his doctors expressed the hope that he would be well enough to conduct a performance of *The Spectre's Bride* at Kroměříž in May, when Magda was to sing the leading rôle for the first time. And indeed by 1 May he was sufficiently recovered from the set-back to take his place at lunch-time at the head of the family dining-table. Half-way through the meal, however, he suddenly collapsed. A doctor who lived just across the street was hurriedly summoned, but it was too late; by the time he arrived Dvořák was dead.

That May Day, as it happened, was one of brilliant sunshine, sunshine which many worthy burghers of Prague were enjoying in the countryside; consequently the sad news did not immediately get around. But although a scheduled performance of Smetana's *Brandenburgers in Bohemia* took place that night at the National Theatre as planned, playgoers found the auditorium draped in black, and were soon made aware that this signified a mark of respectful mourning on the death of a national hero—an even more illustrious national hero than his friend and predecessor, the composer of the evening.

Four days later Dvořák's mortal remains were laid to rest in the citadel of Vyšehrad, the Prague equivalent of London's Westminster Abbey; a great crowd followed the funeral procession, and expressions of deep sympathy for Anna and the family—and indeed for the whole Czech nation—came from all parts of Europe and North America.

Dying when he did, Antonín Dvořák was spared one great sorrow: little more than a year after his own death, came the death of his beloved daughter Otilie at the age of twenty-seven. Her husband Josef Suk went nearly distraught on this tragedy—and his distress was mirrored in much of the music that he wrote during the thirty years that remained to him. Their grandson, another Josef Suk (born in 1929), is an accomplished professional violinist who maintains the family traditions.

Dvořák's widow, like her son-in-law, lived to see Bohemia freed from Habsburg domination—and to welcome a great-grandson into the world; she died on 14 July 1931, at the age of seventy-seven. What a wonderful woman she must have been! To be married to any artist, let alone to one who is a genius, is no easy lot for a wife: she must be ready, when required, to take a back seat on public occasions, and on many private occasions to keep herself to herself without interfering with her husband's activities while at the same time continuing to minister to his material welfare. Anna Dvořáková, with her own experience as a professional singer behind her, had a full understanding of what was required, and she could never have had any cause to reproach herself with the manner in which, over a period of more than thirty years, she had fulfilled the rôle of helpmeet to a great composer.

CHAPTER SIXTEEN

In Conclusion

We have now come to the end of the eventful but for the most part unsensational story of how a humble innkeeper's son from Nelahozeves rose through industry and merit to become not only the greatest composer ever to emerge from Bohemia but also one of the most highly-honoured musicians of his generation in the whole of Europe. It remains only to gather up a few loose threads and try to bind them together.

THE WEAKNESS

It has been said with some truth of Robert Schumann that he was the most unreliable of men and the most reliable of composers: wayward in character to the point of ultimate mental instability, during the course of his life he wrote hardly a bar of music that was not worthy of a sincere and highly-talented artist. Antonín Dvořák was almost his exact opposite: as a man he was utterly reliable, being sufficiently well-disciplined to keep his few capricious human tendencies under control; as a composer, although more highly endowed than was Schumann with the attributes of genius, he failed to keep as tight a rein on the ideas that came into his head and therefore cannot be acquitted of the charge of unreliability.

If this were to imply no more than that he sometimes wrote music that was great and sometimes wrote music that was not so great, it would be of little consequence: the same could be said of Bach, Mozart, Beethoven, Schubert and a host of other illustrious composers. But where Dvořák is concerned the accusation *does* imply something more.

Paradoxically, in view of the certainty and consistency of his attitude towards human relationships, his main weakness as an artist was an uncertainty and inconsistency in his application to the problems facing him at any particular time. It could be plausibly argued that uncertainty as to what the future might hold in store would inevitably affect the outlook (artistic as well as social) of *any* comparatively underprivileged Slav citizen of the contemporary Habsburg Empire. But even if one were to accept this hypothesis, in Dvořák's case something more is needed by way of explanation—and possibly by way of excuse.

That he did not show individuality in youth need not be unduly stressed: very few budding composers do so—and the wiser ones among them don't attempt to. But let us compare Dvořák with Beethoven and Verdi, both of whose creative careers have often been divided by historians into three or more distinct periods, thereby perhaps conveying the notion that (like Dvořák) they shifted their ground from time to time. Nothing could be further from the truth.

The music of early Beethoven is frequently almost indistinguishable from that of late Haydn, and although he began to outgrow Haydn's manner about the time of the piano sonata in C minor op. 13 (composed at the age of twenty-four) yet even in the great works of his full maturity his style remained, to a considerable degree, a logical derivative or development of his predecessor's. Furthermore, one is all along aware, with Beethoven, of a subconscious striving after a definite ideal; although each successive 'period' may contain some poor music as well as much marvellous music, it is all part and parcel of a steady and it would seem inevitable progress towards the ultimate goal. So with Verdi. His early indebtedness to Rossini is writ large on the pages of his first few operas, and however much the character of his music may have changed over the fifty years and more that lay between *Oberto* and *Falstaff* his style remained basically a logical derivative or development of Rossini's, and one feels that his sights, like Beethoven's, were unalterably fixed on a single target. It was this constancy of aim that Dvořák was never able to emulate: from his first few pieces of chamber music, composed when he was nineteen or twenty, until *Armida*, which belonged to the last two years of his life, he was continually roaming down byways—and indeed could never really make up his mind as to what main road he ought to be following.

The root-cause of this life-long indecision was that during his prolonged formative period he was unfavourably placed, as a Czech, to draw nourishment from a single predominating source, as had Beethoven from the Viennese classics and Verdi from a long tradition of Italian opera. In youth Dvořák was not sufficiently self-confident to adopt, other than occasionally, the Slav idiom that came naturally to him, and it is not to be wondered at that for many years he also experimented, sometimes turn by turn and sometimes simultaneously, with pseudo-Beethoven, pseudo-Schumann, pseudo-Wagner and several other pseudos. The varied influences to which he was subject were incapable of acceptable fusion, so that unlike young Beethoven and young Verdi he was unable to establish a basis of style that could be logically developed along individual lines. Although the *Hymnus* of 1872 held out momentary hopes that he might be on the point of achieving a satisfactory measure of integration, they were almost lost to sight in the E flat major symphony of 1873 and reappeared only fitfully in the D minor symphony of 1874.

Therefore every lover of Dvořák's music should be grateful that in his very next important composition, the second setting of the operetta *King and Collier*, he turned over as clean and auspicious a new leaf as had Smetana in *The Bartered Bride* eight years previously. *King and Collier*, like *The Bartered Bride*, may have been a mere *jeu d'esprit*, thrown off in a fit of petulance at the comparatively poor reception given to more serious efforts, but once the work was completed, and indeed while it was still under way, Dvořák began to realize that he had made a big mistake in hitherto neglecting to so great an extent the heritage of traditional Czech folk-music. A year later he composed the admirable symphony in F major which, although perhaps not to be reckoned as a masterpiece, was for the most part genuinely Bohemian in character. But Dvořák was not yet immune from distracting and perhaps subversive alien influences, and his subsequent preoccupation with the ill-starred opera *Vanda* marked a downward rather than up-ward turning-point in the history of his continual fluctuations of approach. And so it went on to the end: even after the 'concentration on Bohemia' of 1896–1901, there came that final and distressing relapse into indecision with *Armida*.

A contributory cause of Dvořák's failure to achieve Beethoven's or Verdi's consistent intensity of artistic purpose lay in his extreme sensitivity: like Bruckner, he was inclined in his uncertainty to pay more regard than he need have done to private and public comment and above all to press comment. When a new work, on its first performance, did not attain the success he had hoped for, instead of taking the disappointment in his stride and trying to do better next time, he was apt to set off in a different direction altogether. For instance, when his predominantly Slav opera *Dimitrij* was received by the critics with something less than rapture, he followed up with a piano trio (op. 65) three out of whose four movements belonged to a different and more muddled world. On the other hand it may have been his admiration for Brahms that caused him to turn aside now and again both from his native Bohemia and from Wagner's idealized Germany and deliberately adopt a *Viennese* style. The most obvious examples of such a divergence were the first two movements of the violin sonata of 1880 and all four of the string quartet op. 61 of the following year, but there were other isolated instances here and there. His flirtation with

Negro and even red-Indian music while in America comes into rather a different category: this was in essence not much more than an attempt to provide local colour, and in any case can be seen in retrospect to have held less significance than was thought at the time.

Despite a lack of self-confidence and a consequent sense of personal mistrust, Dvořák (this time by contrast with Bruckner) had little inclination to submit himself to the rigours of active self-criticism. It is true that in middle-age he revised some of his early manuscript scores before allowing them to be published. It is true, too, that at one time or another he rewrote several scenes of *King and Collier* and *Dimitrij* and *The Jacobin* with new productions in mind, and that by pre-arrangement the violin concerto was touched up by Joachim. But generally speaking, although while actually at work on a score he went to no end of trouble to ensure that everything was 'just right', once it was completed he left it at that; more often than not his attitude was 'what I have written I have written', and rarely did it occur to him that many of his symphonic and chamber-music movements might have benefited from judicious pruning on afterthought. Like Schubert, but perhaps with less excuse, he seems to have acted on the assumption that he could not afford to spend valuable time on the blue-pencilling of repetitive redundancies; in consequence his longwindedness sometimes strains the patience of the most indulgent listener.

I think I have now said nearly all that needs to be said in serious denigration of Dvořák's music taken *en bloc*. I may perhaps have said too much, but it is essential to recognize that his inconsistency of approach and his lack of appreciation of the virtues of self-criticism are weaknesses that must be taken into consideration in any unbiased assessment.

For instance, one comes across curious fluctuations in his normally skilful instrumentation. In most of his important orchestral works, including the 'big five' symphonies and the five later symphonic poems, there is certainly little to complain about: here the scoring is splendid, and according to circumstances either brilliant or tender or descriptive. Yet in the noisier parts of the *Hussite* and *Carnival* overtures, to name only two examples, it is apt to sound perfunctorily crude. And there are a few corresponding lapses, *mutatis mutandis*, in the chamber music. Although as early as the 'double-bass' quintet of 1875 and the E major string quartet of the following year he displayed an admirable understanding of the medium which on the whole served him well right up to the two culminating string quartets of 1895, critical attention has had to be drawn to a huddle of indiscretions in the piano quartet in E flat major of 1889—and this was by no means the only instance of a fall from grace.

THE STRENGTH

And now, for lovers of Dvořák who may be beginning to wonder whether after all their idol had feet of clay, here are four words of consolation: *from weakness sprang strength*. For surely it was to a large extent due to his frequent changes of course that he spread his net as wide as he did and was thereby eventually enabled to establish himself as an *all-round* composer. Certainly, had it not been for his versatility, it is difficult to believe that he could have contrived, in succession, over a quarter of a century, works of such *contrasted* excellence as (say) the *String Serenade*, *The Peasant a Rogue*, the *Symphonic Variations*, the first set of *Slavonic Dances*, the piano waltzes of op. 54, the *Gipsy Songs*, the *Scherzo capriccioso*, the seventh symphony, the piano quintet op. 81, the Requiem, the cello concerto, the string quartet op. 106, and *Rusalka*.

To be an all-rounder is not in itself, of course, a criterion of true greatness: if it were, one would have to put Camille Saint-Saëns and heaven knows who else on the same pedestal as Antonín Dvořák. But if one were to agree that Slavonic dances might be reckoned as ballet music (and why shouldn't they be?) it would be fair to say that Dvořák not merely made his mark but *produced really fine work* in every field of composition. The only other in his own generation of whom the same could be said was his friend and fellow-Slav, Peter Tchaikovsky, and a few comparisons between the two composers may not be out of place.

Tchaikovsky, like Dvořák, was a cosmopolitan artist who wandered all over the place (I am speaking figuratively rather than literally), but he had a clearer sense of direction. Although he never lost sight of his national heritage, he was by no means so pronounced a nationalist as were several of his compatriot contemporaries: generally speaking his symphonies and chamber works were those of a Russian in Vienna, his operas those of a Russian in Milan, his ballets those of a Russian in Paris. As regards quality, there would appear on the face of it to have been a certain amount of level-pegging between Dvořák and himself.

In piano and vocal music, for instance, there was certainly not much, in the long run, to choose between them; perhaps Tchaikovsky had a slight edge with some of his more charming piano pieces and Dvořák with some of his more expressive songs.

Operas? Well, two out of Tchaikovsky's ten, *Eugen Onegin* and *The Queen of Spades*, have achieved considerable success outside Russia, but without further visual evidence I cannot honestly adjudge the former, much though I always enjoy it, to be a better opera than *The Jacobin*, which I have never had the opportunity of seeing; the music of *Rusalka* holds more appeal than that of *The Queen of Spades*, and Tchaikovsky, unlike Dvořák, never ventured into the joyous realm of operetta.

With the symphonies and other large-scale orchestral works it is surely a case of 'everyone to his taste'. Readers will make their guess as to where mine lies; nevertheless, I fully appreciate the great merits of such pieces as Tchaikovsky's *Romeo and Juliet* and all six of his symphonies, not just the last three.

Tchaikovsky's output of chamber music was not large, but what there was of it remains as satisfying as all but the very best of Dvořák's—and furthermore he displayed an equal and perhaps more consistent technical mastery of the medium.

In conventional ballet, Tchaikovsky's frenchified music was *hors concours*, but on the other hand his choral works (there were very few of them) could not stand up in rivalry against Dvořák's *Stabat Mater*, Requiem Mass and *Te Deum*.

If that were all, these two eminent composers might be looked upon as much of a muchness. But to a certain extent the comparisons are superficial, since they fail to take into account one of Dvořák's cardinal characteristics—a sincerity of utterance derived from human experience: whatever his faults as man or musician, he never became an introvert. Tchaikovsky's symphonies no. 4 in F minor and no. 6 in B minor (the 'Pathetic') were genuine works of art—perhaps works of genius—but when set alongside Dvořák's no. 6 in D major and no. 7 in D minor they appear unhealthily morbid. Dvořák rarely exhibited such a tendency and when he did so the phase was a short one.

At this stage one feels inclined to join issue once again with the assertion of Otakar Šourek—and the assumption of other commentators who have followed his trail—that the character of Dvořák's music was often affected by temporary personal or subjective considerations. I disagree, but my own view, conflicting with that of the majority, has already been expounded in preceding chapters and I will not weary my readers by reviving it. In any case, whether Šourek and the others were right or wrong in this particular, the fact remains that while Dvořák's strength as a composer derived partly from his versatility it derived to an even greater extent from his love of humanity (miners and engine-drivers as well as Brahms and Janáček) and of nature (as represented by pigeons and thrushes and the 'beautyful forsts' that surrounded Vysoká).

THE TRUE WORTH

The significance of *King and Collier*, the first composition of importance in which Dvořák adopted throughout an emphatically Bohemian idiom, has already been stressed; those who have come along with me thus far will already be well aware to what a great degree his music was thereafter influenced by the heritage of Czech folk-songs and folk-dances. Although it was only very rarely that he reproduced any actual folk-tune, handed down from generation to generation, he soon became extremely adept at devising tunes of his own that accorded admirably with the tradition.

It is desirable, however, that one should distinguish the works in which the Slav trend was paramount from those in which it was successfully integrated with more cosmopolitan tendencies. To the former category there belong (for example) the four operettas and the opera *The Jacobin* (all set in his native countryside), the *Moravian Duets*, both sets of *Slavonic Dances* (although the second set continually ranged farther afield than Bohemia itself), the *Gipsy Songs*, and perhaps the Mass in D major. To the second category there belong (for example) the operas *Dimitrij* and *Rusalka*, the Requiem, the *Te Deum*, the 'big five' symphonies, the five symphonic poems, the *Symphonic Variations*, the cello concerto, the *Scherzo capriccioso*, the piano quintet op. 81, the string quartets ops. 51 and 106 and 105, the string trio op. 74. It is such works as these, in which the 'national' element is to some degree or other in evidence, that hold Dvořák's quintessence. That is not to deny the excellence, in their own way, of some of his more 'wayward' and less characteristic works. Here, too, one is often conscious of the composer's enjoyment of life, an enjoyment which he strove to impart to his listeners.

So now we can return, with renewed assurance, to where we set out: to the proposition that Antonín Dvořák's true worth lay mainly in the success of his endeavours to write music which, while maintaining the highest artistic standards, would give pleasure to those whom he described as the 'broad masses' of the people. This music, like his outlook on life, was eminently sane and healthy: he was no great innovator, preferring, rather, to consolidate what he found best in the methods of his predecessors. Instead of seeking out a brave new world, he was content to encourage others to share his happiness in the world as he himself found it.

Some Significant Biographical Events

		page
1841	birth at Nelahozeves	21
1848	attends village school	25
1853	attends school at Zlonice	26
1854	sent to the Sudetenland to learn German	27
1857	enters Prague Organ School	29
1862	member of Czech National Theatre orchestra	33
1863	first meeting with Smetana	42
1865	falls in love with Josefa Čermáková but meets no response	35
1869	transfers affections to her sister Anna	39
1873	first performance of a Dvořák choral work (the *Hymnus*)	49
	marriage to Anna Čermáková	51
1874	organist at St. Adalbert's Church, Prague	52
	first performance of a Dvořák symphony (no. 3 in E flat major)	54
	first performance of a Dvořák stage-work (*King and Collier*)	56
1875–	receives State financial award	57
1877	death of all his three young children	63, 75
	first negotiations with publisher Simrock	69
1878	first visit to Vienna	75
	birth of his daughter Otilie	80
	first concert devoted solely to Dvořák's compositions	81
	first visit to Berlin	81
	first meeting with Brahms	82
	start of a long friendship with Janáček	82

1879	first meeting with Joachim	87
	first meeting with Richter	88
1880–1888	birth of five more children	111
1882	death of Dvořák's mother	103
1884	death of Smetana	104
	first visit to London	108
	buys a country property at Vysoká	111
	elected honorary member of Philharmonic Society, London	110
	visit to Worcester	112
1885	first visit to Birmingham	118
1886	visit to Leeds	122
1888	first meeting with Tchaikovsky	139
1889	awarded Austrian 'Iron Crown' by Emperor Franz Josef	138
1890	visit to Moscow and St. Petersburg	139
	elected member of Czech Academy of Sciences and Arts	139
1891	professor of composition, Prague Conservatoire	142
	installation as honorary Doctor of Philosophy, Czech University (Prague)	143
	invitation to New York	148
	installation as honorary Doctor of Music, Cambridge University	143
1892	director of National Conservatory, New York	154
1893	elected member of Berlin Academy of Fine Arts	159
	visit to the Mid-West	164
	death of Tchaikovsky	173
1894	death of Dvořák's father	173
	elected honorary member of New York Philharmonic Society	177
1895	bids farewell to America	179
1896	meeting with Bruckner, not long before his death	189

1897	elected honorary member of Vienna *Musik-freunde*	190
	death of Brahms	190
	appointed member of Austrian State Commission for Music	191
1898	marriage of Dvořák's daughter Otilie	193
	awarded Austrian Medal of Honour for Arts and Sciences	194
1899	visit to Budapest	198
1901	elected life member of Austrian Upper House	204
	director of Prague Conservatoire	205
	death of Simrock	206
1903	meeting with Grieg	213
	marriage of Dvořák's daughter Anna	213
1904	death in Prague	215

A Few Notes on the Bibliography

(with special reference to books published in English)

The first British musicologist to investigate Dvořák's background other than superficially was W. H. Hadow (1859–1937), who in his *Studies in Modern Music* granted three chapters each to Berlioz, Chopin, Schumann, Wagner, Brahms and Dvořák; when the book was first published (two volumes, 1892, 1895) Brahms and Dvořák were both still alive, but in subsequent editions their records were brought up to date. Hadow rather irritatingly referred to Dvořák's works by German titles (*Die Mittagshexe*, etc.), but since he was both a fine scholar and a gifted writer his résumé of the composer's life and music, though inevitably limited in scope, can still to this day be read with profit and pleasure. (Many years after he first became interested in Dvořák Hadow married Emily Troutbeck, whose father had provided the English versions of the *Hymnus*, *The Spectre's Bride* and *Saint Ludmila*.)

Following in Hadow's footsteps came Rosa Newmarch (1857–1940)—always a champion of Slav music—and the erudite and discriminating H. C. Colles (1879–1943). The relevant passages in Newmarch's *Music of Czechoslovakia*, published posthumously, are more illuminating than her earlier translation from the Czech of the somewhat unsubstantial *Antonín Dvořák* (1936) by Karel Hoffmeister (1868–1952), who for several years had been a junior colleague of Dvořák at the Prague Conservatoire. As for Colles, one regrets that he never found time to produce a book wholly devoted to a composer whom he regarded very highly, but he seized many opportunities to make clear his allegiance and a few months before his death wrote an enthusiastic review of Dvořák's operas for inclusion in *Antonín Dvořák: his Achievement* (1943), a symposium edited by Victor Fischl—who himself provided a valuable biographical chapter by way of introduction.

Meanwhile Otakar Šourek was doing some splendid work. Between 1916 and 1933, after dedicating many years to exhaustive study, he completed the first edition of his four-volume *Life and Works of Antonín Dvořák*. Unfortunately even this massive affair (some 300,000 words) tells us comparatively little about Dvořák's family life, and furthermore has never been translated anything like complete from the original Czech: a drastic condensation in German by Paul Stefan (1879–1943) is useful as a work of reference. Several of Šourek's later and less formidable books, however, were published in Prague during the nineteen-fifties *in English:* notably a very much briefer *Life and Works* (only 30,000 words, and again more concerned with the music than the man) and a comprehensive analytical study of Dvořák's orchestral works. Šourek also compiled an interesting collection of *Letters and Reminiscences* and wrote articles on Dvořák for the current editions of both Grove's *Dictionary of Music and Musicians* and Cobbett's *Cyclopaedic Survey of Chamber Music*.

Lastly, we have Alec Robertson's admirable contribution to the *Master Musicians* series, whose general editor at the time was Eric Blom (1888–1959); this was first published in 1945 and reprinted in 1964. Considering that it was written during the uncertain days of the Second World War, when research was not easy, it contains astonishingly few inaccuracies. Moreover, the approach is scholarly without being pedantic; the critical judgments are penetrative and unbiased (although one reserves the right to disagree with some of them); the literary style is faultless, and appropriately enlivened here and there by characteristic touches of humour. Robertson's book should be 'required reading' for any serious student of Dvořák's music.*

* John Clapham's *Antonín Dvořák: Musician and Craftsman* (1966) has been published since these notes on the bibliography were written. Here the composer's working methods are investigated with a thoroughness that compels admiration.

Index of Dvořák's Compositions

(Short piano pieces and songs and some other small-scale works are grouped together under appropriate headings: Part-songs; Piano solos; Songs; Vocal duets.)

Alfred (opera), 39, 44–6, 62, 131, 207
American Flag The, (cantata), 151–2, 154, 159
'American' suite for piano (op. 98), later orchestrated, 171–2
Armida (opera), 206–15, 219–20

Bagatelles for two violins, cello, harmonium, 79–80
Ballade for violin and piano, 117
Bells of Zlonice, The, see Symphonies (no. 1)

Carnival (concert-overture), 145–7, 154–5, 167–8, 198, 222
Cello concertos
  A major, 36, 80, 178
  B minor, 177–80, 188–9, 198, 222, 225
Cello sonata, 39
Cello, other works for, *see* Polonaise; Rondo; *Silent Woods*
Clarinet quintet, 39
Communion Service in D major, *see* Mass in D major
Concert-overtures
  early, 39, *see also Carnival*; *Hussite*; *In Nature's Realm*; *Othello*; *Romeo and Juliet*
Concert piece for violin and piano, 80
Concertos, *see* Cello concertos; Piano concerto; Violin concerto

Cypresses, The, see under Songs
  string-quartet arrangement, 126–7
Czech Suite for orchestra, 84–6

Devil and Kate, The (operetta), 194–8, 206, 225
Dimitrij (opera)
  main discussion, 98–102
  other references, 95, 97, 103, 131–4, 149–50, 172, 193, 200, 206–8, 220–1, 225
Dramatic overture (i.e. overture to *Alfred*), 45
Dumky trio, *see under* Piano trios

Festival March for orchestra, 83
Festival Ode for chorus and orchestra, 198
Four Romantic Pieces for violin and piano, 126, 150
From the Bohemian Woods (piano duets), 107–8, 111

Golden Spinning-wheel, The, see under Symphonic poems

Heirs of the White Mountain, The, see Hymnus
Hero's Song, The, see under Symphonic poems
Hussite overture, 106–7, 109, 111–12, 141, 159, 222

Hymnus (cantata)
  main discussion, 47–9
  other references, 51–2, 69, 112,
    116, 159, 219, 227, 231
In Nature's Realm or *In the Country-
    side* (concert-overture), 145,
    147, 154–5, 167–8
Incidental music for plays, 39
  see also Josef Kajetán Tyl

Jacobin, The (opera)
  main discussion, 131–4
  other references, 135, 139, 174,
    190, 193, 200–1, 206–8,
    221, 223, 225
Josef Kajetán Tyl (overture and
    incidental music), 96–7, 159,
    168

King and Collier (operetta), first
    version, 46–7, 50, 54
King and Collier, second version
  main discussion, 54–5
  other references, 56–7, 72, 80,
    127, 131, 219–21, 225, 227

Legends (piano duets, later
    orchestrated), 94

Masses
  early, 39
  D major, 128–9, 132, 225
  Requiem, *see* Requiem Mass
Mazurka for violin and orchestra, 83
Moravian duets, *see under* Vocal
    duets
My Home overture, *see Josef Kajetán
    Tyl*)

Nature, Life and Love, see Carnival;
    In Nature's Realm; *Othello*
'New World' symphony, *see* Sym-
    phonies (no. 9)
'Nigger' quartet, *see* String quartets
    (F major)

Nocturnes for orchestra (early), 47,
    51
Nocturne for string orchestra (op.
    40), 40, 47, 109
Noonday Witch, The, see under
    Symphonic poems

Octet for a curious combination of
    instruments, 47
Operas and operettas, *see Alfred*;
    Armida; *Devil and Kate*;
    Dimitrij; *Jacobin*; *King
    and Collier*; *Peasant a Rogue*;
    Pigheaded Peasants; *Rusalka*;
    Vanda
Othello (concert-overture), 145–7,
    154–5, 167–8, 189

Part-songs and choruses
  Amid Nature (op. 63), 96–7
  Hymn of the Czech Peasants, 117
  'Lithuanian', 81–2
  'Moravian', 71, 74
  'Slovakian', 76, 82
  others, 63
Peasant a Rogue, The (operetta)
  main discussion, 72–3
  other references, 71, 75, 102, 131,
    196–8, 206, 211, 222, 225
Piano concerto, 70, 109, 116, 130
Piano duets, *see From the Bohemian
    Woods*; *Legends*; Slavonic
    dances
Piano quartets (with violin, viola,
    cello)
  D major (op. 23), 59, 73
  E flat major (op. 87), 135–6, 145,
    222
Piano quintets (with two violins,
    viola, cello)
  A major (early), 49–50, 129
  A major (op. 81), 129–31, 135,
    137, 145, 222, 225
Piano solos
  collectively, 81, 184–5, 223
  'American' suite (op. 98), 171–2
  dumkas, 70–1, 114

Piano solos—*contd.*
  furiants, 71–2, 114
  humoresques, 175
  mazurkas, 90–1, 135
  Poetic tone-pictures, 135–6
  Scottish dances, 71
  Silhouettes (op. 8), 84–7, 90
  Six morceaux pour pianoforte (op. 52), 90–1
  Theme with variations (op. 36), 70–1
  waltzes, 84–7, 135, 222
  other piano pieces, 36, 52, 63, 90–1, 95, 114, 129
Piano trios (with violin, cello)
  early, 47
  B flat major (op. 21), 59
  G minor (op. 26), 63, 110, 150
  F minor (op. 65), 103–4, 220
  Dumky (op. 90), 144–5, 150, 167–8
Pigheaded Peasants, The, (operetta)
  main discussion, 56–7
  other references, 72, 95, 110, 131, 197–8, 206, 225
Polonaise for cello and piano, 83
Polonaise for orchestra, 83
Psalm 149 for chorus and orchestra, 83

Quartets, *see* Piano quartets; String quartets
Quintets, *see* Clarinet quintet; Piano quintets; String quintets

Requiem Mass, 140–2, 149, 151–2, 222, 224–5
Rhapsody for orchestra (op. 14), later entitled Symphonic poem, 55, 76, 80, *see also* Slavonic rhapsodies
Romance for violin and orchestra, 50–1
Romeo and Juliet (concert-overture), 47
Rondo for cello and piano, 150
Rusalka (opera), 198–208, 222, 225

Saint Ludmila (oratorio)
  main discussion, 120–3
  other references, 119, 124, 126, 128, 149, 201, 204, 206, 208, 231
Scherzo capriccioso for orchestra, 104–5, 109, 139, 222, 225
Serenade for string orchestra (op. 22), 58–9, 76, 222
Serenade (op. 44, the 'wind' serenade), 75–7, 81, 85
Sextet (*see* String sextet)
Silent Woods (piano duet, later arranged for cello), 108
Slavonic dances (piano duets, later orchestrated)
  main discussion, 77–9, 124–5
  other references, 80, 82, 84–5, 91, 94, 100, 109, 144, 168, 222, 225
Slavonic Rhapsodies for orchestra, 77, 80–1, 88, 109, 139
Sonatas, *see* Cello sonata; Violin sonatas
Sonatina for violin and piano, 170–1
Songs
  collectively, 52, 81, 88–9, 184–5, 223
  Biblical Songs (op. 99), 171–4, 189
  Cypresses, The (song-cycle), 36–7, 46, 85, 126–7
  Evening Songs, 69–70
  Gipsy Songs, 88–90, 110, 124, 172, 222, 225
  In Folk-song style, 124–6
  'Králové Dvůr' songs, 47, 51
  Love Songs, 36–7
  other songs, 47, 80, 85–6, 117, 129, 178, 205
Spectre's Bride, The (cantata)
  main discussion, 113–14
  other references, 111–12, 117–18, 121, 123, 141, 149, 186, 215, 231
Stabat Mater, 63–5, 109–10, 112, 143, 224

String quartets
  collectively, 3, 83–4, 181, 185
  early, 34–6, 39–40, 219
  F minor (1873), 49–50, 96
  A minor (1873), 49–51
  A minor (op. 16), 55–6, 62, 105
  E major (op. 27 or 80), 63, 222
  D minor (op. 34), 75–6, 82, 90
  E flat major (op. 51), 83–4, 87,
    96, 109, 225
  C major (op. 61), 96, 165, 220
  F major (op. 96, the 'Nigger'),
    165–8, 172
  G major (op. 106), 181–2, 222,
    225
  A flat major (op. 105), 177–8,
    181–3, 191, 222, 225
String-quartet arrangement of The
    Cypresses, 126–7
String quintets
  A minor, 34, 40, 219
  G major (with double-bass), 58–
    9, 61, 131, 167, 222
  E flat major, 166–8
String Serenade, see Serenade for
    string orchestra
String sextet, 79–80, 87, 109
String trio (Terzetto), 126, 225
Symphonic poems
  collectively, 186–8, 191–2, 196,
    200, 221–2, 225
  Golden Spinning-wheel, The,
    186–8
  Hero's Song, The, 191, 198
  Noonday Witch, The, 186, 188,
    199, 231
  Water-Goblin, The, 186–8, 199
  Wood-Dove, The, 187–8, 191, 205
  see also Rhapsody (op. 14)
Symphonic variations
  main discussion, 73–5
  other references, 71, 127–8, 131,
    139, 222, 225
Symphonies
  collectively, 3, 52, 60–1, 173,
    184–5, 221–3, 225

no. 1 (C minor, The Bells of
    Zlonice), 36–7, 85
no. 2 (B flat major), 37
no. 3 (E flat major), 49–51, 53–4,
    57, 63, 66, 219, 227
no. 4 (D minor), 53–4, 63, 150,
    219
no. 5 (F major), at one time called
    no 3
  main discussion, 60–2
  other references, 16, 63, 105,
    131, 139, 173, 220
no. 6 (D major), at one time
    called no. 1
  main discussion, 92–3
  other references, 106, 109,
    111–14, 116, 123, 129, 136,
    139, 161, 198, 224
no. 7 (D minor), at one time
    called no. 2
  main discussion, 114–16
  other references, 53, 124, 136,
    138, 161, 222, 224
no. 8 (G major), at one time
    called no. 4
  main discussion, 136–8
  other references, 139–40, 142,
    144, 161, 167–8, 173, 189
no. 9 (E minor, the 'New World'),
    at one time called no. 5
  main discussion, 160–2
  other references, 163, 165,
    167–8, 171, 176, 178, 182,
    189

Te Deum, 151–2, 155, 159, 182,
    224–5
Terzetto, see String trio
Theme with variations for piano
    (op. 36), 70–1
Tragic Overture (i.e. overture to
    Alfred), 45
Trios, see Piano trios; String trio

Vanda (opera), 62–3, 131, 220

Violin concerto, 86–8, 90, 107, 182, 221

Violin sonatas
  early, 47
  F major (op. 57), 90, 220

Violin, other works for, *see* Ballade; Concert piece; Four Romantic Pieces; Mazurka; Sonatina

Violoncello, *see under* Cello

Vocal duets
  collectively, 88, 184

Moravian duets (op. 32 sometimes called *Airs from Moravia*), 67–9, 71, 77, 110, 225
  others, 58, 67, 71, 85–6, 95, 110

Wanda, see Vanda

Water-Goblin, The, see under Symphonic poems

'Wind' Serenade, *see* Serenade op. 44

Wood-Dove, The, see under Symphonic poems

General Index

Albani, Emma, 118, 122, 149
Albert, Eugen d', 156
Albert Hall (London), 109–10
Alfred, King, 44, 207
American Opera Company, 147
Ančerl, Karel, 161
Andrássy, Gyula, 48
Anger, Mořic, 35, 37, 138, 174
Anne of Bohemia, Princess, 13
Apt, Antonín, 30
Ashkenazy, Vladimir, 79
Austerlitz, Battle of, 17
Austria, political events in, 13–14,
    17–20, 24–5, 32, 38–9, 41,
    48, 94–5, 192–3
Austrian Medal of Honour for Arts
    and Sciences, 194, 229

Bach, J. S., 29, 217
Badeni, Kasimir, 192–3
Balakirev, M. A., 1
Barnby, Joseph, 109
Bayreuth Festivals, 171, 193
Bechstein pianos, 79
Becker, Jean, 83
Beethoven, Ludwig van, 1, 23, 34–5,
    50, 53, 66, 71, 88, 92–3, 96,
    103, 118, 155, 167, 183,
    189, 217–20
Bellini, Vincenzo, 1, 155
Benda, František, 15
Benda, Jiři, 15
Bendl, Karel, 31, 35–6, 49, 138,
    168, 174, 191, 193
Benedict, Julius, 110
Beneš, Eduard, 193
Beneš-Šumavský, Václav, 62
Beringer, Oskar, 109
Berlin Academy of Fine Arts, 159,
    228

Berlin Philharmonic Orchestra, 138,
    205
Berlioz, Hector, 1, 231
Biber, Heinrich von, 15
Bílý, Tomáš, 164, 166
Birmingham Festival
    (1885), 117–19, 173
    (1891), 140, 149
Birmingham Orchestra, City of, 16,
    118
Bismarck, Otto von, 32, 38
Bizet, Georges, 1, 148, 155, 187
Blažek, František, 29
Blom, Eric, 232
Bohemia, Association for the
    Improvement of Church Music
    in, 29
Bohemia/Moravia
    political events in, 12–14, 17–20,
    24–5, 32, 38–9, 41, 48, 94–5,
    192–3
    sketch map, 10
    see also Czechoslovakia
Bohemian folk-lore see Czech folk-
    lore
Boris, Czar, 98–9
Bořivoj, Prince, 119
Borodin, A. P., 1
Boston String Quartet, 156, 172
Boston Symphony Orchestra, 156,
    205
Bote & Bock (publishers), 81, 84,
    91
Boughton, Rutland, 44
Bouhy, Jacques, 148
Brahms, Johannes, 1, 58, 67–9,
    74–7, 81–2, 87–90, 92–4,
    103, 105, 107, 114–16, 129,
    136, 142, 144, 168, 182, 185,
    189–91, 193–4, 209, 220, 227,
    229, 231

Bratislava (Pressburg), Treaty of, 17
Brixi, F. L., 15
Brno Choral Society, 82
Brno Opera House, 174
Bruch, Max, 1
Bruckner, Anton, 1, 185, 189–90, 220–1, 228
Buck, Dudley, 117
Bülow, Hans von, 138, 173
Burney, Charles, 15–17, 25

Café Royal (London), 110
Calvin, John, 13–14
Cambridge University, 143–4, 168, 228
Carnegie Hall (New York), 154, 162, 171
Cavour, Camillo, 32
Čech, Adolf, 30, 35, 93, 135, 174
Čech, Karel, 35, 95
Čermák, Jan, 35, 39–40, 51
Čermáková, Klotilda, 51–3, 153, 158, 176
    (*see also* Dvořáková; Kounicová; Koutecková)
Červinková-Riegrová, Marie, 99, 131, 193
Chabrier, Emmanuel, 1
Chamberlain, Neville, 8, 11
Charles IV, King of Bohemia, 13
Cherubini, Luigi, 1
Chicago Festival Hall, 168
Chicago World Fair (1893), 168
Chopin, Frederic, 1, 91, 156, 231
Churchill, Winston, 8, 11
City of Birmingham Orchestra, 16, 118
Clapham, John, 233
Cobbett, W. W., 232
Colles, H. C., 136–8, 140, 231–2
Columbus, Christopher, 150–2, 154–5
Covent Garden Opera House, 203
Cowen, Frederic, 118
Crystal Palace, 109, 123
Czech Academy of Sciences and Arts, 128, 139, 154, 228

Czech folk-lore, 67, 71, 112, 124, 186–7, 199, 206, *see also* Folk-music
Czech Music Festival (1904), 215
Czech National Theatre, 32–3, 35, 39, 42–3, 46–7, 52, 55–7, 62, 86, 95, 101, 106–7, 127, 149–50, 174–5, 202–8, 213, 227
Czech Philharmonic Society, 161, 175
Czech Society for Chamber Music, 175
Czech String Quartet, 147, 198
Czech University (Prague), 95, 143, 193, 228
Czechoslovakia, political events in, 8, 11–12, 22, 46, 86, 95, 193, *see also* Bohemia/Moravia; Slovakia

Daladier, Édouard, 11
d'Albert, Eugen, 156
Damrosch, Walter, 156
da Todi, Jacopone, 64
Debussy, Claude, 1, 152, 185
de Koven, Reginald, 156
Delibes, Léo, 1, 155
Dmitri, Czar, 98
Dmitri, Prince, 98
Dobrovský, Josef, 18
Dohnányi, Ernö, 129
Donizetti, Gaetano, 1
Drake, Joseph Rodman, 151–2, 159
dumka described, 70
Dušík or Dussek, J. L., 15
Dušík, Václav, 32, 35–7, 39, 51, 54, 82
Dušková, Josefa, *née* Dvořáková, 31–2, 35–7, 39, 51, 54
Dvořák, Antonín
    for significant events in his career, *see* Appendix I, 227
    for index of compositions *see* 235
    interest in railways, 2, 82, 91, 109, 111, 117, 119, 158, 162–5, 168, 177, 180, 205–6, 215, 225

Dvořák, Antonín—*contd.*
love of nature and interest in
ornithology, 2, 111, 117, 119,
157–8, 162–5, 174–5, 177,
202, 205, 225
political views, 27, 190, 193
religious views, 2, 24, 64–5, 128,
141–2, 171, 189–90
Dvořák's children
collectively, 80, 153, 163–4, 168,
174–5, 189, 205, 216, 227–8
Otakar (1), 55, 70, 75
Josefa, 63–4, 75
Růžena, 70, 75
Otilie, 80, 111, 153, 158–9, 168,
170–1, 180, 188–9, 193–4,
213, 216, 227, 229
Anna, 111, 163, 168, 176, 213, 229
Magda, 111, 163, 213, 215
Antonín, 111, 153, 158–9, 170–1,
176
Otakar (2), 111, 163, 176, 179
Aloisie, 111, 163
Dvořák, František (the composer's
father), 1, 21–31, 51, 103,
110, 150, 158, 173, 228
Dvořáková, Anna, *née* Zdeňková,
(the composer's mother), 21–4,
26–31, 51, 103–4, 190, 228
Dvořáková, Anna, *née* Čermáková
(the composer's wife), 39–40,
51–5, 63, 70, 75, 80, 86
111–13, 122–3, 138–9, 153–4,
163–4, 166, 168, 174–6, 179,
184, 193–4, 204–5, 215–16,
227
Dvořáková, Josefa, see Dušková

Ehlert, Louis, 77, 91
Elgar, Edward, 1, 74, 97, 129, 140
Elizabeth I, Queen, 98
Elizabeth (daughter of King James
I), 13
Erben, Karel Jaromír, 112–13, 186–
8, 191, 199
Esterházy family, 23
Ethandune, Battle of, 44

Fauré, Gabriel, 1, 66, 89, 129, 185
Feodor, Czar, 98
Ferdinand, Emperor of Austria, 24
Festival Hall (Chicago), 168
Fibich, Zdeněk, 138–9, 168
Fischl, Victor, 232
Florentine String Quartet, 83
Flotow, Friedrich von, 155
Folk-music
in Europe, 16–17, 21–3, 42–3,
68, 77–9, 124, 128, 160–1,
165, 178, 181, 196, 198, 219–
20, 225
in North America, 156, 160–1,
165–7, 172–4, 178, 181,
220–1
Förster, Josef (the elder), 29, 176
Förster, Josef Bohuslav, 176, 199
Foster, Stephen, 172
Franck, César, 1, 93, 129
Franz II, Emperor, 17–18
Franz Josef, Emperor of Austria, 24,
32, 38, 48, 57, 83, 138, 192–4,
228
Free Trade Hall (Manchester), 128
French Revolution, 17–18, 131
Frída, Emil, see Vrchlický
furiant described, 71–2

Gassmann, F. L., 15
German Provincial Theatre
(Prague), 18–19, 32–3, 44
Gesellschaft der Musikfreunde, 190,
229
Glinka, M. I., 1
Gluck, C. W., 23, 207
Göbl, Alois, 86–7, 97, 111, 148, 158
Godunov family, 98
Göteberg Philharmonic Society, 41
Gounod, Charles, 1, 101, 118, 155,
173, 194
Grieg, Edvard, 1, 145, 156, 185,
213, 229
Grove, George, 53–4, 232
Guldener (Lobeský), Bernard, 46,
54, 56–7, 72
Gyrowetz, Adelbert, 15

Habsburg dynasty, 14, 17–18, 156–7, 216, 218, *see also* Ferdinand; Franz II; Franz Josef; Josef II
Hadow, Emily, *née* Troutbeck, 231
Hadow, W. H., 151, 231
Hálek, Vítězslav, 48, 69, 97
Hallé Orchestra, 128
Hancke, Franz, 28
Handel, G. F., 29, 64, 118, 121, 151–2, 207
Hanslick, Eduard, 58, 75, 94
Haydn, Josef, 3–4, 15, 23, 34, 36–7, 144, 151, 207, 218
Hellmesberger, Josef, 96
Henry VIII, King, 98
Herbeck, Johann, 58
Herbert, Victor, 177
Heward, Leslie, 16
Heyduk, Alfred, 89
Hitler, Adolf, 8, 11
Hlahol Choral Society (Prague), 32, 42, 49, 51, 83, 113
Hlávka, Josef, 128, 154
Hoffmeister, Karel, 231
Hofmeister (publishers), 84–6, 90
Hohenwart, Karl Siegmund, 48
Holy Roman Empire, 13–14, 17–19
Humperdinck, Engelbert, 179, 201
Hus, Jan, 13–14, 106–7
Huxley, Aldous, 23–4

Interim Theatre (Prague), *see* Provisional Theatre
International Exhibition, Vienna (1892), 150
Ivan IV, Czar, 98

James I, King, 13
Janáček, Leoš, 1, 6, 82, 203–4, 208, 225, 227
Joachim, Josef, 87, 97, 107, 221, 228
Josef II, Emperor, 14

Kàan z Albestů, Jindřich, 108, 117, 174
Kneisel, Franz, 156, 172
Kohout, Josef, 15

Kolařová, Kateřina, 41–2
Komzák, Karel, 31–3, 198
Körner, Karl Theodor, 44–5
Kounic, Václav, 91, 106, 111–12, 180
Kounicová, Josefa, *née* Čermáková, 35–7, 39, 91, 111, 180, 227
Koutecková, Terezie, *née* Čermáková, 163–4
Kovařík, Jan Josef, 153, 162–4, 166
Kovařík, Josef Jan, 153, 158–9, 162–6
Kovaříková, Cecilie, 166
Kovaříková, Josefa, 153, 164
Kovařovic, Karel, 175, 202, 214
Koven, Reginald de, 156
Kozánek, Emil, 166
Koželuh, Leopold, 15
Kraft, Anton, 15
Krejčí, Josef, 29–30
Kroměříž Music Society, 166, 215
Krumpholz, J. B., 15
Kubelik, Jan, 198
Kvapil, Jaroslav, 198–200, 204–5

Lachner, Ferdinand, 150
Lalo, Édouard, 1
Landauer, Walter, 79
Leeds Festival (1886), 118–19, 122–3
Lehár, Franz, 147
Liehmann, Antonín, 26, 28–9, 36, 91, 133, 162
Liszt, Franz, 1, 23, 30, 41–2, 50, 53, 55, 66, 80, 135, 156
Littleton, Alfred, 139
Littleton, Henry, 109–10, 112, 116, 118–20, 122, 139, 175, 188
Lloyd, Edward, 122
Lobeský (Guldener), Bernhard, 46, 54, 56–7, 72
Lobkowitz family, 23
Longfellow, H. W., 172, 177
Löwenberg, Alfred, 207
Ludmila, Saint, 119–20
Lully, J. B., 207
Luther, Martin, 13–14

Maas, Joseph, 118
Macdowell, Edward, 156
Mackenzie, Alexander, 116–18
Mahler, Gustav, 1, 89, 150, 185
Malát, Jan, 214
Manns, August, 93, 109
Marina, Czarina, 98
Masaryk, Tomáš, 95, 193
Massenet, Jules, 1, 185
Maturová, Růžena, 205
Medal of Honour for Arts and Sciences (Austria), 194, 229
Mendelssohn, Felix, 1, 40, 50, 61, 118, 137, 172
Metropolitan Opera House, 147, 155, 159, 171–2
Metternich, Klemens, 18–19, 24, 96
Meyerbeer, Jakob, 1, 101, 155
Mikovec, Ferdinand Břetislav, 99
Mnischek family, 98
Moltke, Helmuth von, 38
Moravia, see Bohemia; Czechoslovakia
Moravian folk-lore, see Czech folklore
Mozart, W. A., 14–15, 31, 40, 96, 144, 155, 209, 217
Munich Agreement, 8, 46
Musikfreunde (Vienna), 190, 229
Mussorgsky, M. P., 1, 99
Mysliveček, Josef, 15

Napoleon Bonaparte, 17
National Conservatory of Music (New York), 147–9, 154, 156–8, 162, 170–2, 176–7, 179–80, 228
National Opera Company (New York), 147
National Theatre (Prague), see Czech National Theatre
Nedbal, Oskar, 45, 127, 147, 198–9
Neff, Jan, 67
Neffová, Marie, 67
Negro music, see Folk-music
New York Philharmonic Society, 155, 171, 177, 179, 228
New York Symphony Society, 156

Newman, John Henry, 140
Newmarch, Rosa, 43, 231
Nikisch, Artur, 156, 205
Novák, Vítězslav, 147, 191
Novello (publishers), 109–11, 113, 139–40, 167
Novotný, Václav Juda, 117, 127

Offenbach, Jacques, 1, 42, 197
Ohm family, 27
Ondriček, František, 87, 107
Onslow, George, 58
Opéra Comique (Paris), 148
Organ School (Prague), 29–31, 142, 176, 227
Otropiev, Grischka, 98–9
Oxford University Opera Club, 197

Paderewski, Ignaz, 156
Palácký, František, 18–19, 24, 48, 94, 193
Patey, Janet, 122
Pauer, Emil, 179
Pfleger-Moravský, Gustav, 36
Philharmonic Society (London), later the Royal Philharmonic Society, 108, 110, 112, 114, 228
  for other Philharmonic Societies or Orchestras, see under Berlin; Boston; Czech; Göteberg; New York
Pitsch, Karl, 29
Plevý, Jan, and his family, 29
Prague Conservatoire, 18, 29, 142–3, 147–50, 152, 157, 176, 181, 198, 205–6, 228–9, 231
Prague Organ School, 29–31, 142, 176, 227
Pressburg, Treaty of, 17
Prokofiev, Serge, 188
Prout, Ebenezer, 188
Provesi, Ferdinando, 2
Provisional Theatre (Prague), 33, 43, 96
Puccini, Giacomo, 1, 35, 185
Pushkin, Alexander, 99

Queen's Hall (London), 188–9

Raphael, Günther, 36, 80, 127
Rawicz, Maryan, 79
Red-Indian music, see Folk-music
Revolutions
    (1789), 17–18, 131
    (1848), 19–20, 24, 32, 41, 192
Richard II, King, 13
Richter, F. X., 15
Richter, Hans, 82, 88, 93, 107, 109,
    123, 127–8, 144, 173, 189,
    193, 228
Rieger, František, 19–20, 193
Riegrová, Marie, see Cervinková
Rimsky-Korsakov, N. A., 1, 185
Robertson, Alec, 136–8, 140, 232–3
Rohan-Rochefort, Prince,
    J. A. L. C. P. J. I., 86
Rossini, Giacchino, 1, 31, 105, 172,
    207, 218
Royal Albert Hall, 109–10
Royal College of Music, 16
Royal Opera House, Covent Garden,
    202–3
Royal Philharmonic Society, see
    under Philharmonic
Rubinstein, Anton, 139
Rubinstein, Artur, 79
Rummel, Franz, 116

Sabina, Karel, 44
Sadler's Wells, 73, 203
Sadová, Battle of, 38
Safonov, Vassily, 179
St. Adalbert's Church (Prague), 52,
    227
Saint Cecilia Society (Prague), 30
St. James's Hall (London), 109, 116,
    123, 139
St. Peter's Church (Prague), 51
St. Petersburg Conservatoire, 139
Saint-Saëns, Camille, 1, 129, 185,
    222
Šamberk, František Ferdinand, 96
Santley, Charles, 188, 122
Savoy Theatre (London), 116

Schikaneder, Emanuel, 209
Schiller, Friedrich, 99
Schlesinger (publishers), 84–6
Schopenhauer, Arthur, 190
Schubert, Franz, 1, 23, 37, 52–4, 61,
    76, 88, 92, 96, 113, 129–30,
    143, 167, 217, 221
Schumann, Robert, 1, 30, 37, 63,
    68–9, 85, 88–9, 108, 129, 170,
    217, 219, 231
Schwarzenberg, Felix, 24
Seegr, Josef, 15–16
Seidl, Anton, 155–6, 171, 179
Shakespeare, William, 9, 101, 123,
    146
Shuisky, Prince Vassili, 98–9
Sibelius, Jean, 1
Simrock, Fritz, 60–1, 68–9, 77, 81,
    84–6, 89–90, 94, 97, 108, 111,
    113, 124–6, 138–40, 167–8,
    206, 227, 229
skočná described, 78
Skriabin, N. A., 91
Škroup, František, 19, 96–7
Slavkov (Austerlitz), Battle of, 17
Slavonic Choral Society (Vienna), 82
Slovakia, political events in, 12, 48
    see also Czechoslovakia
Slovakian folk-lore, 76, 89, 124
Smetana, Bedřich, 1, 5, 19, 41–4,
    46–7, 50–1, 54, 61–2, 66,
    72–3, 84, 95, 104, 146, 150,
    156, 168, 181, 185–6, 193,
    197, 215, 219, 227, 228
Smetanová, Kateřiná, née Kolařová,
    41–2
Sobotka, Josef, 213
Sobotková, Anna, née Dvořáková,
    see Dvořák's children (Anna)
sonata form described, 55–6
Šourek, Otakar, 34, 45–6, 62, 69,
    90, 104, 127, 138, 165, 173,
    187, 190, 196, 224, 232
sousedská described, 78
Spic, Josef, 25–6
Srb-Debrnov, Josef, and his family,
    66, 79

Stalin, 11
Stamitz, Jan, 15
Stanford, C. V., 118, 123, 144
Stáry (publishers), 85–7
State Commission for Art and Music
    (Austria), 57–8, 68, 190–1,
    227, 229
Stefan, Paul, 232
Steinway pianos, 79, 154
Stern, Leo, 188–9
Štolba, Josef, 56–7, 72
Strand Corner House (London), 130
Strauss, Johann, 1
Strauss, Richard, 1, 70, 89, 185, 191
Stuart, Charles Edward, 71
Šubert, František Adolf, 106
Sudetenland, 9–11, 27, 86, 192, 227
Suk, Josef (eventually Dvořák's
    son-in-law), 147, 174, 180,
    193–4, 198–9, 216
Suk, Josef (grandson of above),
    50–1, 216
Suková, Otilie, née Dvořáková, see
    Dvořák's children (Otilie)
Sullivan, Arthur, 1, 3, 58, 97, 116,
    123, 185, 197–8
Surzycha, Juljan, 62
Swarowsky, Hans, 104

Taaffe, Eduard, 94
Tasso, Torquato, 207
Tchaikovsky, P. I., 1, 64, 105, 139,
    170, 173, 190, 223–4, 228
Thomas, Ambroise, 155
Three Choirs Festivals, 112
Thun, Leopold, 41
Thurber, Jeannette M., 147–51,
    154–8, 171–2, 176–7, 179–80
Todi, Jacopone da, 64
Tomašek, Václav, 6, 18
Tovey, Donald, 140
Tragy, Josef, 142, 148–9, 198
Troutbeck, Emily, 231
Troutbeck, John, 112–13, 120, 128,
    231
Tyl, Josef Kajetán, 96–7, 194

Urbánek, Velebín, 110, 138

Vanhall, J. B., 15
Venatorini (Josef Mysliveček), 15
Verdi, Giuseppe, 1–4, 20, 31, 64,
    73, 101, 141–2, 155, 185, 208,
    210–12, 218–20
Versailles, Treaty of, 12, 108
Veselý, Josef Otakar, 72
Vienna, Congress of (1815), 17–18
Vienna Conservatoire, 189
Vienna Court Opera, 58, 89
Vienna International Exhibition
    (1892), 150
Vienna Slavonic Choral Society, 82
Villafranca, Truce of, 32
von Bülow, Hans, 138, 173
Vranický, Paul, 15
Vrba, František, 164
Vrchlický, Jaroslav (real name Emil
    Frída), 120–1, 204–9, 214
Vyšehrad, Citadel of, 216

Wagner, Richard, 1, 30–1, 41–6,
    49–51, 53–4, 58, 61, 63, 101,
    105, 115, 118, 134, 145–6,
    155–6, 171–2, 196, 200, 208–
    9, 211, 219–20, 231
Walter, Gustav, 89
Waterloo, Battle of, 17
Weber, C. M. von, 1, 44, 54, 156
Weis, Karel, 174
Wenceslas, 'Good King' and Saint,
    12–14, 19, 32, 106–7, 119,
    193
Wenig, Adolf, 194
Westminster Abbey, 216
White Mountain, Battle of the, 13–
    14, 48
Wihan, Hanuš, 150, 175, 177, 198
Wilson, Woodrow, 108
Wolf, Hugo, 1, 89, 185, 208–9, 211
Worcester Festival (1884), 112–13
World Fair (Chicago, 1893), 168
Wyclif, John, 13

Žak, Benedict, 6, 15
Zakrejs, František, 62
Zdeněk, Antonín, 26, 29, 31
Zdeněk, Josef, 6, 23
Zdeňková, Anna, *see* Dvořáková, Anna, *née* Zdeňková

Zelenka, J. D., 15
Žerotín Music and Choral Society (Olomouc), 120
Zubatý, Josef, 117
Zvonař, Josef, 29, 32